For College, Club and Country

A History of Clifton Rugby Football Club

By

Patrick J. Casey
&
Dr. Richard I. Hale

First published in 2009

ISBN- 9781904312758

MX Publishing Ltd, 335 Princes Park Manor, Royal Drive, London N11 3GX
www.mxpublishing.co.uk

Edited by Richard Savory

The cover of this book is taken from a postcard of Clifton College. It is postmarked Bristol 22nd April 1904.

Dedication

To my family, Debra, Daniel, Kayna and Dulcie from Patrick

To Ian William Hale who taught me the power of rugby football from your son Richard

Foreword

Admiral Sir James Henry Fuller Eberle GCB LLD is the son of Victor Fuller Eberle, who played for Clifton RFC from 1905, was club captain from 1911 to 1913 and went on to become a governor of Clifton College. He is also the grandson of one of the club's founders, Alderman James Fuller Eberle. His two uncles, George and Ellison also played rugby for Clifton.

The Fuller Eberle Family in 1935 together with members of the Wills, Strachan, Fuller, Birtall and Fedden Families. Seated centre, founder, James Fuller Eberle. Standing 5th right George Fuller Eberle, 3rd right Ellison Fuller Eberle, extreme right Victor Fuller Eberle. On the ground in the centre Jim Eberle.

Admiral Sir James Henry Fuller Eberle was educated at Clifton College, the Royal Naval College at Dartmouth and Greenwich. In 1979 he took over command of the British Fleet and NATO Commander in Chief of the Channel and Eastern Atlantic Commands.

He is often remembered for his first signal to the Fleet that he expected his officers and men to have fun, which he regarded as an ingredient of efficiency and not the reverse. Following his Fleet command, he served as Commander-in-Chief of the Naval Home Command during the Falklands War, prior to his retirement from active service in 1983. He was Chairman of the Council at Clifton College from 1984-1994.

In 1984 he was appointed Director of the Royal Institute of International Affairs which he continued to serve until his retirement at the end of the century. In this position he established high-level contacts with many other countries within Western Europe, and also with Russia, Argentina and Japan.

Sir James holds honorary Degrees of Letters at Bristol and Sussex Universities and was for many years Chairman of the Naval Professional journal, the Naval Review. He has strong countryside interests having farmed on Dartmoor. He is a Board member of the Countryside Alliance. He has been Master of the Britannia Beagles at the RN College Dartmouth for forty-six years. He played tennis for the Navy and is a member of the All England Lawn Tennis Club at Wimbledon.

The history of the Eberle family from the sixteenth century in Moravia, Greenland and Bristol, together with the Admiral's service in the Navy from 1944 to 1983 and his subsequent career in international politics, are described in his published trilogy 'Admiral Jim'.

History is often perceived as being about events – but events are created by people. The importance of this book is that it is primarily about people. Among those people were members of my family.

My grandfather, one of the founders of the Clifton Rugby Football Club, was a Clifton man and a distinguished Bristolian. The son of a German-born Minister of the Moravian Church, he had been born in Plymouth and brought up in Bristol. As an elected Councillor for the St Augustine's ward, he served all the citizens of Bristol as a member of the City Council with great distinction for more than fifty years. A weak heart, which developed in his early manhood, prevented him from taking part in active sports.

However he instilled in his three sons a love of sport and a deep understanding of the value of sportsmanship in the wider areas of life. My father, Victor, represented the county of Gloucestershire in rugby, hockey and tennis on no less than fifty occasions; his elder brother George played in an England rugby trial, unfortunately he received an injury that curtailed his top level rugby career during a Bristol match against Bridgwater in 1903; his younger brother Ellison held the record for many years for the most tries scored for the Clifton Rugby Club in one season; and the three brothers held the record of being the only occasion in the country that three members of the same family represented their county, Gloucestershire, in the three-quarter line of a county match.

The value of the personal and lifetime reminiscences of great events whether of war or peace, that impacts on many of our own lives, is brought home on this very day on which I write, when we mark the funeral of one Harry Patch, the last survivor of the trench war in France in WWI.

This book records the deeds of members of the Clifton Rugby Football Club which, over a period of over one hundred years has brought it from the enthusiasm and loyalty of a few like minded Bristol citizens, of what had once been the small suburban village of Clifton on the outskirts of the Port of Bristol. The record is not only that of the substantial contribution to the sport of Rugby Football that has been made by all the club's members, but also to their service to their country in two world wars. "**We shall remember them**".

Admiral Jim
August 2009

Preface

Little did we imagine, back in 2002, that a page on the website of a Clifton under-8s side would metamorphose into a fully-fledged book. The webpage was intended as a short history of the club, and a list of players who had gone on to international status. Everything was taken from the Centenary book; memorabilia were collected from various sources and the website page was expanded until it was too big and needed its own website. To this were added photographs and documents from the club, principally donated by the Clifton players Ellison Fuller Eberle, Gilbert Castle and Tom Burroughs. At a later date the scrapbooks and photographs of Victor Fuller Eberle were donated by his son Admiral Sir James Fuller Eberle. Relatives of former players started contacting me in 2003. Richard Savory was the first; his grandfather played for Clifton from 1908 to 1920. Fortuitously, many of the descendants of those listed on the War Memorial would provide photographs. It was intended to remain only a website until Richard Hale suggested it would make an interesting book. From that point it took another four years to become reality. The website is now one of the largest and most comprehensive rugby club history websites in the world.

The history of Clifton Rugby Club holds a unique place in the history of Bristol. It is the oldest surviving rugby club in Bristol with links to one of the most famous schools in the country, Clifton College.

The history of Clifton Rugby Club has previously been recorded in three books. The first in 1909, "History of Clifton Rugby Football Club 1872-1909" by Frank C Hawkins gave a year-by-year account of the club. The 1922 edition was an extended version of the 1909 book, renamed "50 Years with the Clifton Football Club". In 1972 the Centenary Year was commemorated by a book called "100 Years with Clifton Rugby Football Club". With all this work already done, it was difficult to know what new and interesting facts could be recorded.

In this book we have consciously tried not to replicate previous histories of the club. We have concentrated on its origins - the Founders, the Internationals, the Oxford and Cambridge Blues, the names on the War Memorial and the players and events that have changed the club post-1972, as well as elaborating on what had already been written.

It is appropriate that this season, 2009-2010, is the 100th anniversary of Gloucestershire winning the County Championship for the first time in their history.

Patrick Casey, August 2009
http://www.cliftonrfchistory.co.uk

I was brought up in Bristol with rugby football in my blood, with fond memories of tagging along with my father as he played combination rugby every Saturday, the taste of hot-dogs under big muddy canvas marquees, the smell and eventually the taste of warm beer and the overwhelming sense of camaraderie. I was sent to a rugby school. At Bristol Grammar we were desperate to get our hands on the ball, but had to wait until we were about ten before the masters gave us a taste of it. I developed a love of the game, found my niche and a tremendous community of friends with whom I remain close to this day. I found that, wherever I travelled, if I had my boots I could find an instant group of like-minded, spirited pals. Just standing shoulder to shoulder playing amateur rugby and going into battle together would create an unbreakable bond.

Given the sacrifices of the groups of pals, often recruited as teams from the sports clubs, who not only played together but fought for their country in the world wars, I can only imagine their sense of identity and passion. As a young lad I knew my grandfather, William Hale, and I was always proud of his rugby past, a stalwart of the Bristol team in the period between the wars. What hadn't registered with me until writing this book and discussing it with my father was that he had fought in the trenches, as one of the Glosters. Like so many, he rarely talked about it.

I first became interested in the history of Clifton RFC through my sons playing with the juniors there and attending Clifton College. I was fascinated by the strong and direct link between the formation of the game, Rugby School, Clifton College and Clifton Rugby Club. To me this is not simply a rugby book. Yes, we aim to update and share some of the club history, but I see this also as capturing social history of local and national significance.

Owing to the wonders of web technologies, we have been able to create energy around the club history website, with contributions pouring in from interested parties and families from all around the world. I would like to express thanks to all the contributors, and to my co-author Patrick, for driving this. I would like to think of someone, perhaps in another fifty or a hundred years, being able to draw on this book as a resource to help with their own update. It is work in progress.

Richard Hale, August 2009
http://www.richardhaleassociates.com

Acknowledgements

Without these people and organisations this book could not have been produced:

To Tony Page, who played for Clifton in the 1960s, we owe a huge vote of thanks. He has conveyed loyalty to and passion for the club, and a commitment to support the memory of those who fought for their country. He made a massive contribution by conducting research at locations of battles, burial grounds and memorials, and I hope that he writes up his findings in more detail. The chapters in this book could not have been written without him.

Richard Savory, grandson of Clifton player Harry Savory, who provided so much information, advice and support, as well as editing the final document.

Sheridan Smith, ex-chairman of Clifton RFC, who has provided support, advice and information.

Also:

St. Andrews College, Andrew Mills-Baker, Peter Mills-Baker, Harry Barstow, Roger Bealing, Bedford School, Clive Bevan, Blackheath Rugby Club, Bangalore Rotary Club, Birkenhead Park Rugby Club, Blundell's School, Bodleian Library, Martyn Boot, Keith Bonham, Bradfield College, Diana Biggs, Bristol Grammar School, British American Tobacco, Ian Chard, Chris Bromhead, Leslie Brown, Don Brundrett, John Burrough, Cambridge University Rugby Union Club, Ann Carpenter, Charterhouse School, Kayna Clarke, Clifton College, Bruce Coates, Celia Coleman, James Cridland, Peter Fuller Eberle, Shaun Edwards, Carol Evans, Steven Evans, Georgina Fayle, The Douglas Fairbanks Museum, Nick Gardiner, Robert Gilchrist, Gathorne Girdlestone, Soldiers of Gloucestershire Museum, Peter Greenslade, Trevor Harkin, Judy Harwood, Penny Hiatt, John Hood, Mark Hoskins, Irish Rugby Football Union, Masters and Fellows of St. John's College, Cambridge, Peter Johnston, John Jones, Ben Jordan, Barnaby Kent, King's College Hospital, Darren Lloyd, Robert Lloyd, Robert Kenneth Gillespie MacEwen, The Malvernian Society, Dean Marks, Marlborough College, Meade-King & Co, Colin McFadyean, Narelle Mills, Old Haberdashers, Roger Opie, Otaki Golf Club, Mark Osborn, Oxford University Rugby Club, Richard Pettinger, Royal College of Physicians, David Pontifex, Ray Pontifex, Brian Pugh, University of Queensland, Radley College, John Raine, RFU Museum, Steve Richards, St. Brendan's College, Sedbergh School, Scottish Rugby Union, Sherborne School, Paul Spiring, Ian Tait, Phillip Tardif, Paul Thompson, Dr. M.J. Trew, Keith Trivett, Vestry House Museum, Jonathan Walker, Welsh Rugby Union, Wycliffe College, Malte Znaniecki.

And thank you for buying the book, as all profits support the club's development.

Contents

Roots

There are many views on the roots of the game of rugby football. Whilst its foundation is rightly attributed to Rugby School, variations of football have been tracked back to various sources. Some writers have speculated on the case for links that can be traced back to ball games at the time of the Roman and Celtic invasions through to twelfth century games in London and primitive, often dangerous games in England from the fourteenth to the seventeenth centuries. Regional games have been identified, such as knappan in Wales, hurling in Cornwall and camp-ball in East Anglia. Camp-ball, which was played as far back as the fifteenth century, certainly has characteristics in common with rugby football, with versions of the line-out, scrum, maul, tackle and prohibition of the forward pass. Rather different, however, was that it might involve 300 players a side, and could be played for 14 hours and claim several lives.

For the origins of the game as we know it today we have to look to the public schools of England, which in the eighteenth and nineteenth centuries developed their own forms and traditions of football. In many cases the shape of the game was determined by the shape of the pitch. For instance, at Eton the 'wall game' evolved due to the construction of a wall in 1717 that created a long, narrow pitch, leading to frequent scrums against the wall. Also at Eton, the 'field game', played on a bigger pitch, entailed more running and kicking.

At Rugby there were open fields collectively known as the Close, the same name taken by Clifton College for its playing fields which survive to this day. Prepostors [1]would keep the line, armed with canes.

William Webb Ellis, a pupil at Rugby, is commonly credited with founding the game of rugby football when, according to a granite slab in the Doctor's wall at the School, in 1823 he "with a fine disregard for the rules of football as played in his time first took the ball in his arms and ran with it. thus originating the distinctive feature of the Rugby game."

It is a widely-held view, however, that public schools have a well-developed facility for social engineering, with examples to be found in the traditions and innovations of Rugby School and Clifton College which in many ways contributed to the formation and development of Clifton RFC. It may be that the story of Webb Ellis is indeed more legend than fact.

Why would the school wish to create such a legend? Well, it is important to consider the development of the football game across the nation in this era. Schools were

---

[1] A prefect in a public school.

evolving their own variations of the football game, indeed the rules of the game at Rugby School were subject to regular review before and after matches.

At Rugby School the development of the laws of the game was managed by devolving responsibility to the senior players, who met before games to agree the laws which were to be applied, and again after the game to review learning and to decide whether the laws needed to be changed. This suggests that the experience of the game influenced the laws, rather than the game being governed by the laws. This might be seen as an early example of action learning, with peers learning with and from each other.

There is no doubt that running with the ball in hand did evolve at Rugby, but the Webb Ellis story may also have been a convenient and clever way to create a historical mystique surrounding the origins of the game. One cannot doubt the significance of the connection, because many schools and (from the mid-nineteenth century onwards) newly formed clubs adopted the Rugby School rules. Even if they adopted variations, such as at Clifton Rugby Football Club with 'no hacking[2] or tripping ', then the Rugby system was the benchmark from which variations were developed. By laying claim to having invented the game, and by attributing this innovation to one of its own, Rugby School was to lend its name to the international game it was to become. It even gave the name of one of its apparently unpopular and otherwise undistinguished pupils to the Webb Ellis World Cup.

Here then lies the direct-line relationship with Clifton Rugby Football Club. Clifton College was founded in 1860, and opened on Tuesday 30th September 1862 to provide private education for the sons of gentlemen of the City of Bristol. One should not underestimate the challenge and achievement in establishing, from scratch, a new private school which was to grow rapidly in the following year. A pattern can be seen in terms of how this was achieved, and is one that follows the example of how Rugby School evolved and then laid claim to the game of rugby football. It is the ability to innovate, yet at the same time to draw upon tradition.

Clifton College's most famous Headmaster, the Reverend John Percival, was at the helm from September 4th 1862 until April 1879. He came bristling into the role at the age of 28 from Rugby School, a hurried replacement following the failure to appoint the Reverend Charles Evans who was Headmaster Elect from January 1861 until September 1862. In the meantime Evans had received an irresistible offer to take up the Headship of his old school, King Edward's, Birmingham. Percival had attended Appleby Grammar School and Queen's College Oxford, where he won a Double First in Classics and Mathematics. After his 17 years at Clifton he had built the school's size to 680 boys. He was eventually to return to Rugby as Headmaster at the age of 53 following a period of eight years as President of Trinity College, Oxford.

---

[2] Kicking the shins of an opponent

It was at Rugby School that he insisted boys football shorts be worn below the knee and secured with elastic. He acquired the nickname "Percival of the knees" as a result.

Percival's background as the son of a poor dalesman was humble, yet he was to become a most distinguished and influential man of his time in many ways, not least as cleric and academic. In 1883 he was offered (but refused) the Bishopric of Hereford. His vision and commitment were immense, and he combined these with the ability to construct a school imbued with his spirit which thrives to this day.

There was a sense, in the foundation of the school, of an optimistic desire to establish a new and fresh organisation. How could this be achieved with no history or tradition?

The answer came in part from Rugby School, and the extent to which Clifton has borrowed from the Rugby tradition is considerable: the House system, even the names such as School House and houses named after masters who were Rugby School alumni such as Moberly's, Dakyns' and Tait's, the Close used for sporting matches, the devolution of responsibilities through the Prepostor system, the adoption of the rugby football system, with caps, the Bigside Levee and Puntabout, the punting practice still seen today at break-times - these were all borrowed from Rugby School.

One would, though, be mistaken to view Clifton College as having been founded to create a copy of Rugby School. Systems that worked at Rugby were certainly introduced, but the capacity of Percival to innovate was considerable. He oversaw what must have been bold steps in their time, such as the introduction of the Town House for dayboys, with equal status to those of boarders. He actively sought to develop membership from the mercantile and professional classes rather than pursuing the traditional public school route of currying favour with the aristocracy. The introduction of the Jewish House, so that Jewish boys could follow their own observances, came about in Percival's time. In the curriculum he was ahead of his time in introducing the Moderns rather than simply relying on the Classics and he supported the military and engineering-related innovation. In terms of physical construction he oversaw the opening of the Chapel, fives courts, a racket court, the junior school, the gymnasium, the pavilion, two swimming baths and the Percival Library and Museum. He also presided over the introduction of a structured and disciplined approach to sport, initially in the face of considerable apathy.

Operational management of many aspects of school and sporting life was devolved to boys through the Bigside Levee system. The hierarchy established amongst the different year-groups was seen in the public school system as creating a sound training ground for their future roles in government, the military or public service. The Bigside Levee was a form of council run by the boys of the school and which excluded the Masters. At Clifton it was founded in 1863 and comprised all boys in the Upper School except fags, including all 'Caps' and members of the XI.

The Head of School was clearly in a most influential position, as he was President of the Bigside Levee and School Levee. The Bigside Levee had disciplinary powers, albeit they had to be ratified by the Headmaster. They also had considerable influence on games including the awarding of caps and colours. Presumably the objective was to instil a sense of responsibility for organisation, and this would have been seen as good training for young gentleman. From about 1920 Bigside Levee's role was taken over by those of the Head of School, the Prepostors and the Games Secretaries. The term 'Bigside' remains to this day, with boys being organised into Bigside teams according to standard and seniority.

In these early days Dakyns (who, remember, had come from Rugby School) noted the challenge of instilling core values associated with sport into the boys:

The boys of those days had no notion of games or the respect due to them. I cannot make you understand how difficult it was at that time to create and develop an ardour in all sorts of athletic matters here... You will hardly believe that we used to have to persuade the boys in those days, if it were at all wet in the afternoon, to take their coats off and play football or go on runs (Christie, 1935, p.66-67)

This would appear to be corroborated by an anecdote about Dr Percival's participation in a rugby match held on the Downs, recounted at the Clifton Rugby Club Jubilee Dinner in 1922 when Walter Stuckey Paul (himself a founder member) recalled the foundation of the Club 50 years previously. Paul stressed the debt that rugby in general, and the Club in particular, owed to the public schools for providing the foundations of the game and a plentiful supply of players. Special mention was made of Clifton, and Bristol Grammar School was recognised too. Paul told the story of how Dr Percival was so disgusted with the standard of play that he ran onto the pitch and joined in. He was passed the ball and managed to elude the opposition apart from Paul's brother A.W. Paul, who was Head of School and future member of the Clifton College Council. A.W. Paul had managed to secure a grip of Dr Percival's formal coat tails, and following a fair battle he ripped them from the Headmaster who went on to score a try.

The sense of discomfort that games may have caused young sportsmen who felt pressed into activity by the school is summarised wonderfully by a 'new fag' writing to The Cliftonian (December, 1877), who said:

I want to know why everything here is compulsory. I like football well enough, but when I am forced to play whether I feel inclined to or no is not pleasant. If the Close is too wet I am made to go slipping and slithering across the Downs, scramble through wet hedges and splash along muddy lanes... When I come back I feel too tired to do any work and get into a row the next day.

It can also be seen from this early period that cricket had become an important part of the institution and of the education of boys. Not all were enthusiastic and in June 1869 there was a lobby for a Bicycle Club which might:

... afford occupation to a great many fellows who are now mere loungers, loafers, Pythagorean lookers-on in this Academy, whose sole object at present seems to be the cultivation of cricket.

The concept of fagging is often associated with that seen under the old Rugby School system. This had gained ill-repute as a system for supposedly guiding the development of new boys by assigning them to senior boys, for whom they would have to do chores and by whom they would often be bullied. This was a target of the reforms Arnold sought to establish, as recounted in *Tom Brown's Schooldays* by Thomas Hughes. Fagging at Clifton College appears to have been much more benign, and indeed there are reports of the new fags being assigned to a senior boy who taught them the rules of football - an early example of coaching, perhaps?

When it came to rugby, the boundaries between schoolmaster, pupil, team-mate and even parents seem to have been blurred. It is perhaps worth considering that rugby may have been, even in a most class-based society, a great leveller. Masters would join in House matches at the school in the early days, and the inter-house 'Cock-House' match was established, again imported from Rugby School, where one of the Bigside matches had the Caps of the Cock House - the champion House of the day - and the next house in line playing against the rest of the Caps, with old Rugbeians joining in on each side. There were often 70 or 80 a side. Charles Stuart (Pup) Dakyns, a well-known figure in these games, was noted for his ability to drop-kick with either foot from 50 or 60 yards, and for his skill in running, dodging and tackling. Dakyns entered Rugby School in 1855, one of four rugby-playing Dakyns brothers including the one who became a Master at Clifton College from its foundation until 1890.

Although there was clearly a system for regulating the game, there is no doubt that it could be a brutal experience. Hacking (kicking at the shins of the opposing team), tripping and scragging were acceptable means of tackling, and were exported from Rugby School to Clifton College. In *Tom Brown's Schooldays*, Tom is being inducted into the ways of football at Rugby and asks his companion East why the boys are wearing white trousers in November. He replies:

"Why bless, don't you know? – No, I forgot. Why, today's the Schoolhouse match. Our house plays the whole of the school at football. And we all wear white trousers, to show 'em we don't care for hacks".

When a rare foreign (inter-school) fixture was arranged with Marlborough College in 1864, the Marlborough team was so surprised by the way Clifton played the game that, despite Marlborough's victory, the fixture was dropped until 1891. This match is described in the 'History of Marlborough College', (AG Bradley et al., 1893). It was alleged that the Clifton boys were shouting 'hack him', causing one of the Marlborough team to ask their Headmaster (Bradley himself) whether the game should be stopped. Bradley replied "win the game first, and then talk about stopping if you like". The Clifton College full-back Charles Tylecote, recalling how brutal the game had been, said that it could hardly have been called football, but that after a good supper all were on quite friendly terms.

Clifton College did play an annual match against Old Cliftonians on the Close, but no further inter-school matches for thirty years after the notorious Marlborough match. Clearly there had been some controversy caused by this fixture, and again the roots might be traced back to Rugby School. Whereas Clifton had adopted the more brutal form of the game, Marlborough had its own version. George Cotton, who was the young master at Rugby in Tom Brown's Schooldays, was appointed Headmaster of Marlborough in 1852. Here, where rugby football was seen as a good way of diverting boys from poaching and other illicit activities, hacking was never accepted. Various rules emerged at different public schools and were passed down from one generation of schoolboys to the next. There were variations relating to many aspects of the game, from how the game started, to catching and handling the ball, running in, holding, tripping, hacking or shinning and what constituted out of bounds. Schools like Clifton that were not involved in foreign matches in the 1860s had little reason to conform to a universal set of rules, but there was a need for clubs forming at this time to attain consistency.

In 1863 Cambridge University drafted its own rules, not in an effort to claim the game nationwide, but primarily to bring some order and understanding to its own matches. Its rules were to lead to the formalisation of the rules of association football. The future division of the game from rugby football could be anticipated, and in commenting on the fact that it seemed more civilised than rugby, John Cartwright (Macrory p165), an observer of the first Cambridge game in 1863 after the publication of their rules, commented:

"We do not consider it the best game that might be had, but it is a good one. It is more with the spirit of to-day than those which it is designed to take the place of, now or at some future time".

In November 1863, in the Freemason's Tavern, the Football Association was formed. Only a handful of schools were represented at the meeting, and Charterhouse the only public school. Over the course of ensuing meetings, there were different factions, some in favour of running with the ball and others who wanted to outlaw it. At the same time Cambridge was clarifying its rules, favouring the move against running with the ball. At the early Football Association meetings, the Blackheath club was drawn into a dispute over hacking, which it favoured, and into defending this aspect of the game. The accusation was levied against Blackheath that it could not get fixtures with London clubs because businessmen were unwilling to be hacked. A Mr Campbell, one of the Blackheath representatives, defended the club's position, claiming that those against hacking had begun the game late in life, and were too old for the version of the game played by the public schools and the clubs they formed. He claimed that such players preferred their 'pipes, grog and schnapps more than the manly game of football'. Ultimately the non-hackers and the non-runners with the ball won the day, and on 1st December 1863, the laws of rugby were settled, including:

Law 9: No player shall run with the ball.

Law 10: Neither tripping nor hacking shall be allowed, and no player shall use his hands to hold or push his adversary.

The Association's football rules were thus passed. The rift with Blackheath, now known as 'the hacking men', reflected the diverging courses of Association and Rugby Football for the years to come.

At the same time the London clubs which were forming had even more of a problem as they were attracting not only the public schoolboys but also uninitiated players into their variations of the rugby football game. There was a need for a universally understood code. It was expected that the game would spread to the villages, and rather condescendingly it was considered that village people would need a system of published rules to help control their unruly and ill-disciplined nature. However the decline of the rural communities in the 1870s meant that the anticipated take-up did not materialise in this sector, but it did so in the industrial centres of the Midlands and the North. Clubs that were springing up in the 1860s had consciously to choose their code and, despite the rise of the Association game, rugby football continued to see growth throughout the schools sector. Whereas the Association game had been created to support the adults in the new clubs, rugby had emerged essentially as a public school game and had to adapt through the experiences, actions and learning of the players. Theory tended to follow the action; laws were adapted to meet the needs and experience of the players. However as rugby was spreading there was a call for more control of the game, and a desire to make it a safer and more regulated activity.

If one man could be identified as having the greatest influence on the development of rugby at Clifton, then it would have to be Henry Graham Dakyns. He started rugby at Clifton College in 1862 with the help of Henry William Wellesley, the first head of the school. Henry was the son of Capt. W.H.G. Wellesley of Radstock, and great-nephew of Arthur "the great Duke of Wellington". Henry Wellesley died on January 11th 1878, aged only 33.

Henry Dakyns was born in 1838 on the island of St. Vincent in the West Indies, the son of Dr Thomas Henry Dakyns and Harriet Dascent. He was educated at Rugby School and then at Trinity College, Cambridge from 1856 (BA 1856, MA 1864). He was tutor to the sons of Alfred (later Lord) Tennyson in 1861 at Farringford House, Isle of Wight, before becoming a Master at Clifton in 1862, where he rose to become

Deputy Headmaster and stayed until December 1889. Despite his close interest in the game, he never played for Clifton RFC and had no involvement in the club's foundation. Dakyns, who had a Scots-born wife Margaret, a daughter – also Margaret - and sons Henry and Arthur, had a heart attack and died on 21st June 1911 while waiting for a visitor at Haslemere Station, Surrey on the eve of the Coronation of Edward VII. His brother, C.S. Dakyns, was a founding member of the Richmond club. Another brother was said to have enjoyed playing the game so much that he stayed at Rugby School until he was twenty, and eventually had to be asked to leave.

Henry Graham Dakyns

Dakyns was the first master recruited by Percival. The latter made sure Dakyns didn't delay his move to Clifton College, reportedly asking him "when can you begin, Dakyns?" "Oh. quite soon," Dakyns replied, "in two or three days at most." "There's a train in an hour's time", replied Percival, "they are rather hard pressed down there. I think you had better take it."

Clifton Rugby Club was initially founded in 1869 but disbanded after two seasons because of a lack of players. This first iteration of the club played in mauve jerseys with wide black diagonal stripes and a skull and crossbones on the left breast (Hawkins, 1909, p167). After the club collapsed, several of its players went on to help form the present club. Almost inevitably, the skull and crossbones appeared on a Rugby School badge (School House) and was also used as the first badge of the Barbarians.

Amongst those that played for Clifton between 1869 and 1871 were several members of the **Wills** family, covered in this book's 'Clifton Families' chapter. Others included three Cross brothers born at Merriott in Somerset. **Francis Richardson Cross** was born 26th November 1847. His father, Joseph, was Vicar of All Saints Church, Merriott from 1832-1855. Francis was educated at King's College, London and became a Clifton surgeon and dentist. His first wife Maria died in 1864 and he re-married to Eva Beatrice who also died before she reached her 40th birthday. Francis persisted with rugby and went on to play for the new Clifton club founded in 1872. He became Sheriff of Bristol in 1897 and died on 12th July 1931 at his home, Worcester House in Clifton, Bristol after a bout of influenza. His funeral service took place at Bristol Cathedral on 16th July 1931 and he is buried at Alveston, Gloucestershire.

Dr. Francis Richardson Cross in 1903

Joseph John Cross was born on 23rd February 1849, in Merriott and taught at Newton Abbott School. He played county cricket twice for Gloucestershire CCC in 1870 before studying at Oxford University. He died on 2nd November 1918 at Lambridge, Bath. His brother, **Thomas Uttermare Cross** was born a couple of years after Joseph and followed him into the teaching profession, in his case at Blundell's School from 1876.

Thomas Cross in 1888.
(Photograph courtesy of Blundell's School)

It was reported in the Western Times on 14th October 1893 that he had been suffering from depression and had been advised to take a voyage. He was lost overboard near Madeira.

John Curtis was born in 1851. Like his father (and grandfather) he became an accountant and was another who played for both the 'old' and 'new' Clifton clubs. His brother **Michael Martyn Curtis** appears in the Famous Players chapter, as does another of the original players, W.S. Paul.

Charles Frederick Henderson was the eldest of three sons of a Clifton solicitor, all founder members of the first Clifton club and educated at Ellenborough School, a small private boys' school on Whiteladies Road in Bristol. Charles was born in 1848, and his brother **William** in 1850. William was captain of the first Clifton club and died in 1915. The youngest, **Alfred**, was born in 1852. All three followed their father into the legal profession, Charles and William practising in Clifton and Alfred in Gloucester.

Francis Hastings Martin Atkins was born in 1850 in Kingston Lisle, Berkshire. By the 1860s his family was living in Victoria Square, Clifton. He came from a wealthy background – his father a Landed Proprietor – and by the age of 40 he seems to have been living quietly 'on his own means' back in Faringdon, close to where he was born.

John Edmund Jose was born about 1847 in Clifton and became a tobacco merchant. He left the area in the 1880s to live with his wife Edith in Lancashire.

This 1869-1871 Clifton side did play several games against good opposition, but the only recorded match was a defeat by Blackheath.

On 26th January, 1871, The Rugby Football Union was founded at the Pall Mall Restaurant in Regent Street, London to standardise the rules, removing some of the more violent aspects of the Rugby School game. Several Old Rugbeians were represented and most of the Rugby School rules were formally adopted, with the notable exception that hacking was prohibited - so even with the advent of the rugby code, the Blackheath representative at the Association Football meetings would have lost his fight to maintain this 'character building' practice.

The 21 clubs that attended the first meeting, chaired by the captain of the Richmond Club (E. C. Holmes) included Harlequins, Blackheath, Guy's Hospital, Civil Service, Wellington College, King's College and St. Paul's School, all of which are still playing today. Other clubs now defunct, or playing under other names, were the Gipsies, Flamingoes, Mohicans, Wimbledon Hornets, Marlborough Nomads, West Kent, Law, Lausanne, Addison, Belsize Park, Ravenscourt Park, Clapham Rovers and a Greenwich club called Queen's House. Many famous provincial clubs, in existence before 1871, were not founder members of the Rugby Football Union, although of course the likes of Bath, Bradford, Liverpool and Brighton became members later.

One famous name that was missing, though, was the London club Wasps. Apparently the club somehow contrived to send its representative to the wrong venue at the wrong time on the wrong day, although another version of the story was that he went to a pub of the same name and, after consuming numerous libations, was too drunk to make it to the correct address when he finally realised his mistake.

The game in those early days was very different to todays. In 1892, ex Clifton College and Club player Arthur Budd, who became President of the Rugby Football Union in 1888, wrote in the book *Football - The Rugby Union Game:* (Marshall 1894, p115)

When I played as a schoolboy at Clifton, where the Rugby School game – the progenitor of the Rugby Union game – was adopted in its entirety, the number of players was twenty-a-side in an ordinary match, and, in the Sixth and School game, the latter were allowed forty to the twenty of their sturdier seniors. Old Boys who had gained their caps in bygone days were accorded the privilege of joining in all Bigside matches whenever they pleased, so that it was not at all an uncommon thing to see a dozen supernumeraries ranging themselves on one side or the other. Hacking over the first-on-side was permissible, and tripping over a runner was quite as much practised as tackling. A player who could not take and give hacks was not considered worth his salt, and to put one's head down in a scrimmage[3] was regarded as an act of high treason. We were frequently boxed in a scrimmage for three or four minutes together, only to discover that the half-back had by this time absconded with the ball to the other side of the ground.

The Cliftonian magazine gives more detail on these Clifton College games. They would be played over several days, with players joining in and leaving as they pleased. Old Cliftonians and Masters would also come along and participate. The Clifton College rules of rugby were explained in the Cliftonian magazine of 1875, including:

Rule 25. The match is won by either side obtaining two goals.

Rule 27. All matches are drawn after five days' play, or after three days, if no goal has been kicked by either side.

Rule 31. Masters may play in any match with the consent of heads of the side.

Regular matches were played: Sixth v School, Classical v Modern, School-House v School, Twenty-two v School, Choir v School, with others of a more scratch character, such as A to K v The Rest. There were a few foreign matches, mostly when Old

[3] The old term for scrummage. Scrimmage was derived from the word skirmish.

Rugbeians from Oxford University and Old Cliftonians would put together scratch sides.

After the first International between England and Scotland on 27th March 1871 and the first 'Varsity' match between Oxford and Cambridge on 10th February 1872, there was a surge of interest in the game of rugby amongst the public. This was what prompted the resurrection of the Clifton club. It was Clifton College masters and former pupils who were largely responsible for the foundation of the present club in 1872, and with them they brought the rules, symbols and names borrowed from Rugby School.

Clifton College rugby players in 1872-73. Many of these went on to play for Clifton RFC

Foundation and Early Days

In early September 1872 a notice was circulated among the citizens of the Clifton area of Bristol, which read: "It is proposed to form a Football Club for the ensuing season. A Meeting will be held at the King's Arms, Redland on Friday 27th inst at 7.30 pm to take the necessary steps for arranging same. Your attendance is requested by the undersigned, D. Walsh Jnr, W.S. Paul, W.J.G. Lovell, G.A. Newall, F. Evans, W.R. Webb, M.M. Curtis, W.M. Bird, W.S. Young, E.C. Parker - The Committee pro tem" (Hawkins, 1909, p.1).

That evening 20 people met at the pub on Blackboy Hill and unanimously voted to form Clifton Rugby Club. Ten rules were drawn up, based on Clifton College rules except that an alteration was made to Rule 19 to the effect that "no kicking or tripping be allowed".

The King's Arms, Blackboy Hill in 1885.

The ten signatories to the letter calling for the meeting which founded the club were as follows:

David Henry Walsh, see 'Clifton Families' chapter.
Walter Stuckey Paul and **Michael Martyn Curtis**, see 'Famous Players' chapter

William Joseph Gale Lovell was born in 1853 in Bristol. He was apprenticed as a clerk to a timber merchant. After what must have been a difficult period of unemployment, he was by his late 40s a director of a timber company in Derbyshire, married with two daughters and a son. When Clifton RFC was established he became the club's first secretary. His brother John J. Lovell was also a member of the club from 1872.
George A. Newall was the club's first treasurer and had the distinction of scoring its first ever try. He was born around 1851 in Scotland and spent a few short months at Clifton College in 1863 before becoming a civil engineer.
Frank Evans was born in 1853 in Berkshire. He was the eldest brother of Clifton RFC and Scotland International Herbert Lavington Evans.
William Robert Webb was born on 1st March 1852 in Bristol and was educated at Clifton College from 1865 to 1869. An insurance manager, he and his wife Florence had three daughters and four sons, at least two of which (Wilbert Maitland and Douglas Maitland) also went to Clifton College. William Webb died in 1894.
Walter Montague Bird was born on 20th September 1854 in Masulipatam, India. Educated at Clifton College from 1864 to 1871, he married Edith Wills and became a solicitor and J.P. He died in 1936.
Alexander Stewart Ward Young was born on 14th February 1852, the son of an army surgeon. He was educated at Clifton College from 1863 to 1868 and later rose to the rank of Lieutenant Colonel in the Royal Army Medical Corps.
Edward C. Parker was born about 1853 in Bristol and became a coach painter, married to Sophia and with five children. He died in 1915 in Devonport.

There were twelve Honorary Members elected at that first meeting, two who wished to be anonymous. The ten who 'went public' are listed below.

James Fuller Eberle, born on 11th December 1854 and educated at Clifton College from April to December 1864, was the son of an immigrant Moravian minister. He had a distinguished civil career, serving as an Alderman of the City of Bristol. He was awarded the O.B.E., the Order of the Russian Red Cross in 1918 and was appointed Freeman of the City of Bristol in 1938.

He died on 21st April 1939 at 110 Pembroke Road, Clifton. His Memorial Service was held at Emmanuel Church, Clifton on 25th April 1939 and he was buried at Canford Cemetery, Bristol.

Refer to the 'Clifton Families' chapter for details of his three sons who all excelled in their club careers.

James Fuller Eberle

Alexander Walsh was the brother of signatory David Henry Walsh. He was born on 29th June 1851 and educated at Clifton College from 1863 to 1864.

Edward C. Parker was also a signatory - see above for details.

Edmund Gill was born in Clifton in 1849 and married Anna; they had three sons and three daughters. He worked as a commercial clerk and from 1895 as a secretary's clerk at the Bristol Royal Infirmary.

Albert Hall was born about 1839 and worked as a ship's store merchant and storekeeper.

Andrew John Biggs Weston was born in Bristol in 1846. He ran a lead smelting and ironmongery business, employing 62 men and boys. His sons John Cartland Weston (1871-1932) and Howard Cartland Weston (1872-1947) were both educated at Clifton College, but neither played for Clifton RFC. By 1901 he had moved to Kings Norton, Worcestershire where his wife Miranda was born.

Renault St. John Hall was a stockbroker born in 1845 and based at Liverpool Chambers in Bristol. He was a cousin of the signatory William Webb. He later moved to London and into the world of gold mining. He was convicted of libel at the Old Bailey on 2nd March 1885 and sentenced to 2 months imprisonment. He died in 1918 in Somerset.

Richard Ellison Strachan was born on 25th August 1815 in Bristol. He was the father of Clifton's first captain, Charles Strachan, and worked as an oil merchant. The family – wife Mary, four sons and two daughters - lived at Wick House on Durdham Down. Strachan was the brother-in-law of fellow Honorary Member, James Fuller Eberle, and died on 22nd January 1892.

Above: Richard Ellison Strachan

George H. Newall was born around 1800 in Scotland and married – comparatively late in life – Eliza who was 27 years his junior. Even with this tardy start they managed at least three daughters and a son, George A. Newall, Clifton's first Treasurer. All the family's children were born in Scotland – George had worked as a merchant and it was presumably work that brought him to Bristol in the 1860s.

Frederick Heygate Nunneley was born about 1837 in Boston, Lincolnshire. He was unmarried and worked as a solicitor at Whitson Chambers in Nicholas Street.

The original club badge of 1872 used the club's initials CFC, with the last C mirrored just as the Clifton College badge of CC had the second C mirrored - a badge used by the College until just after the Second World War.

Left: the original Clifton College rugby badge. Right: the original Clifton Rugby Football Club badge.

The crescent moon club crest and the club's motto were adopted in 1873. The origin of the motto is unknown, but at the time of the club's formation the honorary secretary was A.C.St. Paul, who was ex-Clifton College and perhaps a classical scholar. He turned the well known Latin saying *Dum Vivimus Vivamus* "Let us live while we live" (meaning "let us enjoy life") into *Dum Ludimus Ludamus* "While we play let us play" (Giles, 1972, p51). Several crescent moons adorn the buildings around Clifton College so it is not unreasonable to assume a connection. The past president Colonel Castle's view was that it had been a happy flight of fancy, possibly based on the heraldic definition of the crescent as "a bearing in the form of a young or new moon". It is well-nigh certain, in fact, that the Clifton RFC badge was copied from the symbol that Clifton College had in its turn borrowed from Rugby School; after all, the first headmaster and many Clifton College teaching staff came from Rugby School.

There still exists in the town of Rugby today a Crescent School, originally intended, when founded in 1947, to provide a place of education for the young children of Rugby School masters. It was first housed there in the 'Old Sanitarium' on Horton Crescent, and is now an Independent Day School for 4-11 year-olds. However this symbol goes back much further at Rugby. It is the emblem for School Field (Rupert Brooke's House), and has been in existence since before 1852 when the current House was built at the edge of School Close. House crests evolved in the 1840s, when sports uniforms were first introduced. Houses, created by Thomas Arnold, took the name of their Housemaster; when Percival, Clifton College's first headmaster, taught as an assistant master at Rugby School in the 1860s, the first House was named Arnold's (after C.T. Arnold).

Clifton is not the only rugby club to pay homage to Rugby School in this way. The skull and crossbones feature on another Rugby School badge (School House) and were included in the first badge of the original 1869 Clifton club, as well as in that of the Barbarians. Rugby School's symbolic influence runs so deep that the England national team wears all white (as did Rugby School). The England badge featuring a red rose was taken from the Rugby School crest, which in turn borrowed it from the coat of arms of its founder Lawrence Sherriff (c. 1510-1567), an Elizabethan gentleman and grocer to Elizabeth 1. During his lifetime he amassed a great fortune, but remained childless. He stipulated in his will that his estate should be used to found almshouses and a school "to serve chiefly for the children of Rugby and Brownsover... and next for such as be of other places hereunto adjoyneing". This legacy provided for the foundation of Rugby School.

Above: Clifton College in 1872

Having been founded in 1872, Clifton RFC is not the oldest surviving rugby club in the south-west of England; Bath was founded seven years earlier. Clifton in fact stands 31st in the list, jointly with Cambridge University, Lansdowne, Penryn, University College Cork and Exeter which also date back to 1872. The Llanelli club was established in 1872 but neglected to play a recorded game until 1876.

Clifton Rugby Club was founded for the sons of Gentlemen. To become a member one had to be proposed and seconded by existing members, who had been educated without exception at public schools and who came from families that produced well-known, respected and valuable citizens. Its philosophy was one of enjoyment, of playing the game for its own sake; a philosophy reflected in the club motto. The book "50 Years with Clifton Rugby Club" tells us that "if your ambition is to play each week before thousands of spectators, then Clifton is not your club. Clifton never has, and we trust never will, place its spectators' interest before its players' enjoyment. To explain – a Club which has to consider "gates" cannot afford to arrange fixtures with the various Public Schools, and Clifton's list would not be complete without Clifton College, Cheltenham College, Sherbourne, Marlborough, Blundell's etc." Arthur Budd, the ex-Clifton College and Clifton RFC player, who became the President of the Rugby Football Union, would later use this philosophy in his argument against professionalism. According to Budd, "sport" is "a recreation pursued for love of itself and devoid of emolument" (Hawkins, 1922, p.140).

During those early days it was not unusual for children to play the 20-a-side game; it was considered character-building. The Peck brothers, Francis and Herbert, were just 14 and 15 years old respectively when they appeared in the club's 1st XV in 1873.

William Proctor Baker

At the December 1872 meeting of the club it was proposed that the Mayor of Bristol be asked to accept the position of Club President, William Proctor Baker started a tradition that would last until the position became more permanent with the appointment of Harry Beloe on 11th May 1891.

The club finished its first season undefeated, and in fact during the first five seasons only five matches were lost. Until 1875, games were decided solely on the basis of the number of goals scored. The scoring of a try merely gave the team the opportunity to kick at goal.

Clifton 1st XV in 1873-74. (L-R) Back Row: W.G. Gribble, F. Allen, W.R. Webb, A.S.W. Young, W.S. Paul, F.S. Peck, C. Strachan (captain), W.F. Bence-Jones, A.H. Allen, A.C.S. Paul, E. Phillips, H.W. Peck. Front Row: F. Morris, H.A. Francis, W.N.Tribe, T.R. Barnes, C.A. Badcocke.

This was the first ever photograph of a Clifton RFC team, and included nine players who had been Clifton College pupils. James Arthur Bush was away for most of this season on tour with the MCC in Australia, a trip that also served as a honeymoon for W.G. Grace and his wife.

The fixture list in 1873-74 included several teams that no longer exist, namely Sydney College, Bedminster, Bath Rovers, Ashley and Swindon Rangers.

Clifton 1st XV in 1874-75. (L-R) Back Row: E. Townsend, F. Allen, J.G. Thomson, E. Phillips, J.H. Powell, W.R. Webb, A.H. Allen, W.S. Paul, J.G. Budd, W.R. Gribble, A.K. Butterworth. Seated: E.J. Taylor, M.M. Curtis, C. Strachan, A.C.St. Paul, J.A. Bush. On the ground: F. Morris, C. Chamberlain, J. Curtis, J.D. Miller.

On 6th March 1875, the West of England played Oxford University. The West were represented by: J.A. Bush (captain), A.K. Butterworth, J. Curtis, J.D. Miller, W.S. Paul, E.J. Taylor (all Clifton), W. Boughton and J.P. Riddiford (both Gloucester), J.S. Udal (Birmingham), A. Bailey and C. Grindron (both Worcester), W. Carless and P. Giles (both Hereford), C. Barton and P. Goodwin (both Kidderminster). M.M. Curtis (Clifton) and J. Hartley (Gloucester) were both selected but unable to play. The following Monday Clifton played Oxford University in their last match of the season and lost by six tries to nil. However because rugby results were based on goals scored the match was deemed a draw. The season ended with Clifton unbeaten.

Clifton 1st XV in 1875-76. (L-R) Back Row: E.P. Warren, H. Nash, W. Fairbanks, E. Phillips, W. Strachan, E.J. Taylor, W.S. Paul, W.R. Webb, J.H. Dunn, J. Curtis, M. Curtis, F. Morris, J.G. Thomson. Seated: R.E. Bush, C. Strachan, A.C.St. Paul, J.D. Miller. On the ground: W.R. Gribble, J.A. Bush.

The above photograph shows E.J. Taylor, J.D. Miller, and M.M. Curtis, who took part in the North versus South England trial match at Whalley Range, Manchester, wearing South of England shirts. This trial also featured Alexander Butterworth of Marlborough Nomads who was later to join Clifton. The match ended with a victory for the North, courtesy of a try scored by J.R. Hay Gordon of Liverpool. J.A. Bush, wearing his England shirt, is joined in this photograph by his brother Edwin Bush as well as by Cambridge Rugby Blue Walter Fairbanks.

This season was one of the most successful in the club's history. Of 23 games played, 17 were won, five drawn and only one lost, away to Rugby. Clifton scored 40 goals and 50 tries against two goals and four tries.

Clifton 1st XV in 1877-78. (L-R) Back Row: F.S. Peck, E.P. Warren, A. Fry, A. Nash, W.N. Tribe, G.M. Butterworth, J.C. Gilmore, A.U. Plant, H.W. Ward, E.J. Taylor, W. Strachan, E.W. Ball. Front Row: A. Francis, J.D. Miller (Captain), C.A. Badcocke.

The above photograph shows John Miller in his first season as captain.

It was on 28th September 1878 that the Gloucester County Football Union was formed at The Bell Hotel in Gloucester. The meeting was instigated by T.F. Brown of Gloucester and J.D. Miller of Clifton. A trial match took place on November 13th 1878 at the Gloucester Spa ground between a XV selected from the North of the County (nine Gloucester players, three from Cheltenham and three from Stroud) and a side from the South of the County (eight Clifton players, four from Rockleaze and three from the Royal Agricultural College) . From this trial a Gloucestershire County side was selected to play Somerset on 2nd January 1879, with six Clifton players including the captain John Day Miller. All the captains of Gloucestershire were to be Clifton men until 1889 (Hutt, 1978, p2)

Clifton 1st XV 1879-80. (L-R) Back Row: H.L. Evans, G.V. Cox, H.C.M. Hirst, G.M. Butterworth, H.W.R. Gribble, J.P. Bush, E. Leonard, H.W. Peck, J.C.R. Scott, W. Strachan, F.S. Peck, W.O. Moberly. Front Row: E.W. Ball, J.E. Bush, J.D. Miller, E.P. Warren.

Clifton's status is reflected in the presence of England International W.O. Moberly, Scotland International H.L. Evans and Oxford Rugby Blue Graeme Vassall Cox in this team.

Prospects were good, but the club's performance fell away in 1885. Despite efforts to improve matters, the club was forced to move to a new ground which did at least allow it to start charging for admission. The club won only four matches out of 15 in 1885-86, compared to 13 out of 17 the previous season. The main problem was that the club ground was outside the City of Bristol and it was difficult for spectators to get there. Closer to the city were the Downs where the majority of the other rugby teams in Bristol played. The quality of rugby here was getting better and the Carlton club in particular was improving quickly.

The Bristol Harlequins Football Club, in its first season, held a dinner in April 1886 at the Don Cossack Hotel in Redcliff Street, at which one of the Carlton Football Club's representatives first proposed that a town football club be established. During the 1887-88 season the Carlton 1st XV had only lost two matches of 20, and its 2nd XV lost not one of its 17 matches. The newspapers were calling for a city side. The Carlton club decided to invite Redland Park and Westbury Park to join forces with them to form a town club at its monthly meeting at the Montpelier Hotel on 11th April 1888. At the

Queen's Hotel in Clifton on May 3rd 1888, Redland Park met Carlton and agreed to amalgamate to form Bristol Football Club.

The Clifton 1st XV in 1887-88 with Clifton, Gloucestershire Captain and England International Hiatt Cowles Baker.

Before the start of the season, on the 26th September 1888 the Bristol Mercury commented

last season convinced authorities that there really was talent in Bristol of an exceptional nature, only it was scattered amongst various clubs, the consequence being that we really had no first-rate team but two or three very good second-rate teams. Clifton have always been recognised as the team, but after the close matches played between them and the Carlton and Redland Park Clubs, it seems that there was a distinction with very little difference amongst the three teams. But now Clifton must beware! The time has come, I think, when there will be a distinction with a great deal of difference, and all doubt will be removed as to which club is entitled to represent Bristol. The Carlton and Redland Park Clubs have amalgamated and forced the nucleus of a long felt want – a Bristol team.

It then made the proposition

it is hoped support will be accorded the club, and that inter-club jealousy will be laid aside. I say let every man who is a promising player join the Bristol Club, and if he is picked play for his town. Surely this would be strengthening football in Bristol much more than going on in the old style, where each club possessed half-a-dozen good men and the remainder of the team not so good.

On the same page, in a preview of the Clifton season, the newspaper said

Mr H.C. Baker will again captain this club, the members of which will, unfortunately, still retain their field at the end of Westbury Down, which being so much out the way, is a great drawback. Mr W.H. Birch, the secretary, has a strong list of fixtures waiting to be published, including Cardiff, Gloucester, Wellington, Swindon, Bristol and Weston-super-Mare. Mr Baker will doubtless be able to select from his 100 men a strong XV, and he will, I believe, try some new men; but it is doubtful whether they will compensate him for the loss of E.D. Lace, who played so well at full back, and that wonderful little half-back Troup, who, to the regret of footballites and cricketers generally is leaving Bristol.

The Bristol team trained every Tuesday, working on skills such as passing, dribbling and kicking, and again every Thursday with a cross-country run for fitness training. The matches they had lined up were tough, and included a northern tour against some of the leading clubs in the country.

The first match between Bristol and Clifton was postponed, but on 23rd March 1889 they finally met at Clifton's ground, Leach's Field in Westbury-on-Trym. Clifton was a team combining youth and experience - Gloucestershire county players, including the captain and England International, Hiatt Cowles Baker, and England triallists - against a team with very little experience that had only played together for seven months, moreover a team that had been outplayed the previous season when Clifton took on a Bristol United side of mostly Carlton, Redland Park and Westbury Park players. Bristol had no internationals and no county players, but won the match. Some Clifton supporters swapped allegiance.

It wasn't just the Clifton Club that was troubled, but English rugby in general. There were ructions at the Rugby Football Union, with ex Clifton College and Clifton RFC player Arthur Budd, who had become Vice President of the RFU from 1886-1888 and President in 1888-89, being one of the instigators. England had refused to join an international board, taking the lofty view that the numerical predominance of English clubs meant that English administrators could not be expected to join such a board on equal terms. Deadlock ensued and England played no matches with other unions in

1887-88 or 1888-89. The RFU still selected and awarded caps to players for non-existent matches. Some players who were awarded caps never played for England.

Arthur Budd would be a vocal supporter of amateurism to his dying day. He enjoyed great success when he coached Oxford University in the 1880s. Harry Vassall, the England captain, recalled that he had demanded "constant practice...crowds of men [were] ready to play six days a week. If given the chance, the difficulty was to stop them getting too much practice". A columnist from the left-wing weekly *Clarion* asked why losing was so unacceptable if the game was supposed to be enjoyed for its own sake. This philosophy of amateurism was one that Clifton had adopted from the beginning, but which would split English rugby (Richards, 2007, p77).

At the Full Moon, North Street, on 19th May 1890, representatives of Bristol, Oakfield, Hornets, Knowle, Lodway, Clifton Crusaders and Carlton Rugby Clubs met to discuss the formation of a Rugby Union for Bristol and a more representative city team. One proposal agreed at this meeting was that 25 per cent of all subscriptions would go to Bristol Football Club, and another agreement gave the club the right to ask any player from the other union clubs to play for Bristol, which further strengthened the finances and playing strength of the Bristol club. Although Clifton supported the Bristol Rugby Union, it refused to join.

The Clifton 1st XV in 1892-93. (L-R) Back Row: ?, Frederick Charles Belson, ?, W.P. Gwynne, ?, T. Jones, B.H. Belson. Seated: F. Borwick, Edward Panter-Downes, Henry Lawrence Weekes Norrington, Edward Payne Press, William Wyamar Vaughan, Edward Barff, C. Parkes-Smith. On the ground: Albert Stewart Hume. The original of the above photograph (entitled Clifton Rugby Football Club with A.S.H 1893) is part of the Hume Collection (UQFL10) and is reproduced courtesy of the Fryer Library, University of Queensland, Brisbane, Australia.

During the 1890s things only got worse. Clifton struggled to find a permanent home, playing on five grounds during this decade. Perhaps the worst season was 1892-93 when the club had to move to the suburb of Fishponds to play. The club was in debt, and the bad weather at the start of the season meant cancelled fixtures and the loss of revenue. Throughout this decade the 1st XV would sometimes struggle to field a full side. First team players Birch, Ford and Hunt moved to Bristol.

At a general meeting of the club there was a motion to wind it up because of the debts of £24 17s. 10d. The motion was voted out and a fund was started to clear the club's debts, after which things started to improve. Eventually 21 matches were played and only eight were lost.

The Clifton 1st XV 1893-94. (L-R) Back Row: (L-R): W. James, F. Belson, N. Cooper, H.B.F. Bingham, W. Bunbury, W.P. Gwynne, A.B. Cridland, T. Jones. Front Row: W.W. Vaughan, B.H. Belson, W.J. Lias, H.L. Norrington, H. Bacchus, C. Rogers. On the ground: C.W.W. James.

Between 1893 and 1896 Clifton's home ground was Buffalo Bill's Field. Ironically the only known photographs of the ground during this period were taken at matches when Bristol borrowed the ground because its own home ground at the County Cricket Club was unavailable.

The second game at Buffalo Bill's Field, the following week, produced a 5-3 win against Bath. Later in the season the club would beat Bath 6-0 away at Henrietta Park, but results were a little erratic and included a rare loss to Clifton College by 2 goals to 2 tries.

A complaint levelled at Clifton by the local newspapers at this time was its use of guest players to bolster the side for important fixtures. Unfortunately these same newspapers seemed conveniently to ignore the fact that Bristol was indulging in its own spot of bolstering of Bristol Rugby Union players from the Oakfield, Hornets, Knowle, Lodway, Clifton Crusaders and Carlton clubs. Even Clifton would periodically help out its rival by the loan of players to Bristol.

Rugby in England changed dramatically in 1895 when the Northern Union was formed, an event prompted by the RFU declaring payments to players to be illegal. This declaration had its origins in the RFU General Meeting nine years previously, when Arthur Budd was a member of the sub-committee set up to draft new laws to outlaw all forms of payment. 200 delegates attended this meeting at the Westminster Palace Hotel on 4th October 1886. Budd is quoted as saying in 1897 "the Northern Union is a most admirable drainpipe. A man who would cook accounts would steal your watch, and is capable of any kind of inequity. We are well rid of such persons." The consequence of the Northern Union's birth was that England lost the majority of the country's clubs and players; total RFU membership almost halved, from 481 clubs in 1893 to 244 a decade later (Richards, 2007, p81). In the fifteen seasons leading up to the schism, England had won twenty-three matches and lost nine against the other three nations, winning three Triple Crowns along the way. Over the next fifteen seasons, it won twelve and lost twenty-nine, with no Triple Crown or championship until the fifteenth year, 1910.

Moving to the North View ground in 1899 provided much needed stability for Clifton, but the club's record remained erratic. The 1900-01 season was one of the poorest on record, with only four games won out of 20. However, the advent of a new era at the club was marked with the appointment of key committee members and new players. Before the 1901-02 season commenced, players began to join in large numbers with the result that, rather than it continuing to be difficult to raise two teams (indeed sometimes even one), three XVs had to be organised in order to find games for the younger members. One of the highlights of this era came on September 26th 1903 when Clifton beat Gloucester at Kingsholm (see the Famous Matches chapter).

The Clifton 1st XV in 1906-07. (L-R) Back Row: T. Miller, F.L. Mullaly, E.W. Baker, F.T. Boucher, A.J. Gardner, P.T. Rowe, V.F. Eberle, F.J. Hannam. Seated: G.F. Matthews, E. Briggs, P.H. Thomas, P.J. Slee, E.J.G. Higham, E.N.N. Sellman, A. Reid. On the ground: L.G. Dimmer, Cecil W. Baker, A. Gardiner, E.F. Eberle.

After 1912, for various reasons there was a decline in English rugby. The three southern hemisphere countries, Australia, New Zealand and South Africa, shared between themselves the top IRB World Ranking until the rise of Clive Woodward's England side in 2002, excepting one day's leadership by France in 1987 and two weeks' by England in 1995. Either South Africa or New Zealand led for 77 of the 79 years between 1912 and 1991 (Richards, 2007, p111).

During the seasons 1912-13 and 1913-14 there had been a decline in the club's fortunes. There were plenty of playing members, and in the final season before the war the club ran four sides, but the club had however lost several high-quality players who were not being replaced by players of the same ability. The 1913-14 season was very disappointing, with only four games won against town clubs and the 1st XV's leading scorer notching only four tries.

The Clifton 1st XV in 1913-14. (L-R) Back Row: F.D. Andrews, E. Taylor, C.M. Welsby, N. Durant, H.V. Thomas, F.S. Woodley, A.B. Sellman. Seated: G.H. Gibbs, V.F. Eberle, J.A. Dommett, Mr.H.W. Beloe, R.S. Witchell, H.H. Hutchinson. On the ground: G.E. Cripps, G.C. Watson, E.H. Addenbrooke, R.I. Hawkins.

The future may not have been looking good for the club, but events abroad were about to change history and put Clifton's troubles firmly in perspective.

By the beginning of the August Bank Holiday in 1914, the worsening news had started panic-buying in Bristol. Players who were members of the Bristol Territorials were set to leave for a fortnight's training camp. On Sunday 2nd August 1914 the 4th (City of Bristol) Battalion of the Gloucestershire Regiment paraded at 7am. Half an hour later their train left Temple Meads station to take them to their camp in Minehead. On Bank Holiday Monday they were called back to Bristol and all camps were cancelled. Large crowds assembled at Temple Meads. The following day it was clear to most people that war was imminent; news of the invasion of Belgium by Germany was in all the papers, and Britain had given Germany an ultimatum to withdraw. The appointed time passed, and Britain declared war on Germany following her 'unsatisfactory reply' (Lloyd George's description of the response). The Army immediately took over Avonmouth Docks and the city's railway stations. All Bristol's Territorial's were now in the regular army and a huge recruitment drive started.

Rugby's response across the country was rapid: the RFU suspended all matches with immediate effect. Many other sports continued, causing outrage in some quarters. The Football Association held off from suspending fixtures until after the 25th April 1915 FA Cup final when Sheffield United beat Chelsea (Richards, 2007, p.106). The only concession made to the war was to move this final from London to Manchester. The cup was awarded by the Earl of Derby whose speech, largely drowned out by a noisy crowd of young supporters, noted that all present needed to join together and play "a sterner game for England". A local Sheffield newspaper branded the team "a disgrace to the city".

Imperial Tobacco was one of the first companies to announce that any employee required to join the Army, Navy, or any national service would receive from the company whatever money was necessary to top up his service pay to the same level as his Bristol wages. The company also announced that it would hold open every single serviceman's job until their return to Bristol.

The British Expeditionary Force landed in France on 17th August. Everyone said it would be over by Christmas.

World War I Roll of Honour

It was on 28th June 1914 in Sarajevo that Gavrilo Princip, a Bosnian Serb student, killed Archduke Franz Ferdinand, the heir to the Austro-Hungarian throne. The assassination set in motion a series of fast-moving events that escalated within two months into a full-scale European and eventually worldwide war. Austria-Hungary demanded action by Serbia to punish those responsible and, satisfaction not having been provided, declared war. Conflict between the major European powers broke out within weeks because of overlapping agreements for collective defence and the complex nature of international alliances. Great Britain declared war on Germany on 4th August 1914 and sent a relatively small force to France and Belgium. It was almost Britain's entire standing army at the time, perhaps 120,000 men, and small in relation to the French and German armies which were each in the process of mobilising five million men. The Kaiser was so disparaging about the tiny British Army contribution that he declared he would not bother to engage his army with it but would send his 'gendarmerie' to arrest it!

This photograph was mailed as a postcard on 25th August 1914. On the reverse the names are shown as 'back row Ellis (*perhaps 17 year-old Francis Arthur Ellis, ex Clifton College*), Cripps (*Clifton player George E. Cripps*), Sainsbury, Eberle (*Clifton player Victor Fuller Eberle*); front row Mortimer Savory (*younger brother of the Clifton player J.H. Savory*), Ellerton (*Clifton player Frank Ellerton*), Robinson'. The card was sent from their training camp in Chelmsford prior to leaving for France and Belgium.

My dearest M——, this is just to show you what a nights work is like. You start from the hut about 6 o/c & having got the waggons loaded with tools & material you start off along the road out of the village. After 2 miles you get to the X roads beyond which the carts may not go & then you have to carry all the stuff & the carts go home. You may soon pass a burning farm house, as you pass the firing line blazing away & lighting all the country round. The road soon gets very bad with shell holes & the signal coy. have a way of pulling their wires to the trenches rather too low for comfort. Shortly after that you get into the danger zone & branch off the road into fields over muddy paths towards the trenches. Thus you have to be v. careful when the lights go up & plop

These are not tortoises!

shell shell

Down in the mud at once, the whole lot of you. Well, you might start on some old trenches & start baling knee deep in mud. I got v. badly stuck in a field drain the other day & R—— had to pull me out or I might still be there.

JHS R.

G Trenches

our Trenches

Some of your men wd. go in front of the trenches putting up wire entanglements. This is an unpleasant job as you see the enemy's rifles firing in your direction. With luck you find ten minutes to smoke a welcome cigarette in a handy dug out. On the way back you report at Batt. H.Q. One isn't there & the "dining room" is of the top rooms the ceiling of like this owing to an erstwhile shrapnel shell. On the way up yesterday, some shrapnel came unpleasantly close, so we all hopped into the road side ditch for cover till it was over. Then at the X roads you find an empty pontoon waggon waiting to carry you home an excellent institution & you smoke a pipe of contentment.

You reach "home" a regular scarecrow of mud & damp just about cock crow. M—— gives you a splendid hot breakfast & raises perhaps some warm water for a wash & then you spend the rest of the day like this. H.S.

March 1915. CHEER-O!

Clifton player Harry Savory's illustrated account of life as a sapper, a letter sent to his mother on 15th March 1915. During the small hours of 1st April he was shot through the neck by a stray bullet but fortunately survived and was invalided home; the situation and injury sound eerily similar to the circumstances of Hugh Parr's death the following month.

A large number of Clifton players joined the 4th Glosters as privates, and for several months a platoon in "D" Company was almost entirely composed of club members who wanted to fight together as they had played together (Hawkins, 1909).

On the following pages we provide an account of those members of Clifton Rugby Football Club who made the ultimate sacrifice. These accounts are drawn from research we have conducted over several years, and we are most grateful to families and friends of those named who have been so willing to help in providing information and photographs. We recognise it will never be a comprehensive history, but in our research we have uncovered several facts which had not previously come to light. In some cases we have also come closer to understanding events which may have previously been misunderstood or confused in the heat and aftermath of the war.

1914

Lieutenant Colonel Edward Martin Panter-Downes 26th August 1914
Edward Panter-Downes was born on 3rd December 1872 at Rushford Rectory, Thetford, Norfolk and was educated at Clifton College from 1885 to 1890. He trained at Sandhurst, and joined the Royal Irish Regiment.

Having joined Clifton RFC in the 1890-91 season, he was a regular 1st XV player from 1892 to 1894 and its Vice-Captain in 1892-93. He played in the first match on the new Clifton ground at Fishponds against Taunton on 24th September 1892 and for Clifton v

Bristol at Buffalo Bill's Field on 23rd September 1893, in what was the first rugby match ever played there.

Lt.-Colonel Panter-Downes, C.O. of the 2nd Royal Irish Regiment died on 26th August 1914 during the retreat from Mons, only three weeks after the start of World War 1. He was killed in action at the Battle of Le Chateau. General Smith-Dorrien decided to turn around the retreating British Expeditionary Force and make a stand. The greatly fatigued condition of his troops – they had been fighting a retreat for several days by this stage - convinced Smith-Dorrien that, psychologically as well as tactically, a fighting stand was appropriate.

Germany artillery began the action at dawn the next day, 26th August, across the eight miles of essentially open ground held by Smith-Dorrien's forces. The barrage continued until noon before German infantry began to advance. Fighting predominantly with rifles fired from shallow trenches prepared hastily (a tactic similarly employed with great success at Mons), the British managed to greatly slow the advance of the German infantry, to the extent that Smith-Dorrien was able to organise a strategic retreat during the late afternoon despite overwhelming odds and in the absence of flank protection.

Losses however were high on both sides, including 7,812 British casualties. Nevertheless the German forces suffered not only losses inmanpower but, crucially, a further delay of their planned advance on Paris.

The British Expeditionary Force's Commander-in-Chief, Sir John French, had specifically ordered a continued retreat on the evening of 25th August and, despite the relative success of the action, resented Smith-Dorrien's decision to fight. An acrimonious argument sprang up between the two men, ultimately leading to Smith-Dorrien's removal from command on the pretext of ill-health.

Edward is remembered on the La Ferté-sous-Jouarre Memorial located on the south bank of the River Marne, on the outskirts of the commune of La Ferté-sous-Jouarre, 66 kilometres east of Paris. His name is missing from the Clifton RFC War Memorial.

His daughter Mollie, who was only eight years old when he died, became a writer. For 50 years she wrote a regular feature called 'Letter from London' for the *New Yorker*, as well as book reviews and over 30 short stories.

Lieutenant William Stanley Yalland 23rd October 1914
Stanley Yalland was born in Bristol on 27th June 1889 at The Manor House, Fishponds. His father Thomas was a building contractor. Stanley was educated at Clifton College from 1903 to 1906 and joined Clifton Rugby Club in 1910-11; his younger brother Robert had already joined in 1903-04. He played cricket on one

occasion for Gloucestershire on 1st - 3rd August 1910, v Somerset at the County Ground in Bristol. The match was drawn – Stanley scored a solitary run.

He was commissioned in December 1912, a Lieutenant in the Gloucestershire Regiment 1st Battalion ("Glosters") and was drafted to Belgium in the early days of the war. On 23rd October 1914 a surprise German advance had ousted the Coldstream Guards from their positions at Langemarck, and they were stubbornly fighting back in a turnip field. Two platoons of Glosters under a Captain Rising moved to assist them. Exposed on one flank, the Glosters were repeatedly attacked but fought off every assault. Stanley was killed whilst leading an attack on a German trench; the Germans were repulsed but the battalion lost three officers and 51 men. By that evening the Coldstream trenches had been re-taken.

Stanley Yalland is commemorated on the Ypres (Menin Gate) Memorial and his name is also recorded on the War Memorial at Fishponds. His name was moved on the Clifton Rugby Memorial from the bottom to replace the name of Warren Chetham-Strode.

Captain Arthur Edward Jeune Collins 11th November 1914

Arthur Collins was born on 18th August 1885 in Hazaribagh in the eastern state of Jharkhand, India. His father was Arthur Herbert Collins, a judge in the Indian Civil Service who died when his four children, three boys and a girl, were still young. His mother, Esther, brought the family up at 29 Beaufort Road in Clifton, and on the strength of her pension Arthur was educated at Clifton College from 1897 to 1902. He became famous as a cricketer in June 1899 when, as a 13 year old schoolboy, he scored 628 not out, spread over four afternoons, in a Junior House match between Clark's House and North Town, to this day the highest recorded individual cricket score.

Arthur was gazetted 2nd Lieutenant in the Royal Engineers in 1904, and promoted Lieutenant in 1907. He married Ethel Slater in the Spring of 1914, and was sent to France when war broke out later that year.

On 11th November 1914 his company (5th Company, Royal Engineers, of which he was then in command, his senior officers having been killed or wounded), was called up to help thrust the enemy back at Polygon Wood, near Ypres. It was whilst signalling for reinforcements during this action that he was killed at the age of 29. Like so many others, his body was never found but his name is recorded at the Menin Gate Memorial in Ypres. His name is missing from the Clifton RFC War Memorial.

Tragically both his brothers, Herbert and Norman, were also killed in the war.

1915

Major Ernest Gardiner 2nd March 1915
Ernest was born on 16th March 1880 in Bristol. He was the son of Thomas Chapple Gardiner and Sarah Bishop Gardiner, of "Waratah", Beaufort Road, Clifton, and husband of Kathleen Eleanor. He joined Clifton Rugby Club in 1900-01.

His father owned several ironmongery businesses in Bristol called Gardiner & Sons Ltd. In 1972 the company merged with Haskins Furniture to become Gardiner Haskins Homecentre, one of the largest stores in Bristol. Ernest was an assistant in his father's firm.

He joined the South Midland Royal Engineers (SMRE), 1st Field Company. He was killed at St Eloi, near Ypres, during skirmishes between the first and second major battles in the area. Ernest has no known grave.

You will have heard by now of our misfortunes during that
Scrap at the beginning of the week. (Richards & I were of
Course in for the first night as we finished up the last
spell.) The following morning the men brought back the
news of Gardiner's death, I think it was from a bomb
We can still hardly realize it & it is much too sad for me
to try to write about just now. We all feel rather mournful
but of Course have to keep ourselves & the men as cheerful
as possible under the circumstances. Cyril Haygood wrote
his people the following day & by now I think they must
have heard about it. Please on no account let this
letter be the means of their getting the news.
Then you will have heard too that Crewe has left here
he got hit across the nose, thank God it is not serious

An account of Ernest Gardiner's death was included in a letter home from Clifton RFC team-mate JH (Harry) Savory. It says *You will have heard by now of our misfortunes during that scrap at the beginning of the week. (Richards and I were of course in for the first night as we finished up the last spell.) The following morning the men bought back the news of Gardiner's death. I think it was from a bomb. We can still hardly realize it and it is much too sad for me to try to write about just now. We all feel rather mournful but of course have to keep ourselves and the men as cheerful as possible under the circumstances. Cyril Hosegood wrote his people the following day and by now I think they must have heard about it. Please on no account let this letter be the means of their getting the news. Then you will have heard too that Owen has left here. He got hit across the nose, thank God it is not serious.*

Ernest Gardiner is commemorated on the Ypres (Menin Gate) Memorial.

His nephew Christopher Gardiner went on to become Managing Director of Gardiner & Sons and to play for Clifton Rugby Club.

Lieutenant Hugh Wharton Myddleton Parr 5th May 1915

Born on 14th October 1881, Hugh was the youngest child of the Rev. Robert Henning Parr, first Vicar of St. Martin's, Scarborough, who died when Hugh was still a student. His mother Henrietta (née Watson) had sufficient means to see him educated at Clifton College from 1891 to 1901, and at Oxford University where his brother Eustace also studied. He taught at Clifton College from 1909 to 1914 and joined Clifton RFC in 1903-04. He also played golf for the Bristol & Clifton Golf Club.

He joined the 5th Battalion South Staffs Regiment and was killed at the 2nd Battle of Ypres. Hugh is buried at St Quentin Cabaret Military Cemetery.

When he died, he was under the command of a school colleague who related his death:

About one o'clock this morning he was out in front of his trench with a party of men fixing some barbed wire entanglements. A chance bullet, fired at random by a German sentry, who may have detected the noise of men at work, hit him in the neck, and he died almost immediately. I need not tell you what a valuable officer he was. He was one of the very best. Everyone loved him, and his men would do anything for him. Some of them fairly broke down when they knew he had gone. His Captain is inconsolable. It is a grievous bitter loss, and hard to bear, but the war is taking toll of our best, and before it is over will drain the best blood in England very deep. We must steel our hearts and set our teeth to face much more than we have so far endured before the end will be in sight. We are fighting nothing less than Satan and all his angels, and must comport ourselves accordingly.

His brother, Captain Wilfred Wharton Parr, also a Clifton rugby player, was killed in France almost two years later (see the 1917 section).

Second Lieutenant Frederick Cecil Banes Walker 9th May 1915
Frederick Banes Walker was born on 19th June 1888 at North Petherton, Somerset. His father Harry owned a brewery. Cecil was educated at Mr Coplestone's School at Exmouth and afterwards at Tonbridge, and joined Clifton Rugby Club in 1912-13. He played cricket for Bridgwater Cricket Club (and five times for Somerset) and was a member of the Gloucester County Hockey team.

After enlisting, he completed a machine-gun course and went out to France as a machine-gun officer (2nd Lieutenant) in the 2nd Devonshires a little over two months before he died.

He was killed at the Battle of Aubers Ridge. This was in support of a much larger offensive carried out by the French around Arras, one of the French objectives being Vimy Ridge. Many shells in the preliminary bombardment were either too light to cause much damage or were defective. Many of the French shells were also 'duds', made in the USA and filled with sawdust. In consequence, when the whistles blew for the infantry to 'go over the top' they were massacred. "Fire until the barrels burst" was the German order. The battle only lasted one day but the casualties were in total 458 officers and 11,161 men, the majority within yards of their own front-line trench. Mile for mile, division for division, this was one of the highest rates of loss during the entire war and yet it is not generally renowned. The battle was an unmitigated disaster for the British Army - no ground was won, no tactical advantage gained.

During the battle in which Banes Walker was killed, Lance Corporal Adolf Hitler, a runner in the 16 BRIR, was billeted in the Regimental HQ base at Fournes, about two miles as the crow flies from the 2nd Devonshire's starting positions, south of Rue Petillon. He would certainly have been heavily involved in the same action on the 'other side of the bags'. Hitler spent virtually his entire military service in this sector of the Western Front, winning the Iron Cross First Class on 4th August 1918, 'for personal bravery and general merit' which he wore for the rest of his life. Ironically, the regimental adjutant who recommended him for the award, Captain Hugo Guttman, was a Jew.

He is buried at Le Trou Aid Post Cemetery, Fleurbaix.

Lieutenant Henry Wyndham Goodden 9th May 1915
Henry was born on 11th September 1883 in Swindon, Wiltshire, the son of Dr. Wyndham C. Goodden; having moved to Bristol, the family lived at 14 Berkeley Square, Clifton, now the Berkeley Hotel. Henry was educated at Clifton College from 1892 to 1899 and joined Clifton RFC in 1901-02.

He received his medical training at Bristol Royal Infirmary, and in Paris and Vienna. After the outbreak of war he was with the Royal Army Medical Corps, attached to the 2nd Battalion, Royal Irish Regiment and had previously been wounded during the Battle of the Aisne.

Henry is believed to have been killed in the Ypres Salient. His body was never recovered, and like Ernest Gardiner he is commemorated on the walls of the Menin Gate.

Lieutenant Arthur Norton Hickling Churchill 7th September 1915
Arthur Churchill was born on the 23rd April 1891 in Bridgwater, Somerset, the son of Edward Hickling Churchill. His father owned the Wembdon brewery in Bridgwater. During the war it became the Quantock cannery, providing tinned food for the troops. Arthur was educated at Clifton College from 1905 to 1908 and joined Clifton RFC in 1909-10.

Arthur went to British Columbia in 1913 and settled at Salt Spring Island as an agriculturalist, but enlisted in the Victoria Brigade on the day that war was declared. He came over to England with the 1st Canadian contingent as a private in the Royal Canadian Dragoons. On 4th May 1915 he was drafted to France with the Canadian Cavalry Brigade, which was hastily converted to infantry.

He was subsequently selected to command the machine gun section; every officer who had commanded the section before him had been killed.

On the same day that his parents received a letter from him to say that he was about to be allowed some leave, they received a telegram informing them that he had suffered a bullet wound. Vain hopes were expressed that he would recover, but he died two days later at Ploegsteert. He had been wounded by machine-gun fire from German trenches whilst placing a machine gun on top of the parapet of his own trench the battalion were holding Gloucester House and Showery trenches.

Two other brothers were also in service: Edward Archibald Hickling Churchill of the 5th Somerset and Private Harold Archer Hickling Churchill of the 2nd Canadian Brigade. All three had been educated at Clifton College and were very capable rugby players, and for a number of seasons had assisted at Bridgwater Albion, both having served as captain of the club.

Arthur Churchill is buried in Maple Leaf Cemetery, Romarin. His father was so saddened by the death of his son that he sold his business and put his money into stocks and shares just in time for the 1920s crash.

After his death, the road on which Arthur lived in Salt Spring Island was renamed Churchill Road in his honour. It is still called that to this day.

Lieutenant Burnet George James 26th September 1915
Burnet James was born late in 1886 in Clifton, the son of Sir Edward Burnet James, and joined Clifton RFC in 1908-09.

A prominent Bristol citizen, his father had a partnership in the company of tobacco manufacturers Edwards, Ringer & Bigg (which later became part of W.D. & H.O. Wills). In public life he served as a Councillor and then Alderman from 1891 to 1913; he was High Sheriff in 1900-01 and Lord Mayor of Bristol in 1904-05, and again in 1907-08. In 1898 he was Master of the Society of Merchant Venturers, and was knighted in 1908 during the royal visit to open the Royal Edward Dock.

Burnet was a talented sportsman and played cricket for Gloucestershire on three occasions in May and June 1914 – a left-hand bat, he must have made a nervous start to his truncated career, scoring only 27 runs in six innings with a top score of 10.

In 1907 he joined the 1st Gloucestershire R.G.A. Volunteers, resigning in 1912. On the outbreak of war he rejoined his old corps, which had since become the 1st South Midland Brigade R.F.A. (T.F.). In July 1915 he was attached to the 7th Squadron R.F.C.

He flew regular reconnaissance missions with Pilot 2nd Lt. Louis William Yule. On 26th September 1915 the pair were flying in BE 2c 1719 of No 7 Squadron RFC when engine problems caused a fatal crash near Helvele. Louis Yule was only 18 years old.

Yule and James were initially buried beside each other, near to where they crashed, by the German Army. Their bodies were later reburied in adjacent graves in the Cement House Cemetery at Langemark-Poelkapelle, Flanders.

1916

Captain George Carr Watson 8th March 1916
George Watson was born in early 1887 in Sunderland, the son of Edward George, a Schoolmaster, and Emma Watson. He spent his early years with his elder sister and younger brother at Monk Wearmouth Shore in Sunderland, later taking a degree at

Cambridge University before becoming a classics tutor at Colston's School, Bristol. He joined Clifton Rugby Club in 1912-13.

Upon the outbreak of war he joined the 6th Devonshire Regiment, which was initially based at Barnstaple, and sailed to India on 9th October 1914, landing at Karachi on 11th November 1914. On the 5th January 1916 his regiment reached Basra and remained in Mesopotamia for the rest of the war.

Originally planned to begin on 6th March, but postponed on account of heavy rainfall, the Battle of Dujaila was fought on 8th March 1916 between British and Ottoman forces. The Ottoman forces, led by 72 year-old Colmar Freiherr von der Goltz (who died in Baghdad a little over a month later), were besieging Kut. The British forces, led by Fenton Aylmer, attempted to relieve the city. The attempt failed, British losses in the course of the action being 4,000 killed and wounded: half the force was lost without ever seeing the enemy. There was once again a complete breakdown of medical arrangements owing to the overwhelming number of casualties, the weather and the ground conditions. Some units were so reduced by casualties that they had to merge temporarily with others.

Watson was one of the casualties. He is commemorated on the Basra Memorial, until 1997 located on the main quay of the naval dockyard at Maqil, on the west bank of the Shatt-al-Arab, about eight kilometres north of Basra. Because of the sensitivity of the site, the Memorial was moved on the orders of President Saddam Hussein. The move, carried out by the authorities in Iraq, involved a considerable amount of manpower, transport costs and engineering on their part, but the memorial was re-erected in its entirety. The Basra Memorial is now located 32 kilometres along the road to Nasiriyah, in the middle of what was a major battleground during the first Gulf War of 1991. It commemorates more than 40,500 members of the Commonwealth forces who died in the operations in Mesopotamia from the Autumn of 1914 to the end of August 1921.

Lieutenant Norman Durant 12th March 1916
Born on 29th April 1893 in Hadleigh, Suffolk, Norman's father was the Reverend William Friend Durant of South Woodland Road, Tyndall's Park, Bristol. Norman was educated at Clifton College from 1907 to 1911 and then at Bristol University. He joined Clifton Rugby Club in 1911-12. His twin brother, Maurice, also played for Clifton.

He was with the Gloucestershire Regiment 1st Battalion when killed near Loos. He had been supervising digging parties which were trying to rescue 20 soldiers buried in an old mine which was being used as a dugout. Working in an entirely exposed position, he was hit by high-explosive shrapnel that the Germans were continually sending over. They succeeded in getting all but three of the buried men out alive at about 6.30 a.m. on the next morning.

Captain Philip Arthur Edwards 18th March 1916
Philip Edwards was born on 22nd June 1888 in Henbury, Bristol, the third son of Herbert George and Eleanora Edwards of Oakfield, Stoke Bishop. He was educated at Clifton College from 1899 to 1906 and joined Clifton RFC in 1906-07, five years after his brother, George Dall Edwards. His father, Herbert George Edwards, was also educated at Clifton College and joined Clifton RFC in 1872-73. He was Master of the Society of Merchant Venturers in 1899 and a member of Bristol City Council.

Philip Edwards went to the Royal Military College at Sandhurst and was gazetted 2nd Lieutenant North Lancashire Regiment on 19th September 1908, promoted Lieutenant on 1st April 1911 and Captain on 3rd February 1915. He joined the 1st Battalion of his regiment in Mauritius in 1908 and served with them in Poona and Bangalore. He was home on leave when war broke out in August 1914 and was subsequently sent to Salisbury Plain to train one of the battalions. He served with the Expeditionary Force in France and Flanders from 16th July 1915 when he rejoined his old battalion.

He was shot dead by a German sniper in the trench known as the North Arm of the Double Crassier, near Loos on the 18th March 1916 aged 28.

He was also a member of Clifton Rowing Club along with seven other Clifton Rugby players who lost their lives in World War 1: Down, Durrant, Fry, Gardiner, Haycroft, Rowe and Rudman. Clifton Rowing Club is now known as Avon County Rowing Club.

Philip Edwards is buried at Maroc British Cemetery, Grenay. His name is missing from the Clifton RFC War Memorial.

Lieutenant Harold Alfred Llewellyn 14th June 1916
Harold Llewellyn was born on 22nd May 1891 in Melbourne, Australia, the son of James Davies, a physician, and Mary Llewellyn of Gorphwysfa, Glamorgan. He was educated at Cheltenham College from 1905 to 1909 and played rugby for the college 1st XV in 1908. He joined Clifton RFC in 1909-10 at which time he was employed by Downing and Hancock, solicitors, in Cardiff. After the declaration of war he joined the South Wales Borderers. His regiment was first in action on the Somme from May 1915

and he was wounded in a German counter-attack in September of that year in the Peronne area. His battalion, the 8th, was in action against the Bulgarians in Salonika between December 1915 and June 1916, by which stage sickness and disease were causing more deaths than enemy action.

The regimental history of the South Wales Borderers states that he was accidentally killed at Thessalonika. There are no details of the incident.

He was originally buried two miles south of the village of Sermenli and reburied at the Sarigol Military Cemetery, Kristoni, Greece.

His estate passed to his sister, Elsie Margaret Llewellyn of Brynhyfryd, Sully, Glamorgan.

Lieutenant Edouard Herbert Allan Goss 1st July 1916
Edouard was born on 13th June 1877 in Rangoon, the son of Louis Allan Goss (Inspector of Schools in Burma) and his French wife Marie Leonie Goss, a native of what is now Réunion Island. He grew up at Oakfield Grove in Clifton and was educated at Clifton College from 1889 to 1895. He joined Clifton RFC in 1896.

He was gazetted in December 1914 and served with the 7th Battalion, The Buffs (East Kent Regiment). On 1st July 1916, the 55th Brigade held the line in front of Carnoy, where its objective was a trench about two hundred yards north of the Montauban-Fricourt road. The battalion lost 51 soldiers that day, including Edouard.

Captain AG Kenchington reported his death thus:
At zero [7:30 a.m.] the three sections of each platoons [sic] advanced as arranged round the flanks and the other two sections with snipers went over the craters which were very muddy. The left-hand party entered the enemy trenches with only one casualty, the platoon Commander Lieut. E.H.A. Goss, who was killed instantly by a shell. This platoon found the rear portion of the crater area quite knocked out of recognition, and soon overcame two bombing parties and three or four snipers who opposed them.

He was buried in a crater on the Carnoy-Montauban Road. In 1920 his parents were informed by the War Office that his remains had been exhumed and re-interred at the Dantzig Alley British Cemetery.

His name is missing from the Clifton Rugby War Memorial, but is included on the memorial in the Cathedral of the Holy Trinity, Rangoon, Burma, which is dedicated to the everlasting memory of members of the Bombay Burmah Trading Corporation of Burmah who died fighting for their King and Country."

Captain Francis John Hannam 5th July 1916
Francis Hannam was born in the Summer of 1880 in Bristol and grew up in Westbury-on-Trym. He was the only son of Samuel J. Hannam, a timber merchant, and Laura, who also produced two daughters, Maude and Mabel. Francis was educated at Bristol Grammar School, joined Clifton Rugby Club in 1898-99 and was captain from 1901 to 1903. His rugby career was ended by a serious injury sustained playing for Gloucestershire.

He married Edith Boucher, a tennis player who won gold medals in the Ladies Singles and Mixed Doubles competitions at the 1912 Stockholm Olympics, and was twice a finalist at Wimbledon. Three of her brothers played for Clifton RFC.

Francis served with C Company, 2nd/4th Battalion of the Gloucestershire Regiment. He was killed carrying out a night time raid on German trenches at Aubers, and is buried at Laventie Military Cemetery, La Gorgue.

A memorial service was held for him on 23rd July 1916 at St Mary's, Tyndall Park. As well as his family, rugby players and officials from all over Bristol attended. At the service the Reverend F. Norton, in his impressive address, said that "just as the battle of Waterloo was won on the playing fields of Eton, it is true, in a measure, that Frank Hannam's energy, courage and coolness, daring and self sacrifice was learned in no small degree upon the playing fields of Bristol."

'"They had assembled that afternoon" he said "to take off their hats - if I might use the term - to a brave man and a gentleman. Known throughout Bristol as Frank Hannam, his death has caused a tremendous loss in their lives. Few sacrifices in this war could have been greater than his, for he was in the prime of his life, mentally, physically and - let us not forget it - spiritually. Ever since he went into the trenches he never forgot to go to God's altar for strength and help."

Captain Harold Ewart Rudman 19th July 1916
The son of Emily and James Rudman, Harold was born on 30th October 1883 in Redland, Bristol. His father was an oil importer and paint manufacturer, and Harold enjoyed a comfortable upbringing with two brothers and a sister in Clifton, although his father died before the turn of the century.

He was educated at Clifton College from 1891 to 1901. Harold joined Clifton Rugby Club in 1903-04 and after war broke out served as an officer in the Gloucestershire Regiment, 6th Battalion 'D' Company.

He was killed at Fromelles carrying out an attack on German trenches. No man's land became so congested by dead and wounded soldiers that the attack was aborted. In total 178 men of the 2/6 Glosters died. The action, at a point known as Sugar Loaf, was an unmitigated disaster for the Australian 5th Division, in particular, which suffered 5,533 casualties and 400 captured in a single night. This attack was a diversion for the renewed offensive taking place further south on the Somme, intended to prevent the Germans from sending reserves to replace their casualties in 'the main event'.

Harold Rudman's body was never found and he is listed on the Loos Memorial. He was also a member of Clifton Rowing Club and is listed on their memorial.

Lieutenant Noel Alexander Target 4th August 1916
Noel Target was born on 23rd November 1895 in London, the son of Felix Alexander Target, a civil engineer with the Indian Public Works Department, and the great-great-grandson of General Baron Target, Governor of Warsaw. Noel was educated at Haileybury School, Hertfordshire from 1909 to 1912 and joined Clifton Rugby Club in 1913-14.

He originally applied to join the Indian Police when war broke out, but was first commissioned as temporary 2nd Lieutenant 13th (Service) Battalion Durham Light Infantry on 22nd September 1914 and as a temporary Lieutenant on 3rd March 1915. He was commissioned into the regulars as 2nd Lieutenant, Durham Light Infantry on 4th April 1916.

Noel Target was killed in action on the Somme in a sector called Munster Alley, while defending a section of trench under heavy machine gun fire. He was buried where he fell. His body was later lost and his name is commemorated on the Thiepval Memorial.

Lieutenant Robert Hayward Down 17th August 1916

Robert Down was born the son of Henry and Grace in the Summer of 1888 at Woburn Sands, Bedfordshire and educated at Bedford School. Robert lived subsequently with his wife Gladys at 6 Apsley Road in Clifton and was Manager of the Westbury-on-Trym branch of Lloyds Bank. He first appeared for Clifton RFC in 1912-13.

Having joined the Gloucestershire Regiment 1/4th Battalion in August 1914, he was part of the attack on Pozières Ridge, a subsidiary attack of the Somme offensive. The battle was launched on 23rd July 1916 and saw the Australians and British fight hard for an area that provided a first rate observation post over the surrounding countryside, as well as the additional benefit of offering an alternative approach to the rear of the Thiepval defences.

The attack on Pozières Ridge lasted from 23rd July to 3rd September 1916. The village of Pozières itself was captured on 25th July, but it was the Australian Divisions that were instrumental in taking it. The 1/4, 1/5 and 1/6th Glosters were in the same Division (the 48th) attacking on this sector, although they actually occupied the line running a little to the north-west of Ovilliers at this stage of the Battle of the Somme. By 17th August, the day Down died, the fighting had reached the area around Mouquet Farm, known to the British as 'Mucky Farm', a powerful German stronghold. The Germans counter-attacked in this area on the 18th, causing many casualties before being repulsed. Down was killed in the artillery bombardment preceding the German attack.

Robert is buried at Puchevillers British Cemetery. His name also appears on the Lloyds Bank War Memorial at the bank's headquarters at Canon House, London.

Captain Friedrich Wilhelm Bartelt 11th September 1916

Friedrich Bartelt was born on 23rd September 1887 at Corston Lodge, Somerset. His father, Friedrich Ludwig Bartelt, originally came from Prussia and founded the Polysulphin Company, first in Brislington and then at Keynsham, manufacturing soap for laundries; the firm was sold around 1965. The factory was sited by the river, accessed from where the Keymarket roundabout is now situated at the end of the Keynsham by-pass. The company offices were the other side of the river, in what is now Matthews, next door to Portavon Marina. The factory premises constantly flooded and the stock washed away on a regular basis.

Friedrich was educated at St Christopher's Bath, Bath College (1900-04) and at Bristol University. He was in the Bath College rugby XV, the cricket XI and the 2nd rowing IV. Directly after leaving school he joined the 1st Battalion Somerset Light Infantry in which he held a commission, retiring in 1911. When war broke out he rejoined his regiment. His family because of their German background were shunned and excluded.

He died on 11th September 1916 from food poisoning in Calcutta, leaving a widow Gertrude. It is not known if his body or ashes were repatriated but he is now buried in Corston (All Saints) Church, Somerset.

Corston All Saints still rings its bells in his honour every year on his birthday.

Rifleman John Harold Bacchus 15th September 1916
Harry Bacchus was born on 11th February 1875 in Sarawak, Borneo, the son of Mary Constance Bacchus, and the late George Henry Bacchus.

Harry was educated at Clifton College during 1887 and 1888. He lived at 20 Vyvyan Terrace, Clifton. He appears in the 1893-94 Clifton XV photograph and played for Clifton with his brother during this season. The family emigrated to Australia in 1899. They sold their property at South Sydney Harbour and moved to Otaki, New Zealand in 1902 and he became a farmer.

Harry Bacchus. Image courtesy "Adopt an Anzac Project".

He served with the New Zealand Rifle Brigade and died with his brother, Ralph Lancelot Bacchus, on the Somme battlefield. The brothers were detailed from the front line to carry the wounded back to the casualty station and, while doing this, a shell exploded very near to them killing both brothers and the man they were carrying. They had only arrived on the Western Front six weeks before their death.

He is commemorated on the Caterpillar Valley New Zealand Memorial, Somme, France. He left a wife Sabie Ruth (née Skerman)

Rifleman Ralph Lancelot Bacchus 15th September 1916
Ralph Lancelot Bacchus was born on the 5th December 1877 in Sydney, Australia, the brother of John Harold Bacchus, and attended Clifton College from 1887 to 1889.

He played for Clifton during the 1893-94 season.

Ralph died with his brother on the Somme and left a wife, Enid Blanche Dorcas (née Harnett). He is also commemorated on the Caterpillar Valley New Zealand Memorial, Somme, France.

Ralph Bacchus. Image courtesy "Adopt an Anzac Project".

Both Ralph's and his brother Harry's names are missing from the Clifton Rugby War Memorial.

Major Geoffrey Dennis Browne 19th September 1916
Geoffrey Browne was born on 10th May 1888 in Notting Hill, London, the son of the Rev. Ernest Alfred Browne and his wife Maria, and grew up in Apsley Road, Clifton.

He attended Clifton College from 1901 to 1905 and joined Clifton RFC in 1906-07. His elder brother, Michael Ernest Browne, a solicitor, also attended Clifton College and played rugby for Clifton RFC from 1905-06.

He joined the Royal Field Artillery (C Bty, 240th Brigade) and was killed in action at Ovillers, just to the west of Pozières, during the Battle of the Somme. He was mentioned in despatches, London Gazette 4th January 1917, by General (later Field Marshal) Haig for gallant and distinguished service in the field.

Major Browne, right, departing with the 3rd Battery (Gloucester) 1st South Midland Brigade of Field Artillery.

He is buried at the Aveluy Communal Cemetery Extension in a village immediately north of the town of Albert.

Captain Barcroft Joseph Leech Fayle 24th October 1916
Barry Fayle was born on 18th November 1888 at Devonport, Devon, the son of Lt. Colonel Robert Fayle, born in Ireland, and wife Mary (née Leech) who later lived at 51 Canynge Road. Clifton. His elder brother Disney had joined Clifton in 1909-10.

Barry was educated at Clifton College from 1899 to 1907 and took a degree in Natural Sciences at Emmanuel College, Cambridge in 1911. Returning to Bristol to work at Bristol General Hospital, he joined Clifton RFC in 1912.

When war broke out in August 1914 Barry joined the Royal Army Medical Corps and was part of the British Expeditionary Force sent to defend Belgium.

Barry Fayle with his mother Mary.

Attached to the 2nd Battalion, Prince of Wales's Own West Yorkshire Regiment, he was later involved in the Battle of the Somme which lasted from July to November 1916. He was killed instantly by a shell whilst tending wounded men in the trenches on October 24th 1916 between Lesboeufs and Flers, to the south of Bapaume, France. During this offensive 58,000 British troops were killed, a third of them on the first day of the campaign.

Barry is buried at the London Cemetery, Longueval.

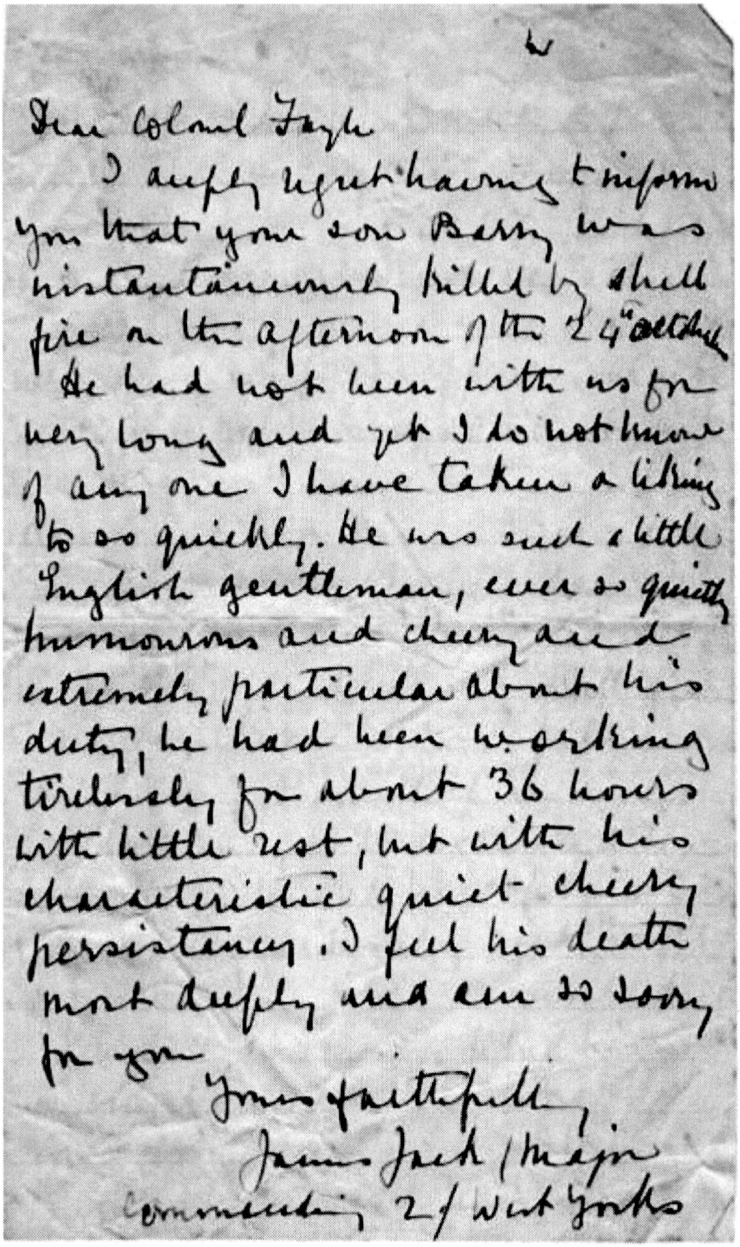

Dear Colonel Fayle

I deeply regret having to inform you that your son Barry was instantaneously killed by shell fire on the afternoon of the 24th October. He had not been with us for very long and yet I do not know of any one I have taken a liking to so quickly. He was such a little English gentleman, ever so quietly humourous and cheery and extremely particular about his duty, he had been working tirelessly for about 36 hours with little rest, but with his characteristic quiet cheery persistency. I feel his death most deeply and am so sorry for you.

Yours faithfully

James Jack (Major

Commanding 2/West Yorks

Letter from Major James Jack, Commanding Officer 2nd Bn. West Yorkshire Regiment to Barry's father Robert informing him of his son's death.

Lieutenant Henry George Phippen 9th November 1916

Henry Phippen was born in early 1892 in Easton-in-Gordano, the son of Albert Henry Phippen, a mason, and Ada. His parents met when they became next door neighbours in Easton-in-Gordano. His father was 17 years older than his mother and died in 1901.

When his mother died two years later, Henry became the ward of the Bristol solicitor Edward Meade-King, whose firm of solicitors still exists and has an office in Queen Square, Bristol. He was educated at Blundell's School in Tiverton, Devon from 1904 and joined Clifton RFC upon leaving school in 1910.

When war came Henry joined the 4th Glosters. He died of wounds received almost at the end of the Battle of the Somme, somewhere just to the south of Bapaume, where the Allied advance petered out.

He is buried at Bécourt Military Cemetery on the road between Bécourt and Albert.

Captain Alan Caldicott 7th December 1916
Alan Caldicott was born in Coventry on 19th March 1887, the eldest of three children of Richard Botham Caldicott, a ribbon manufacturer, and his wife Annie. He was educated at Lindley Lodge near Nuneaton, and at Bradfield College from 1901 to 1905. He worked for W.D. and H.O. Wills Ltd in Bristol and briefly in Blantyre, Nyasaland. He joined Clifton RFC in 1907-08.

He enlisted in September 1914 and was gazetted to the Loyal North Lancashire regiment. After service at the front, he was invalided home at Christmas 1915 and returned to the firing line the following summer. He was subsequently posted to the King's African Rifles (attached 1st/2nd).

In December 1916 General Smuts launched an offensive in German East Africa designed to prevent a merger of the two main German forces and to trap General von Lettow-Vorbeck, or at least to bring him to the elusive engagement that might decisively end the campaign.

The allied commander General Jacob van Deventer, operating south of Iringa, was slowed by mountains covered with dense bush and valleys that the rains had filled with water. Thus delayed, von Lettow-Vorbeck slipped through his fingers once again, this time by crossing at Rufugi. As von Lettow-Vorbeck once said "there is always a way out, even of an apparently hopeless position, if the leader makes his mind up to face the risks".

During this attempt to confront the German forces in German East Africa, Captain Alan Caldicott was killed. Regrettably, the regimental history does not note the circumstances.

Alan Caldicott is buried in Dar es Salaam Cemetery in what is now Tanzania, and commemorated in War Memorial Park, Coventry (opened by Field Marshal Haig in 1927) and on the Clifton Rowing Club Memorial.

1917

Flight Sub-Lieutenant Ronald Victor Knight 12th March 1917
Ronald Knight was born on 30th March 1894 in Wells, Somerset, the second son of John Knight, an oil merchant of Milton Hill, Wells, and his wife Marie. He was a pupil at Wells Cathedral School and from 1908 to 1911 at Bedford Grammar School, and then studied at Bristol University.

He joined Clifton RFC during the 1912-13 season, when he headed the list of try scorers with eight, five of which were scored in the match versus Clifton College on 26th October 1912, the final score being 59-3.

When still only 18 years old, he played for Somerset against South Africa on 3rd October 1912 at The Recreation Ground in Bath. South Africa won 24-3. The following year he was a reserve for the England team, but never won a cap.

Studying medicine at Guy's Hospital in London at the outbreak of war, he abandoned his career and joined the 8th Battalion City of London Regiment (Post Office Rifles). He was commissioned as a 2nd Lieutenant and underwent six months' service in the trenches at Festubert and Loos in France.

At his own request he transferred to the Royal Naval Air Service in 1916 and was killed at RAF Cranwell on 12th March 1917. He was an assistant flying instructor and died when his aircraft crashed owing to engine failure. He is buried in Wells Cemetery,

Somerset and his name is recorded on the war memorial in the town. He was survived by his wife Gwendoline and daughter, Beryl.

Private Morton Leonard 5th May 1917
Morton Leonard was born in late 1879 in Bristol, the son of Frank, a flour merchant, and Alice, and grew up with his brother and twin sister at 50 Belmont Road in the parish of St James & St Paul Out.

He was educated at Bristol Grammar School from 1891 to 1894. He joined Clifton Rugby Club in 1899-1900, and before the war he worked for John Watson & Co. corn merchants.

He was killed at the Battle of Arras with the Gloucestershire Regiment 12th Battalion, known as 'Bristol's Own'. Yet another soldier with no known grave, he is commemorated on the Arras Memorial.

Captain Wilfred Wharton Parr 8th May 1917
The elder brother of Hugh Wharton Myddleton Parr (see above), Wilfred was born in 1873 in Clifton, the son of the Reverend Robert Parr. He was educated at Uppingham School and joined Clifton RFC in 1890-91. Before the war he married Katharine Margaret of Bathford, Somerset and worked as a coal merchant in Bristol.

He enlisted in the Gloucestershire Regiment 12th Battalion 'Bristol's Own' in 1914, allegedly aged 34 years eleven months. According to the census he was actually 42 when he joined up, and so outside the age limit for active service at the front, He somehow persuaded the authorities to let him in.

Wilfred was commissioned in February 1915 and was awarded the Military Cross in the New Years Honours list of 1917. Serving in "B" Company of the Glosters, he was killed at Fresnoy.

An account of his death relates that "on the 4th May 1917 the battalion relieved the 1st Canadian Battalion in the trenches to the east of Fresnoy which had been captured only the day before. The captured village and its defences had not yet been consolidated and the enemy seemed to regard it as a position of the highest importance and one which they were determined to recapture. The Glosters were heavily shelled and bombarded by aeroplane and on May 8th the enemy made a fierce attack.

The enemy opened an exceptionally heavy barrage on the lines and battalion headquarters at 3.45 am, when there was a thick mist which made observation difficult even at fifty yards distance. By four o'clock there was no doubt about the matter; the enemy were attacking in force. It was afterwards learned that they had brought up the Bavarian Division with the object of re-capturing the village and its defences. The preliminary barrages had taken a heavy toll of the Glosters even before the German infantry came on; in fact "A" Company had practically ceased to exist before the infantry attack began and the brunt of the attack was borne by "B" Company. Captain Parr of that company was last seen surrounded by the enemy and fighting desperately with a shovel. The remnants of these two companies stood their ground valiantly and, though surrounded, fought to the last."

Captain CS Petheram wrote to his wife as follows:

B.E.F. May 12th 1917,
Dear Mrs Parr, It is with the deepest regret that I have to write and tell you that your husband, Captain W.W. Parr, is missing. He took his Company over in a brave attempt to gain, by an immediate counter-attack, some ground which had been lost. The last seen of him was by an NCO who saw him walking about among his men, helping and encouraging them. His men absolutely worshipped him, and would follow him anywhere. Every single officer loved him, and he was absolutely the life and soul of the Mess, always he was ready to make jokes at any time. When I first joined the Battalion in Sept. last I was posted to his Company, and was his only subaltern for a long time. I went over the top first with him, and stayed with him nearly all the time in this Battn. In this way I may say that I got to know him, and count him as one of the best friends I have ever had. I am now commanding the Company he last took over, and shall endeavour to run it on similar lines to what he did. I do not know what to say, Mrs Parr, to give you any hope. I leave that to God and the future. I can only sincerely console with you in such especially distressing circumstances. If he is dead, he died, as he always lived, like a hero, and if he is alive - I cannot hold much hope of that - no one will be more glad than I. If I can do anything to help in any investigation, or can assist in any way out here, please command me. Believe me, yours very sincerely, C.S. Petheram. (courtesy of Stephen Lewis of Cheltenham)

Wilfred is listed on the Arras Memorial, Pas de Calais.

Lance Corporal William John Rogers 9th May 1917
William Rogers was born in the Spring of 1888 in Clifton, the third of six children of Francis Edward and Kate Rogers.

He served in the 1st/14th Battalion London Regiment (London Scottish), the same Regiment and Battalion as Arthur Simpson Littleton-Geach, the brother of Hugh William Littleton Geach. He died in the Battle of Arras.

William Rogers is buried in the Faubourg d'Amiens cemetery near Arras.

Lieutenant-Colonel Courtenay Talbot St. Paul 31st July 1917
Courtenay Paul was born 18th November 1881 in Clifton, the eldest son of Walter Stuckey Paul, one of the original signatories that established Clifton Rugby Club in 1872. Courtenay was educated at Clifton College from 1891 to 1898 and joined Clifton RFC in 1905-06.

He received his first commission in the Royal Field Artillery in January 1900. Shortly after the outbreak of the War he was drafted to France with his battery and promoted to the rank of Major. He was twice mentioned in despatches and in September 1916 was awarded the DSO "for conspicuous gallantry and devotion to duty during the operations near Lavantie July 1916".

Courtenay was the officer, by now a Lieutenant-Colonel, commanding 36th Battery, 45th Brigade, Royal Field Artillery 8th Division when he was killed during the Battle of Pilkem, which formed part of the 3rd Battle of Ypres. The 8th Division were attacking astride the Menin road in a north-easterly direction through Hooge and Bellewaarde.

He was buried at The Huts Cemetery, Dikkebus and his name also appears on the base of the St. John's Memorial on Whiteladies Road, Clifton. His death was a second tragedy for his parents, who had previously lost another son, Hugh Beresford, at the Battle of Jutland in May of the previous year.

Captain William Edgar Paul 31st July 1917

William Paul was born on 23rd March 1874 . He was the fourth of six children – three girls, three boys - of Charles, a Bank Manager, and Elizabeth Paul. Charles was a Bristolian, but Elizabeth and their first two children were born in Chile; William and the next two siblings were born in Argentina and the youngest – by seven years – was the late arrival born in Somerset.

Apsley Road in Clifton appears to have been a fertile recruiting ground for Clifton players. In the 1890s the Paul family lived at No. 23; over the years at least four other club colleagues and fellow casualties lived in the same road – Edgar Sellman's parents at No. 41, Robert Down at No. 6, Geoffrey Browne at No. 8 and Harold Rudman at No. 3.

William was educated at Clifton College from 1882 to 1891. He joined Clifton RFC in 1890-91 and was captain in 1896-97. In common with his father and brothers he was a member of the Society of Merchant Venturers.

He trained as an architect, working at first in public service and subsequently in private practice in Baldwin Street, Bristol. Shortly after the outbreak of war he was instrumental in the formation of the Bristol University OTC, but was then offered and accepted a commission as Captain in the Royal Scots Fusiliers. After training in Bristol, he was drafted first to France and then to Salonika, where he served for 18 months and was invalided home in the winter of 1916. After recovering from his wounds he again went to the front but was killed in action.

William died on the first day of the 3rd Battle of Ypres and is commemorated on the Menin Gate at Ypres. He left a wife, Lena, and three children.

Captain Dudley Allen Pontifex 31st July 1917
Dudley Pontifex was born on 26th August 1890 at Parkstone, Dorset, the second of five sons of the Reverend Septimus Edmund and his wife Helena; three of his brothers became monks at Downside. Dudley was named after his uncle, who played 17 first-class cricket matches for Somerset and Surrey between 1878 and 1896 and was apparently a very fine billiards player; another uncle, Alfred, played a single match for Gloucestershire.

The family moved to Bristol and Dudley grew up in All Saints Road, Clifton; He attended Clifton College from 1898 to 1907 and joined Clifton RFC in 1908-09.

Dudley joined the 3rd Battalion, Scottish Rifles in 1911 and left just over a year later to become Director of Physical Training at Rugby School. He rejoined the Scottish Rifles (the Cameronians) after war broke out.

He died in the Battle of Pilkem Ridge, Ypres and is commemorated on the Ypres (Menin Gate) Memorial.

Second Lieutenant Frank Alexander Haycroft 10th August 1917
The elder child of Charles, a hide merchant, and Alice, Frank Haycroft was born in the Spring of 1890 in Bristol and joined Clifton RFC in 1908-09. He grew up on Sion Hill in Clifton.

Frank fought with the 10th King's Royal Rifle Corps, detailed to carry out the operation of crossing the Steenbeek at 4.15am on 11th August. The crossing was to be made by two companies of the Battalion, which were to form up in the open within 200 yards of the stream. Unfortunately, an enemy patrol which had crossed the river detected the troops in the act of forming up, and turned a machine gun on them. The operation failed, only small parties managing to cross the stream, and they were never seen again. Frank Haycroft died from his wounds after being captured by the Germans. In total 130 soldiers were killed, wounded or taken Prisoner of War in this small action.

Frank is commemorated on the Ypres (Menin Gate) Memorial; his name is also on the War Memorial at St. Paul's Church, Clifton.

Captain Frederick Dudley Andrews 14th August 1917
Born in the Spring of 1887 in Lichfield, Staffordshire, Frederick Andrews was the son of Thomas and Edith of Old College House, Lichfield, Staffs. He was educated at Rossall School in Lancashire and joined Clifton Rugby Club in 1911-12. He married Gladys Ethel Abrahall, of Shustoke, Warwickshire, only a year before he died.

When war broke out he was Second Brewer at Messrs. Rogers of Bristol but immediately enlisted in the Gloucestershire Regiment. He obtained a commission on February 14th 1915 and went out to the Front the following July. During the Somme offensive he had many miraculous escapes, his obituary in the Lichfield Mercury reporting him as 'on more than one occasion being the only officer in his Battalion to return without a scratch'. He was awarded the M.C. in January 1917.

He was killed during the 3rd Battle of Ypres and is buried at Track X Cemetery, St. Jean-les-Ypres. Two brothers survived the war.

Major Henry Clissold 28th September 1917
He was born on 12th February 1871 in Nailsworth, Gloucestershire; his father, William George, owned Nailsworth Brewery and his mother Julia died in the late 1880s. He was educated at Wycliffe College, Stonehouse and Clifton College from 1885 to 1889, and at Trinity College Cambridge, where he took a first-class degree in Natural Sciences, from 1889 to 1893. He became an assistant master at Marlborough College in 1893 and then at Clifton College in 1894, joined Clifton RFC in 1894-95 and was made Captain in 1900-01.

Harry taught at Clifton College until the outbreak of war, when he was given leave of absence to train a field company of Engineers. He went to the Front in April 1915. In July 1917 the Royal Engineers moved northwards to take part in the 3rd Battle of Ypres, which began on 31st July and continued for three months. They remained in this area until the early part of October and sustained heavy casualties. He was killed sheltering in a dug-out when a heavy shell came through the roof and exploded inside.

Harry Clissold is buried at Duhallow A.D.S. Cemetery, Ypres.

Captain Richard Guy Titley 13th October 1917
Richard Titley was born in the Summer of 1893 in Clifton. He was the son of William and Isabel who later lived at Wynton Lodge, Durdham Down in Bristol. Richard joined Clifton RFC in 1911-12.

He fought with the Gloucestershire Regiment 1/6th Battalion and was awarded the M.C. in 1916. He was wounded at the Battle of Poelcapelle on 9th October 1917, dying of wounds four days later aged 24, and is buried at Dozinghem Military Cemetery, northwest of Poperinge.

Before the major British-led offensive around Ypres began in June 1917 (the 3rd Battle of Ypres, sometimes known as Passchendaele after the village which became its final and much reduced objective) the responsible medical authorities, in anticipation of the expectedly large casualties, set up three entirely new casualty clearing stations behind the starting lines, to the west and north west of Ypres. The local troops, noticing that many of the surrounding Flemish villages ended in "ghem", and in tune with the trench humour which had by now developed, named these treatment centres as 'Bandagehem', 'Dozinghem' and 'Mendinghem', names which were eventually accepted by the authorities as official. An American volunteer orderly working in Mendinghem, dismayed at the number of casualties who did not survive the operating tables, suggested, half-seriously, that the CCS should be re-named 'Endinghem'. It wasn't.

Captain Percy Trevellyn Rowe 30th November 1917
Percy Rowe was born on 2nd September 1879 in Exeter, the youngest of at least six children, and very much an afterthought with a dozen years between him and his next youngest sibling. His father was Thomas Rowe, a lead manufacturer, and his mother Emma was some 48 years old when he was born. He was educated at The Leys School, Cambridge and joined Clifton RFC in 1901, by which time he was also a lead merchant living with his sister Gertrude at 'Linthorpe' in the Parish of St Michael, Bristol.

He was drafted to France on 2nd November 1914 and gazetted 2nd Lieutenant Royal Field Artillery (1st South Midlands Gloucester Brigade) on 8th June 1915. Percy had been slightly wounded with the Expeditionary Force on 18th May 1915, but returned to the front and was killed in action at Wailly in the Battle of Cambrai. This was the first battle in which the British Army successfully used tanks. It started off well with major land gains, including the crossing of the Hindenburg Line, and with low casualties.

Less than two months later, Percy died on the day of the German counter-attack. On 3rd December Haig ordered a retreat, and by the 7th all the British gains were abandoned except for a portion of the Hindenburg line. The Battle of Cambrai was seen by British as a success, but casualties were around 45,000 on each side, with 11,000 Germans and 9,000 British taken prisoner. In terms of territory the Germans had recovered their early losses and a little more. Despite the outcome, the battle was seen as evidence than even the strongest trench defences could be overcome by a massive tank attack. The British had seen the advantage of tanks whilst the German command had seen the potential of new infantry tactics, such as storm-troopers.

Percy lies buried at Orival Wood Cemetery, Flesquières, some six miles south-west of Cambrai.

1918

Captain Henry Ryan Bennett 23rd March 1918
Henry Bennett was born on 13th October 1892, the son of John Ryan and Florence Bennett of 3 Upper Belgrave Road, Clifton. The family owned collieries in the Easton, Bedminster and Kingswood areas of Bristol. Henry was educated at Clifton College from 1906 to 1909 and at the Bristol University Engineering School. He was in his 2nd year at Caius College, Cambridge when war broke out and had joined Clifton RFC in 1909-10. His brother, John Piers Bennett and uncle, Alfred Henry Bennett also played for Clifton.

He obtained his commission in September 1914, was gazetted Captain in the 11th Bn., The King's (Liverpool Regiment) in January 1916 and went to France the following August.

He is remembered on the Pozières Memorial, but his name is missing from the Clifton Rugby War Memorial.

Second Lieutenant Edgar Nevill Newmarch Sellman 4th April 1918
Edgar Sellman was born in the Summer of 1876 in Taunton, Somerset, the son of Edward George and Ellen E. Elizabeth Sellman, who at the time of his death were living at 41 Apsley Road, Clifton. He was educated at Rugby School, and then at Lincoln College Oxford from 1896 to 1900.

Edgar taught at a school in Exeter and then set up private schools in Burnham and later in Oxford. He joined Clifton RFC in 1902-03. Edgar's brother, Arthur Beresford Sellman, survived the war and was the club's first post-war 1st XV Captain.

Having given his school up and joined the 5th Oxfordshire & Buckinghamshire Light Infantry in 1915, at the time of his death Edgar was with the Gloucestershire Regiment's 3rd Battalion. He was involved in defending against the German Spring Offensive, which began from their Hindenburg Line positions between the south of Arras and the town of St Quentin on 21st March 1918. This was Germany's last-ditch attempt to finish the war before the Americans (who had declared war on Germany in April 1917) could make the crucial difference. However, the attack ran out of steam by the beginning of April, mainly because the German supply lines were defeated by the scale of the advance, and, ironically, because the main thrust was across the old Somme battlefield areas which they had laid to waste during their retreat to the Hindenburg Line in March 1918.

Edgar Sellman was killed when the German advance was halted and partially reversed in front of Villers Bretonneux, about ten miles from Amiens. The official final figure for British casualties between 21st March and 5th April 1918 was 160,000 killed, wounded and missing. Of this total, some 22,000 had been killed and approximately 72,000 captured by the enemy. German casualties were similar, but with a much smaller number of prisoners.

He is buried at Villers-Bretonneux Military Cemetery, Somme.

Lieutenant Leslie Harrington Fry 9th August 1918

Leslie Fry was born on 25th January 1893 in London, the son of Charles Alfred Harrington Fry and Eleanor Fry, of Long Ashton, Bristol. He was educated at Marlborough College and at Clare College, Cambridge, and joined Clifton RFC in 1913-14. He was gazetted to the North Somerset Yeomanry in 1913.

Leslie joined his regiment at the outbreak of war and went to the Front on November 1st 1914. In October 1915 he obtained a permanent commission in a Hussar regiment, and in 1916 was selected as a Signalling Officer to a Cavalry Brigade. He remained at HQ until April 1918 when he was transferred again as Signalling Officer to another brigade; he was in that position, and had been mentioned in despatches, when he was killed in the early stages of the Allied advance to victory, which began from their positions just to the east of Amiens on 8th August 1918, a date which Major-General Erich Ludendorff referred to as 'The Black Day of the German Army' in his memoirs.

Leslie is buried at Caix British Cemetery, south-east of Amiens.

Lieutenant William Jackson Haggart 31st August 1918
Born in the Spring of 1883 in South Shields, William Haggart was the son of William and Elizabeth and the husband of Ivy. He was educated at South Shields High School and worked for the National Provincial Bank of England, firstly in Newcastle and then Bedminster. He joined Clifton RFC in 1913-14.

William joined the Gloucestershire Regiment 4th Battalion upon the outbreak of war. At the time of his death, he had been transferred to the Gloucester 12th Battalion 'Bristol's Own' and was killed in the final Allied advance which, by the end of August 1918, had pushed the lines forward over the old Somme battlefields to within a few miles of Bapaume.

He is buried at the Achiet-Le-Grand Communal Cemetery Extension, Pas de Calais.

Lieutenant Claude Bostock Smith 5th October 1918
Claude was born early in 1891 in Bristol, the son of Samuel Smith, a sugar merchant, and Anna Elizabeth. By 1901, their children seem to have abandoned the simple surname in favour of the grander, un-hyphenated Bostock Smith. Claude was the baby of the family and had at least five siblings upwards of eleven years his senior. His elder brother would go on to become the Chairman of Bristol Rugby Club and was one of the people to open the Clifton War Memorial.

The second phase of the last and decisive Allied advance took place on 28th September 1918 from the Ypres Salient, with King Albert of the Belgians in overall command. In a single day they succeeded in capturing the infamous Passchendaele Ridge. However the offensive was held up, as usual in that sector, by rain, mud and the consequent impossibility of supplying troops with food, ammunition or reinforcement, and little further progress was made before 14th October. It was during this hiatus that Claude was killed. He is buried at Potijze Cemetery, north-east of Ypres.

Captain Charles Holbrook Rosling 22nd October 1918

Charles was born on 24th May 1882 in Derby, the only son of the Reverend Charles Douglas Rosling and Madeline. His father was Headmaster of Horwells School in Launceston and his parents later lived at Caerhays Rectory, Gorran in Cornwall. Charles followed in his father's footsteps and became a schoolmaster. He joined Clifton RFC in 1912-13.

He enlisted in August 1914. Formerly a Trooper in the Royal North Devonshire Hussars, he died of wounds received at the Battle of the Selle (17th-25th October in Picardy) whilst serving with the 3rd Battalion, attached to the 7th Battalion, of the Duke of Cornwall's Light Infantry.

He is buried at Rocquigny-Equancourt Road British Cemetery, Manacourt, 12km south-east of Bapaume, and is also listed on the War Memorial in Caerhays.

Captain Frederick Stanley Hill 4th November 1918

Frederick Hill was born in the Summer of 1888 in Bristol. Whilst the Commonwealth War Graves Commission and the club memorial record him as SF Hill, he was born Frederick Stanley and appears as Frederick S in the 1891 and 1901 censuses. He was the son of William, a clothing manufacturer, and Hester, and grew up at Knowle House in Knowle Road, Bedminster. His parents later moved into Bristol and lived at 1 Upper Belgrave Road, Clifton. Frederick was educated at Bristol Grammar School and joined Clifton Rugby Club in 1909-10.

By 1918 he was with the Gloucestershire Regiment 4th Battalion. At the front the German resistance was falling apart and unprecedented numbers of prisoners were being taken. At dawn on November 4th, 17 British divisions headed the attack to cross the 60 to 70-foot wide Sambre canal and the flooded ground around it. It was there that the British Expeditionary Force had fought over four years previously. The XIII and IX Corps reached the canal first; German guns quickly ranged the attackers, and bodies piled up before the temporary bridges were properly emplaced under heavy fire. The 1st and 32nd Divisions of IX Corps lost around 1,150 men in the crossing. Even after the crossing the German forces defended in depth amid the small villages and fields, and it was not until midday that a two mile deep by fifteen mile wide breach was secured. Hill was one of the casualties.

Frederick Stanley Hill from the Bristol Grammar School Cricket XI July 1906.

At the Battle of the Sambre Canal on the 4th November four Victoria Crosses were won. In this battle the poet Wilfred Owen also died.

Frederick Hill is buried at Landrecies British Cemetery in the Département du Nord, 40km south-east of Valenciennes.

By 1918 there were strikes and demonstrations in Berlin and other cities protesting about the effects of the war on the population. The British naval blockade of German ports meant that thousands of people were starving. Socialists were waiting for the chance to seize power in Germany as they had in Russia. The northern Allies were advancing relentlessly, sometimes more than five miles a day. In October 1918 Ludendorff resigned and the German navy mutinied: the end was near. Kaiser Wilhelm II abdicated on 9th November 1918. Two days later the armistice was signed at the 11th hour of the 11th day of the 11th month.

Germany signed The Treaty of Versailles on 28th June 1919.

A war memorial was first suggested in 1919, but it was another twelve years before it was unveiled,

In gathering the names of the players that died in the War there was no government assistance. The government had neither the time nor the resources to help to gather the names for private memorials, so the club had to send a letter to members asking if they knew the name of any players who had died.

In the World War I section of the memorial there are some errors; the following have been identified and in some cases resolved.

It is an established fact that Warren Chetham Strode, born on the 28th January 1896 in Henley, survived the war, but his name had already been included on the Memorial. His name was removed and the name of W.S. Yalland moved up from the bottom - hence the Memorial is in alphabetical order apart from Yalland.

Above Warren Chetham-Strode in the1912 Sherborne XV.
Image courtesy Sherborne School

Warren Chetham Strode was educated at Sherborne School from 1910 to 1913 and played in the school cricket XI in 1913. He joined Clifton Rugby Club for the 1913-14 season. Strode later became an author and playwright, best known for the play 'The Guinea Pig' (1946), whose stage production provided the acting debuts for Ronnie Barker, Honor Blackman and Peter Barkworth. The film version, which starred Richard Attenborough and was directed and produced by John Boulting in 1948, caused controversy at the time for using the word "arse" in the script. It was filmed at Strode's old school, Sherborne. He went on to write the screenplays for several films including 'Odette' (1950) and 'The Lady with a Lamp' (1951).

Warren's brother, Edward Randall Chetham Strode, was killed in World War I and probably caused a case of mistaken identity. They were both in the 2nd Border Regiment and the same battalion; Warren was the youngest son of Dr Chetham-Strode, Edward the eldest. Their father died on 7th August 1943; born in New Zealand, he played cricket against England in 1879 and came to England to train as a surgeon at the University of Edinburgh.

Warren Chetham Strode in 1949. Image courtesy of the National Portrait Gallery.

Warren was invited to write the screenplay for the Noel Coward play 'Brief Encounter'. He reluctantly refused and explained his reasons to Noel Coward in a letter in 1948. "It would need a good deal written in to bring it to a full length picture...Your work cannot be messed about." Noel, however, was clearly in favour of someone else adapting in this case and wrote urging the playwright to reconsider. This brought a fuller explanation. "It's not a matter of taking your play and adding twenty minutes. Whoever did the script of Brief Encounter [Noel himself] didn't only throw in a few extra trains...I feel that since the war we have come to hold more firmly to the values and security of work and friendship - rather than to the temporary enchantment and excitement of sex."

Warren Chetham Strode would later spend his life writing the TooToo children's books about siamese cats. When he died on 26th April 1974, he was living in Playden, Sussex.

It is well documented that Hugh William Littleton Geach survived the war. He was born in St. Agnes, Cornwall in 1895; his father William Geach was a solicitor. Hugh was educated at Blundell's School from 1905 to 1914. He joined Clifton RFC in 1912-13 and gained his county rugby cap whilst still at school. The Times announced his marriage on 15th June 1925.

The Somerset side that played Monmouth on 6th March 1913 at Newport with William Littleton Geach standing 3rd from the right. It was at the start of this season that he joined Clifton RFC.

The entry on the club memorial was probably another case of mistaken identity - his brother, Arthur Simpson Littleton Geach, was killed on 23rd November 1917.

Robert Rowatt, listed on the War Memorial, also survived the war. He was born in early 1892 in Crosby, Liverpool. His grandfather, David Allison Rowatt, founded the firm of Rowatt & Lyon, Tobacco Importers, in Glasgow.

Robert joined Clifton Rugby Club in 1913-14 when he had started work at British American Tobacco in Ashton Gate, Bristol as a factory pupil before being posted to Liverpool. When war broke out he joined the King's Liverpool Regiment and was discharged in February 1919. Although badly wounded he survived the war, but his two brothers David and Edmund did not. After the war, Robert Rowatt joined his father at Rowatt & Lyon, where he took over as Company Secretary.

In 1924 British American Tobacco's Ships' Stores organisation took over Rowatt & Lyon, which ceased as an operating concern. Robert Rowatt was posted to Bangalore, India, as Assistant Factory Manager. He spent the next 20 or more years in Hyderabad, Calcutta and Monghyr as well as Bangalore. Robert Rowatt was one of the founders of the Rotary Club of Bangalore which was chartered on 27th October 1934.

Robert Rowatt who died in June 1959.

It has not yet proved possible to identify W.H. Lambert who joined Clifton Rugby Club in 1912-13. There are several candidates, one of whom survived the war.

The death of four players is not recorded by the Commonwealth War Graves Commission:

L. Caulfield (joined 1913-14)
W.G. Laxton (joined 1912-13)
W.E. Pane (joined 1911-12)
G.F. Puckle (joined 1912-13)

Assuming their names are spelt correctly, they possibly also survived the war.

A G. Caulfield is listed in a newspaper report as attending the annual club dinner on Saturday 5th April 1913. If this is correct then it seems likely that the L. Caulfield on the memorial was confused with 2nd Lieutenant Gordon Caulfield who belonged to the Somerset Light Infantry (3rd Battalion, attached to 7th Battalion), and was killed during the Battle of Cambrai on the 30th November 1917. He is commemorated at Cambrai Memorial, Louveral. Gordon Caulfield was born on the 25th February 1885 at Classa, County Cork in Ireland. His father Captain John Caulfield was JP for County Cavan. Following a famous murder case, the Coachford Poisoning which involved their governess and a local doctor, the family moved to Midsomer Norton, near Bath, in about 1890 as they had several relatives already living in the South West at the time.

W.G. Laxton is thought to be Warren George Laxton, the father of Mathew Henry Laxton who played for Clifton from 1908-09. He died on the 4th July 1914 at 6 Iddesleigh Road, Redland, Bristol. However the date of death is exactly a month before the war started and he is not listed by the Commonwealth and War Graves Commission.

It has not been possible to identify W.E. Pane, who joined Clifton in 1911-12, as there is no-one with the surname and initials listed in CWGC records as having died in the war. It seems probable that his initials on the War Memorial and in the book '50 Years with Clifton Rugby Football Club' are incorrect.

There are two men with the surname Pane listed by the CWGC as having died in the war. One, Private Harold Alfred Pane, is too young to have played for Clifton; the other, Rifleman Cyril Ernest Pane, of the Rifle Brigade, the son of Leonard and Elizabeth Pane, of Birmingham, died on 1st August 1915. There are 1,068 men with variations on the name Pane, such as Payne, Paine, Panes and Paneta, who are listed as having died in World War 1 by the CWGC. Twelve had connections with the South West.

G.F. Puckle was a 1st XV player in 1912-13 and there were only four soldiers with that surname that died in the war. They do not have the correct initials and the only one who had a connection with this area was Captain Thomas Norman Puckle, 2nd Leicester Regiment (attached West African Frontier Force), killed in action on 30th August 1914 near Gurua in German West Africa (now Cameroon), aged 39. He is one of 93 names printed in the Gloucestershire Echo on 26th July 1915 as "Cheltenham men who have fallen in the war".

Seven names are missing from the War Memorial: E.M. Panter-Downes, P.A. Edwards, J.H. Bacchus, R.L. Bacchus, A.E.J. Collins, E.H.A. Goss and H.R. Bennett. This is probably because they had left Clifton many years before war broke out, and contact with the club had been lost.

The War Memorial was unveiled at the Eastfield Road Ground in Westbury-on-Trym on the on 21st November 1931.

At the unveiling, Walter Pearce, the President of the Rugby Football Union and an ex-Bristol player, who played in the 3rd fixture for Bristol against Clifton in 1890, said in his final words:

> "For though the dust that's part of them,
> To dust again be gone,
> Yet here still beat the hearts of them,
> The game they handed on."

Newspaper cutting from the 'Bristol Times and Mirror', Monday November 23rd 1931.

There are twelve Old Cliftonian names on the World War 1 section of the memorial and seven missing. In total 578 Old Cliftonians lost their lives, and over 3,100 served in the war.

Names missing from war memorials in this country are not uncommon. Several reasons have been suggested, but relatives may have requested that they be omitted. It is for this reason the authors would like to think that this book serves simply as one form of memorial to all those associated with the club who made the ultimate sacrifice.

Between The Wars

Sixty thousand regulars and volunteers, soldiers, sailors and airmen, had left Bristol to fight in the Great War – "the war to end all wars". Four thousand never returned. Those that did come home were left with the mental and physical scars of the bloodiest conflict in history. The Battle of the Somme alone had claimed the lives of nearly 1.5 million men, and on the first day of that battle 60,000 British soldiers were killed.

The British government had introduced rationing in February 1918. In the immediate aftermath of the war, Britain, unlike central Europe, was not starving even if food was in short supply.

Most soldiers returned with little prospect of returning to their old job, despite the pre-war undertakings. Bristol initiated a programme of road building and construction to provide employment. For a while, the country seemed to prosper despite various privations. Many thought that the transition from war to peace would be difficult, but fears of an immediate post-war depression proved unfounded: 1919 and early 1920 saw a strong worldwide inflationary boom.

It was not until the Spring of 1919 that the majority of club members were demobilised, and discussion of resurrecting the club began. At that time the club's ground at North View was still being used for allotments. There were practically no club funds, and of the members of the three XVs run prior to the War only three agreed to play again. A meeting was held on September 18th 1919 in the Fortts Rooms on Queen's Road, which some 30 prospective players attended.

A number of fixtures were subsequently arranged, mainly against public school teams. On 4th October 1919, the first game since 28th May 1914 took place against Bristol Grammar School, resulting in a 33-3 victory. The following week Clifton College was beaten 25-0. All matches of course had to be played 'away' until a new ground was found; Gloucester and Bristol did offer fixture dates, but the club committee felt that it would be better to wait until a side could be raised that would be good enough to provide serious opposition.

On November 23rd 1919 a service was held at St. Mary Redcliffe to honour those who had died. The vicar began his address with the words "let us remember with thanksgiving and with honour before God and men the rugby footballers of Bristol and Clifton who have died giving their lives in the service of their country, and who numbered over 300".

Finally, a ground was found at Redland Green. Fixtures re-commenced from November 1919, but the facilities were atrocious. What could be salvaged from the old ground at North View was brought over by club officials, who also prepared the pitch because no groundsman was as yet available.

This first season was a struggle at times. The away match against Bridgwater on 6th December 1919 was perhaps, on the face of it, a farce, but the events preceding the match explain much about the situation. The night beforehand, only seven regular 1st team players had declared themselves available. On the Saturday morning, telegrams were sent to members who had only just joined the club that same week. In all, 33 were asked and 15 travelled. Alwynne B. Fricker was one of the recent recruits and received his telegram at 9.30am. He turned up at the regular meeting-place ready in his Clifton kit, assuming it was a home fixture. Nevertheless Fricker made it to Bridgwater in time to play the game of his life – alas in vain since Bridgwater fielded a side with seven county players and ran out 53-0 winners. Later that season, the match arranged against Bath had to be cancelled following the death of a Bath player in a match against Cross Keys the previous week.

Clifton 1st XV of 1919-20 Back Row (L-R): E. Seymour-Bell (Hon.Asst.Sec.), M.A. James, W.F. Gaisford, B. Whitolow, J.P. Hitchings, E.S. Bromhead, K.O. Bathgate, G.V. Gibbs (Hon.Sec.). Middle Row: H.

Pyrke, M. Durant, E.C. Ball, A.B. Sellman (Captain), J.H. Savory, A.N. Carruthers. Front Row: H.H. Apted, V.E. Rogers, M.E.K. Westlake, E.C. Evans

Manley Angel James, in the 1919-20 photo, was awarded the Victoria Cross during the World War I when he was only 21 years old.

In terms of results it was far from a successful season, but most importantly it was completed. There were certainly a few obstacles, notably the ground. At the end of the season 93 men had been tried, of which 49 played for the 1st XV. On one Saturday, the club had to invite 53 members to play before two full sides could be fielded.

At this distance it's difficult to appreciate in full the challenges faced, but somehow - despite being decimated by the men killed, wounded, psychologically damaged and just grown too old to play again - the club survived and, in time, flourished.

The Clifton 1st XV towards the end of the 1920-21 season. (L-R) Back Row: E. Seymour-Bell, G. Hasler, W.F. Gaisford, E.C. Ball, T.N. Bowerbank, E.G. Everett, J. Dommett, R.D. Just. Seated: G. Ellis, T.D. Lewis, A.N. Carruthers, Mr.H.W. Beloe, F.M. Arkle, B.S. Chantrill, J.L.W. Ewens. On the ground: J. Bromhead, J.P. Hitchings, L.C. Waters.

The Clifton 1st XV in Jubilee year 1922-23. (L-R) Back Row: A.N. Carruthers (Hon.Sec.), J.A. Dommett, J.P. Hitchings, J. Bourne, V.E. Rogers, G.S. Castle, R. Huntly, L.H. Hatcher, H. Pyrke, L.C. Waters. Seated: C.N. Hatcher, E.H. Esbester, F.M. Arkle (Captain), H.W. Beloe (President), H. Bromhead, W.F. Curtis, W.A. Thomas. On the ground: R.D. Evans, G.A. Rose.

The Jubilee Dinner to celebrate 50 years of rugby at Clifton was held at the Grand Hotel, Broad Street, Bristol on Saturday March 25th 1922. The chief guest was Mr E. Prescott, the President of the Rugby Union. Six players from 1872-73 were present - Walter Stuckey Paul and his brother Arthur Clifford St. Paul, Edmund Judkin Taylor, Francis Morris, Herbert George Edwards and James Arthur Bush. The founder and first honorary member James Fuller Eberle also attended, as well as all the captains from 1903 onwards. Walter Stuckey Paul spoke of the debt of gratitude that rugby football owed to the public schools, and owed by the Clifton club specifically to Rugby School, Marlborough, Blundell's, Lancing, Leys, Bath, Cheltenham as well as to Bristol Grammar School and Clifton College which had fostered and nurtured so many of the club's players.

The Clifton 1st XV in 1924-25. (L-R) Back Row: F.T. Pollinger, E.O. Lambert, T.D. Corpe, D. McArthur, H.S. Holman, T.D. Harris. Seated: B.O. Foster, E. Esbester, H.W. Thomas, J.H. Bromhead, F.M. Arkle, C.N. Hatcher, J.A. Dommett. On the ground: H.R. Wirgman.

On September 11th 1926 Clifton Rugby Club at last moved to a new ground at Eastfield Road in Westbury-on-Trym. It had taken three years to get the site cleared, to lay the pitches and to erect the new stand. The first match was against Bristol, resulting in a 35-6 defeat. During the post-match celebrations, the Bristol captain Len Corbett, whilst replying to the toast to his club, advised Clifton to take the game more seriously if the glories of past days were to be revived.

Members of the Clifton and Bristol clubs who took part in the special match to open the Eastfield Road Ground on 11th September 1926 (Bristol in white). (L-R) Back Row: W. Saunders (Clifton's groundsman), J. Pippin of Bridgwater (Referee), J.S. Tucker, T.F. Hood, A.T. Hore, D. McArthur, F.G. Pratten, T.D. Corpe, J.H. Bourne, R. Thomas, H. Shreman, H.R. Wirgman, R. Ling, R.G.B. Quick, H.L. Shepherd, W.G. Francis, W. Rossiter, J.K. Morman. Seated: G.D. McMurtie, J.A. Tucker, R.D. Evans, L.J. Corbett (Bristol captain), C.N. Hatcher (Clifton captain), M.V. Shaw, A.M. Stotesbury, E.L. Stinchcombe, C.F. Crinks. On the ground: T. Babington, J.H. Bromhead, C.B. Carter, A.F.B. Ham, F.J. Coventry.

During the 1930s the club's playing fortunes gradually improved. As well as the regular opponents - Bristol, Bath and the public schools, the fixture list included Moseley, Neath and Wasps.

It was in April of 1931 that the reporter John Rickman moved to Bristol to work for the 'Bristol Evening World'. His nom de plume at the time was Trymdon, which he chose because some of his friends lived in Westbury-on-Trym, the location of the Clifton RFC ground. Trymdon was also the name of a famous racehorse. A regular at the ground, he was occasionally persuaded to play for the club. On one occasion the team was two men short for a match at Weston-super-Mare, and probably against his better judgment he agreed to turn out as a centre three-quarter. This caused him to be an hour late with his report, and a severe reprimand from the newspaper's editor inevitably ensued. John Rickman went on to become a famous horse-racing commentator in the 1970s on ITV's 'World of Sport' programme. He died at Midhurst in Sussex on 13th October 1997.

The 1932-33 season was notable in that 17 games were won, the highlights including the matches against Bristol (8-6) and Bath (14-3). The victory over Bristol was the first in eleven years, the last occasion having been in 1921, the year the Memorial Ground was opened.

A week after that Bristol game, the Clifton team flew from Bristol Airport to Cardiff on 1st October 1932 to play Glamorgan Wanderers. Seven aeroplanes were used to fly club officials and players. Although an 'early adopter', Clifton was not the first team to take to the air, as Harlequins had done so on 9th February 1923 from Croydon to Cologne to play The British Army of the Rhine.

Clifton 1st XV taken March 1934. (L-R) Back Row: H.M. Evans, H.C. Russell, G.W. Davey, P. Gardiner, A.T.G. Neale, E.P. Mortimer, G. Osmond, S.J. Carwardine, C.A.L. Richards. Seated: H.S. Pamto, K.O. Cottee, D.C. Osbourn, A.F.B. Ham, T.H.B. Burrough. On the ground: H.S. Robinson, E. Robertson.

FEBRUARY 23 1935 · 7

A Spotlight on the Clifton v. Weston Match at Eastfield

A local newspaper's view on how to improve the Clifton side prior to the Weston match on 23rd February 1935.

Clifton XV taken on 12th February 1938. Clifton beat Bridgwater 24-8. (L-R) Back Row: J.H.N. Moss, G.J. Dillon, D.A.?, R.A. Garrett, B.G.?, G.?. Seated: W.T. Gresham, T.H.B. Burrough, C.D. Garrett (Captain), R.G.?, M.?. On the ground: F.W. Grant, D. Fleming, D.B.E. Paine, ?.

1938 saw the spectre of war looming once again. Anderson shelters were issued to people in Bristol - free to those with an income of under £250 a year, and £7 for everyone else. Gas masks were issued in September 1938.

Minutes of the September 1938 club meeting record a request to display a recruiting notice for the Territorial Army on the notice board. Bristol was preparing for the worst.

World War II Roll of Honour

The Treaty of Versailles that followed the Great War caused Germany to lose a significant portion of its territory, prohibited the annexation of other states, limited the size of the German armed forces and imposed massive reparations upon a country that was starving. It was against this background that extremism flourished. A bare 15 years after the Great War ended, the 'war to end all wars', the National Socialists were in power, Germany began the process of re-armament and the world slid inexorably towards another devastating conflict. On 1st September 1939 Germany invaded Poland, and two days later Great Britain declared war on Germany.

Three members of the Clifton RFC committee promptly met and cancelled fixtures on the 4th September, although the club did go on to play seven matches, mainly against service sides, before the ground was let for soccer matches and grazing. It was then requisitioned by the War Office in 1941 and used as a gun-site for an anti-aircraft battery. The Football Association acted more quickly than its rugby counterpart this time, suspending its league programme on 8th September whilst the Rugby Football Union waited until the 15th to impose suspension notices (Richards 2007, p.146).

Evacuees arrived in Bristol from London thinking that they would be safer, but on 20th June 1940 Bristol was to suffer the first of 548 bombing raids.

Pupils from Clifton College's preparatory school were evacuated to Butcombe in Somerset, which was thought less likely to be the target of German bombs than Clifton. For the same reason, the senior school occupied several of the requisitioned hotels at Bude in Cornwall. Clifton College itself was later used by the US Army, and it was here that General Omar N. Bradley of the U.S. 12th Army Group planned the D-Day assault on the Normandy beaches, codenamed Operation Overlord.

'The Holmes' in Stoke Bishop, the former home of ex-Clifton captain Hiatt Cowles Baker, was used by General Bradley and his senior staff as their residence during this period. Photographs of the six senior officers who lived here, as well as a signed statement by General Eisenhower, now hang in the hall.

The following pages document the 16 Clifton RFC players known to have fallen in the Second World War. Once again, we would like to express our grateful thanks to those families and friends who have been so generous with their time, information and photographs.

1940

Flight Lieutenant Edward Patrick Mortimer 7th August 1940
Edward Mortimer was born on 17th March 1911 in Keynsham, near Bristol.

Edward Patrick Mortimer in the Clifton 1st XV, March 1934.

He joined the RAF and was the pilot of a Blenheim MkIV P4902 that stalled and spun into the ground near Cranfield on the evening of 7th August 1940. Aircraftsman Vivian Hollowday, a member of 14 FTS (Flying Training School), was walking back home when he saw the accident. He attempted to rescue the crew but was beaten back by the flames. He was awarded the George Cross for conspicuous gallantry.

The Public Record Office holds the following abridged accident report:

Mertlands Farm, North Crawley, Bucks, at 2235hrs on 7th August, 1940.

The pilot's instructions were to fly from Upwood to Bicester 53 miles, Bicester to Northampton, 25 miles and back to base 33½ miles. At a time when the aeroplane should have been near Northampton it was seen flying in an easterly direction 20 miles SE of the scheduled course and close to Cranfield aerodrome where night flying was taking place. When opposite the wireless telegraphy station the machine was seen to stagger. Five seconds later at about 1500 ft and while still in flying position it lost speed and spun to the ground.

The aeroplane struck the ground at a moderate speed and came to a stop pointing east, the engines were not on at the time. From its position and the proximity of trees immediately behind it could be judged to have been flattening out, probably in a left hand spin. Fire occurred immediately and destroyed all the centre of the machine. All safety belts were burnt. One body was found in the navigator's compartment and one in the gunner's cockpit. The third, that of the pilot, was lying face down 72 yards east of the wreckage and he had evidently fallen from a considerable height. His parachute was unopened and was on the ground 4 ft away; the harness was free. The rip-cord had not been pulled. No parts broken or otherwise were found to show the circumstances under which he left the machine.

The engines, extensively damaged by fire, were stripped but appeared to have been in good order at the time of the accident.

Examination of the pilot's parachute harness showed that the release ring had not been turned and while in the locked position had been driven back by direct impact on the front. This had forced the spin-loaded plunger out through the aluminium casing and had released the catches and then the harness. From this it may be seen that the harness was in position on the pilot's striking the ground.

The investigation concluded that the pilot may have lost his way, was trying to identify Cranfield aerodrome and on suddenly becoming aware of the risk of collision with the night flying machines stalled the aeroplane while climbing. Alternatively it was thought possible that on losing sight of the aerodrome flares he lost control in the "black-out".

Edward Mortimer is buried in Bury Cemetery near RAF Upwood.

1941

Pilot Officer Robert William Sloan 17th January 1941
Robert Sloan was born in 1915 and educated at Prior Park College, Bath, a Catholic boarding school.

He was the son of Samuel Hugh and Catherine Ann Sloan, of Pembroke Road, Clifton, and became manager of T. Buxton & Co. Ltd, chemists on Queens Road, Clifton. He joined Clifton RFC in 1937.

After the outbreak of war he trained as a Pilot Officer and his appointment was confirmed on January 2nd 1940 in the Equipment Branch of the RAF. His base was the RAF Central Flying School at Upavon, which began life in 1912 as an RFC base and is sometimes referred to as the birthplace of the RAF.

The circumstances of his death are unknown. He left a wife, Barbara, whom he married just three weeks before his death.

Robert Sloan is buried at Upavon Church Cemetery in Wiltshire. On the Clifton RFC war memorial his name is incorrectly spelt Sloane.

Robert William Sloan

Arthur Acraman Greenslade 28th February 1941
Arthur Greenslade was born in early 1894, the son of William Acraman Greenslade and Eliza Shipley (née Bromiley). His debut for Clifton RFC came in the 1913-14 season. He was also noted as an inventor. He registered two patents, in 1930 for a tressle and 1937 for a moving sign.

During World War 1 he was a captain in the 3rd South Lancs, RFC and RAF. When war came again, Arthur joined the Home Guard, 11th Gloucestershire (City of Bristol) Battalion. Prior to his death his mother and son, who was part of the same Home Guard Battalion as Arthur, were killed during the bombing of Bristol. It is believed that he died after a raid on Eastville and East Bristol sometime during 26th or 27th February 1941. He is buried at Canford Cemetery with his parents and son.

Ordinary Seaman John Dennett Burrough 21st April 1941
J.D. Burrough was born on 30th July 1914 in Reigate, Surrey, the son of Hedley and Caroline (née Potter). His brother was the Clifton and Gloucestershire player Tom Burrough.

John was educated at Clifton College from 1924 to 1928 and married Kate Guest on 10th August 1940. He was a schoolmaster who lived in Frenchay, Bristol. Kate's parents lived at Frenchay House, next door to Grasmere (later The New House) where John and his wife lived.

John Burrough on his wedding day

John was killed in a German bombing raid concentrated on the Royal Naval Dockyards and Barracks at Devonport on 21st April 1941, during the worst period of the Plymouth Blitz. He was killed instantly on a street while walking back to his ship, H.M.S. Mackay, during the raid and was picked up by a civilian party. He is buried at the Plymouth (Weston Mill) Cemetery.

HMS Mackay

Sub-Lieutenant John Arthur Osborn 29th May 1941
John Osborn was born in late 1917 in Bristol, the son of Iver Dennis and Dora (née Aldridge) and the brother of Clifton player Dennis Osborn.

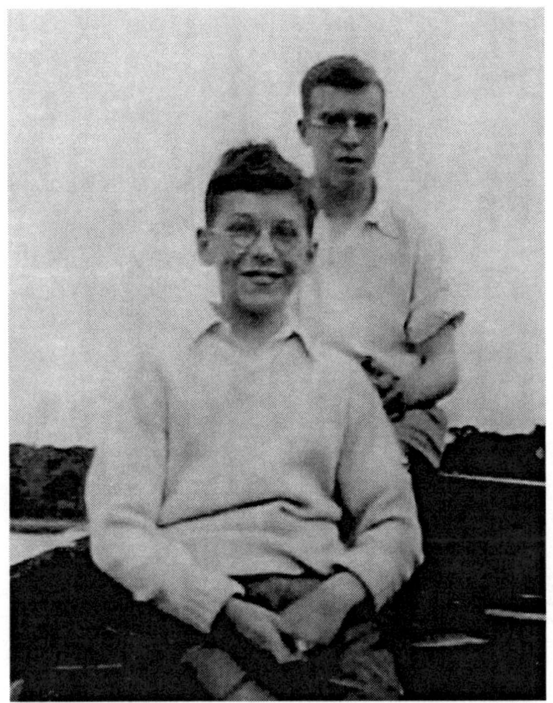
John Arthur Osborn, aged 12, (foreground), with his brother Dennis Charles Osborn in 1930.

He was commissioned RNVR (Severn Division) in 1939, joined HMS Orion the 1st September 1939 (the day Germany invaded Poland) and served as a Sub-Lieutenant on the ship which was badly damaged after being bombed on 29th May 1941 during the evacuation of Crete.

After the Crete evacuation HMS Orion left Heraklion Bay and headed for the Kaso Strait. Orion expected to be five miles south of the Strait by dawn on 29th May, but the destroyer Imperial suffered damage to her steering gear and had to be sunk, forcing Orion to reduce her speed by 14 knots for two hours. Instead of entering the Strait during the night, she found herself there at dawn. She was soon spotted by enemy reconnaissance planes and shortly afterwards bombed by Stukas. HMS Orion eventually limped back to Alexandria where the clean-up began. The ship was so badly damaged that repairs were only fully completed in San Francisco some ten months later. Orion was later used by Winston Churchill and his staff from 30th January to 2nd February 1945 in Grand Harbour, Malta, whilst holding talks in preparation for the Yalta conference

In all 262 people lost their lives on Orion during the evacuation of Crete, of which 112, including Osborn, were from the ship's company.

John Osborn is commemorated on the Plymouth Naval Memorial.

HMS Orion, May 30th 1941, the morning after the action in the Mediterranean.

Captain John Frederick Giles 27th December 1941
Johnny Giles was born in the summer of 1917 in Long Ashton, the son of Frederick William and Margaret Mary Maud Palin (née Evans). He was educated at Bristol Preparatory School and at Kelly College, Tavistock.

On 27th July 1936 he was commissioned 2nd Lieutenant, 6th Battalion the Gloucestershire Regiment of the Territorial Army (Bristol), and later transferred to the Royal Tank Regiment Royal Armoured Corps. He was mobilized on 24th August 1939, promoted to Lieutenant on 27th August 1939 and to Captain on 9th December 1940. He was the Army heavyweight boxing champion, Southern Command.

Having already been prominently involved in the commando raid on Lofoten on 1st March 1941, he was killed during a successful action by British commandos on the Norwegian coast at Vaagso on 27th December 1941. This raid was known as Operation Archery. It was the first time all three services combined their resources to mount an amphibious raid against a defended coast.

It was said that the men he commanded held him in such awe that it bordered on worship, and that they would follow him anywhere, without question.

An account of his death appeared in the book 'Commandos and Rangers of World War 2':

South Vaagso lies on a narrow strip of shoreline beneath a sheer rock face several hundred feet high, the town's unpainted wooden buildings struggling along the three-quarters of a mile of main road running parallel to and some 50 yards from the shoreline. Down this road No. 3 Troop were led by their Troop officer, a giant of a man, making a series of wild charges. They had taken several houses when the Troop officer - Captain Johnny Giles - was working his way room by room through another. He and his men had killed three Germans in this house when he burst into the back room and was probably killed by a fourth German hiding there, although he may have been hit from across the street. Such is the confusion of street fighting that bullets can appear to come from anywhere and everywhere.

Johnny Giles

Johnny Giles' body was taken aboard HMS Prince Charles by the soldiers he commanded of 3 Troop, and he was buried at sea. He is commemorated at the Brookwood Cemetery, Bagshot.

The aftermath of the Raid on Vaagso was swift. Within 48 hours the Germans had sent two full companies of soldiers and a Gestapo detachment to the area. Nearly 70 townspeople had left with the landing force. The German headquarters in Oslo ordered that the eldest male relative of each of the Norwegians who escaped to England with the landing forces should be arrested and shipped to the concentration camp at Grini.

With every incident of sabotage by the underground, Hitler became more convinced that Norway would be the place where the Allied Invasion would take place. Between the end of 1941 and the 6th June 1944 the Germans reinforced the number of troops. Consequently, on D-Day 372,000 German troops were sitting idly by in Norway, guarding against an invasion that never came.

More than twenty years after the raid a former member of 3 Troop reminisced about Captain Giles, recounting incidents that typified the manner in which Giles inspired every man of the troop to give everything he had to the task at hand. He concluded his account this way:

I remember my old captain very well and, whenever I can, in November I place a small cross in the Commando Field of Remembrance at Westminster Abbey for him. He had high standards and was a first-class officer and gentleman. I would have followed him anywhere and, thank goodness, I eventually shall.

1942

Ernest Henry Broadbent Usher 23rd April 1942
Ernest was born on 9th September 1892 in Bristol, the son of Ernest Lawes and Martha Ann (née Broadbent). His father – who also played for Clifton RFC from 1897 - was part of the Usher family that had a brewery in Trowbridge until taken over by Watney Mann in 1960. Ernest was educated at Clifton College from 1907 to 1909 and joined Clifton RFC the year he left school.

During World War 1 he was a battery commander with the Royal Field Artillery, and from 1928 onwards served with the Regular Army Reserve of Officers. Research has as yet failed to elicit details either of his Military Cross award or of the circumstances of his death.

Ernest Usher is buried with his parents at Canford Cemetery. His name is missing from the Clifton RFC memorial.

Wing Commander Murrey Vernon Peters Smith 27th July 1942
M.V. Peters Smith was born on 15th April 1916 and joined the RAF on 16th April 1935 on a six-year short service commission. He was graded Pilot Officer on 16th April 1936, rose to the rank of Squadron Leader by 1st June 1942 but was killed less than two months later. He was awarded the DFC on 21st November 1941.

Whilst Commanding Officer, 57 Squadron RAF, based at RAF Feltwell, Norfolk, his Wellington III bomber took off at 1530 hours on 27th July 1942 in an attempt to use the cloud cover to reach Bremen, but crashed; cause of loss and crash-site were not established.

All five servicemen on the flight were re-buried in Becklingen War Cemetery. The cemetery location was chosen because it overlooks Lüneburg Heath where Montgomery accepted the German surrender from Admiral Dönitz on 4th May 1945.

1943

Major Joseph John Wagstaff 12th April 1943
J.J. Wagstaff was born in the Spring of 1919 and educated at Bristol Grammar School from 1929 to 1936. He joined Messrs Hudson-Smith and Briggs, accountants, after school and was a member of the Territorial Army, joining the Regulars just before war broke out. He was subsequently promoted to Major in the Royal Artillery 349 Bty, 76 Heavy Anti-Aircraft (H.A.A.) Regiment.

Allied troops made a series of landings on the Algerian coast in early November 1942. From there they swept east into Tunisia, where the North African campaign came to an end in May 1943 with the surrender of the Axis forces. Bejaia, formerly Bougie, was the landing place of the 36th Infantry Brigade Group on 11th November 1942.

He married Doreen (née Hunter) in the summer of 1940, and they made their home at Chew Stoke, Somerset. JJ Wagstaff died of wounds and left his widow and a daughter. He lies buried at La Reunion war cemetery, south-west of Bejaia in Algeria.

Wing Commander John Ryan Cridland 31st May 1943
John Cridland was born on 3rd December 1910 in Bristol, the son of Henry James and Rachel Mary, and educated at Radley College from 1924 to 1928. After school, he joined the family firm Cridland and Rose which made boots and shoes. The factory was bombed out in the Second World War and the company folded.

John Cridland married Jean Patricia Croom-Johnson on 29th June 1940. His wife gave birth to a son, Alastair Ryan, on 17th January 1943.

He joined the 4th (City of Bristol) Battalion of the Gloucestershire Regiment in 1931. On 5th July 1938 he joined the RAF and served with the old 501 Squadron at Filton. During the war, as service no. 90459 in the Royal Air Force (Auxiliary), he fought in the battle for France, trained fighter pilots near Chester, and then became a liaison officer in North Africa. He was killed on 31st May 1943, aged 32, when his Hurricane came down, and is one of 2,903 Commonwealth servicemen to be buried in Mediez-el-Bab in Tunisia.

Wing Commander John Ryan Cridland

Lieutenant-Colonel John Richard Easonsmith 16th November 1943
J.R. Easonsmith was born on 12th April 1909 in Bristol, the son of George and Daisy. He was educated at Mill Hill School in London.

Photograph taken when Easonsmith played for Clifton RFC against Clifton College on 1st October 1927, aged 18.

Before the war he was a travelling wine salesman with the Emu Wine Company, based in Bristol. In the summer of 1935 he married Honor Gertrude Marsh; they had one daughter.

John Easonsmith joined the old 4th Glosters (66th S.L. Regt.) at the outbreak of war and was transferred to the Royal Tank Regiment. In December 1940 he was transferred to the Middle East theatre and joined the Long Range Desert Group, nicknamed The Scorpions, an elite Special Forces outfit that operated behind enemy lines. The unit was established in Egypt following the Italian declaration of war (June 1940) by Major Ralph A. Bagnold with the assistance of Captains Clayton and Shaw, acting under the direction of General Wavell, who bestowed a second nickname – the 'Mosquito Army'. The group specialised in mechanised reconnaissance, intelligence gathering and desert navigation and Special Air Service soldiers would refer to it as 'the Libyan Desert Taxi Service'. The unit was assigned 150 New Zealand volunteers; Bagnold had reasoned that New Zealanders, being mostly farmers, would be more adept at using and maintaining machinery. In October 1943 Easonsmith became their Commanding Officer.

In May 1943 the LRDG was sent to the Lebanon where it was trained for a new role in mountain warfare. Unexpectedly, however, the unit was then posted to the Aegean and took part there in the battle for the island of Leros, where Easonsmith was killed whilst leading what was described as a pointless patrol.

His name is incorrectly spelt Eason-Smith on the Clifton RFC War Memorial. John Easonsmith is buried at Leros War Cemetery on the shore of Aghia Marina Bay.

Captain Anthony Frederick Price 28th November 1943

A.F. Price was born in the Spring of 1910 in Bristol, the son of Stephen Alfred and Lillian Maud.

Tony Price in the 1931-32 Clifton RFC 2nd XV

He was killed whilst serving as a captain in the Royal Fusiliers (City of London Regiment). Two months after invading Italy, the Canadian and British forces of General Bernard Montgomery's Eighth Army were south of the Sangro River, at the edge of the Germans' heavily-defended Bernhard Line.

Montgomery planned a two-pronged advance which would bring his troops up the coast to Pescara, then swing west to cut across the Italian peninsula and reach Rome.

One of the objectives just south of Pescara was Ortona, a coastal town which had both a port and a railway marshalling yard. Capture of the port would facilitate landing supplies for Montgomery's troops as they moved forward. This point also occurred to the Germans, who quickly brought in engineers to ruin the harbour facility, denying the use of the port to the Allies.

The first stage of Montgomery's offensive was to cross the Sangro River, some four hundred metres wide. The attack went in on November 28th and was a success. Formations of British, New Zealand, and Indian troops were able to get bridges across the river and seize the opposite banks after tough fighting. Over the next few days they drove the Germans back about eight miles to the Moro River - about five miles south of Ortona. There the fighting petered out, the front-line formations of both sides worn down.

Tony Price is buried at the Sangro River War Cemetery (together with Llewellyn Campion Wood of the same Regiment, killed the following day).

Lieutenant Llewellyn Campion Wood 29th November 1943
L.C. Wood was born in early 1914 in Wandsworth, Surrey, the third son of Percy Thornton and Lucy Florence (née Enright). Having joined the North Somerset Yeomanry at the outbreak of war, he was drafted overseas early in 1940. He was commissioned in 1941 and fought in the Syrian campaign, where he was captured but escaped. For his work in Syria he was mentioned in despatches. Lieutenant Wood was a keen member of the Scouting movement and a junior partner in Glover's Advertising, Bristol.

1945

Trooper Ronald Henry Gardner 18th January 1945
R.H. Gardner was born in Gloucester in the Spring of 1923, the son of Leonard and Fanny (née Money).

He joined the Royal Tank Regiment after leaving school. By the end of January 1945 the Allies had driven up from the 'D' Day landings through Northern France, Belgium and Southern Holland, pushing the front line from the Schelde Estuary near Antwerp eastwards as far as Nijmegen on the Waal; then across to the Maas, which it followed down as far as Roermond, from where the U.S. forces joined up. The task facing the British and Canadian troops in the north was to reach the Rhine, but the attempt was halted by the winter weather - first by snow and hard ice, then by a prolonged thaw which turned the ground into glutinous mud covered by slush. The British tried to edge forward in January, but only vehicles with special armour could make any headway. It seems likely that Gardner's tank was blown up, either by a mine or anti-tank fire, during this stage of the offensive.

Ronald Gardner is buried at Nederweert, Eindhoven. In the same row of graves as Gardner's lie another five men from the Royal Tank Regiment, all killed on the same day - perhaps fellow crew in his tank?

Captain Charles Andrew Rennie 17th March 1945.
C.A. Rennie was born in early 1915 in Newport, Monmouthshire. He was the son of John and Lucy (née Knight) of Clevedon, Somerset and the husband of Annie (Nan) Taylor, whom he married in 1939.

He was commissioned in the Royal Armoured Corps in 1942 and seconded to the Indian Army in April 1944. At the time of his death he was attached to the 16th Light Cavalry (Indian Armoured Corps). On the 27th and 28th February 1945 he was part of a patrol on the Meiktila to Rangoon road. He was awarded the Military Cross immediately after the action.

His citation for gallantry read as follows:

Capt. Charles Rennie
This officer on the 27th and 28th February 1945 led two patrols down the Meiktila-Rangoon road. Little was known of the enemy dispositions at this time, particularly the placing of his anti-tank weapons. Despite this, Capt. Rennie completed both the patrols which went out to a distance of 23 miles into the enemy occupied territory. His skill and boldness produced excellent results. On the first day, apart from producing the information required, by a skilful series of traps, he destroyed three enemy trucks full of personnel and one staff car, killing a total of 24 Japanese. On the second day he killed another 12 Japanese. He was recommended for an immediate award of the Military Cross.

On the 17th March 1945 Captain Rennie was sent with a troop along the Meiktila to Rangoon road. While searching the village of Kandaung a Japanese sniper in a tree shot and wounded Captain Rennie through the back of the head. He was immediately evacuated to a casualty clearing station where he died.

His Military Cross was posthumously awarded four months later.

Charles Rennie is buried at Maynamati War Cemetery, now in Bangladesh, far away from where he died. Graves from isolated places in the surrounding country, and some from as far afield as Burma, were moved into the cemetery by the Army Graves Service and later on by the CWGC. He is also commemorated on the memorial at St Quiricus and St Julietta Church, Tickenham (near Nailsea), and listed as a World War II casualty by the Clevedon Civic Society.

Able Seaman George Hamilton Turner 20th March 1945
GH Turner was born in Axbridge on 1st September 1911, the son of Edward Algernon and Edith Mary (née Cotgrave). He was educated at Clifton College (1922 to 1927), as were his two brothers William and Robert. After Clifton he moved to the Royal Naval College at Pangbourne and joined the Royal Naval Volunteer Reserve, serving on HMS Lapwing at the time of his death.

HMS Lapwing

HMS Lapwing was a British sloop of 1,250 tons torpedoed and sunk in the Kola Inlet off Northern Russia while on escort duty with the outward bound convoy JW-65. It was her ninth voyage to Russia. After giving support to the Normandy landings the Lapwing joined the 7th Escort Group based on the Clyde in Scotland. During the morning of 20th March 1945, U-968 attacked the convoy off Northern Russia, north of Murmansk, in position 69º26'N, 33º44'E, and reported a destroyer and a Liberty ship sunk and another Liberty ship torpedoed. In fact, the sloop HMS Lapwing of the 7th Escort Group and the Liberty ship Thomas Donaldson were sunk. Lapwing was hit amidships at 10:58 and sank 12 minutes later with the loss of 158 of the crew, including Turner; 61 survived. Many that died were frozen in the icy Arctic waters. The ship broke in two but the stern section remained afloat for 20 minutes and enabled some survivors to be rescued.

George Turner in the 1932 Clifton 2nd XV

George Turner is the last Clifton RFC player known to have died on military service. He is commemorated on the Plymouth Naval Memorial.

The U-boat U-968 surrendered on 16th May, 1945 at Loch Eriboll, Scotland. During Operation Deadlight, a post-war Allied operation, she was sunk on 29th November

1945 in position 55.24N, 06.22W. Operation Deadlight was the codename for the scuttling of the unwanted German U-boats which the Allies captured at the end of the war.

Grand Admiral Karl Dönitz announced on the radio on 8th May 1945 the unconditional surrender of the German forces.

The two names missing from the Clifton memorial, those of Usher and Greenslade, would have brought the total of club men recorded there to 16, of which 15 are described above. Mystery continues to surround the identity of the last, J.E. Bush, because there are three servicemen of that name who died during the war, two of which definitely had Bristol connections. One intriguing possibility is that the club mistakenly included Brigadier-General John Ernest Bush, who fought in both the Boer War and the Great War. He died on 28th October 1943 at Berkhamsted and is not listed by the CWGC as having died in the 2nd World War – his years of active service were of course far behind him. He was a regular for the club in the 1870s and 1880s and there is more in the Famous Players chapter. The likeliest fit, if the extra initial is ignored, is with Lieutenant-Commander John Edward Scott Bush, born on 2nd April 1909, the son of Clifton player Robert Edwin Bush and the nephew of John Ernest Bush, one of the more famous Clifton RFC players of the 19th century. He was educated at Clifton College from 1922 to 1927 and served on HMS Hood between 1928 and 1929. He was killed on HMS Kipling on the 23rd May 1941, aged 32, during the evacuation of allied soldiers from Crete after the German invasion of the island, and is commemorated on the Chatham Naval Memorial.

Lacking the obvious Clifton 'pedigree' but with exactly the right initials, a John Eric Bush was born on 10th November 1921, the son of Herbert John Sholto Bush of Knowle, Bristol. He was in the RAF Volunteer Reserve, died on 25th March 1943 aged 21 and is buried at Kirklee Cemetery in Mumbai.

We may never know his true identity, but his name stands proudly with his fellow Clifton players who made the ultimate sacrifice.

The War Memorial at Clifton Rugby Football Club. Photograph by Kayna Clarke.

Up To The Present Day

The re-establishment of the club after the Second World War was a lot easier than in 1919, although it took several years (until the 1948-49 season, in fact) to get the Eastfield Road ground de-requisitioned with only one pitch and limited changing accommodation being made available.

The first game of the season was played against Clifton College on 6th October 1945. The team included Jim Bryan of Bristol, three university men and three lads from HMS Vansittart, a depot ship in the harbour. Putch Beloe was on leave and played despite a broken finger.

The Clifton side that played Clifton College on 6th October 1945 in front of the Pavilion at Clifton College.

Rationing persisted for some years after the war and the club needed permission from the RFU to allow them to buy three new balls and five bladders with 36 clothing coupons. The 75th Anniversary of the club was celebrated with a special dinner at Wills Recreation Hall.

In 1949 the club officially changed its name from Clifton Football Club to Clifton Rugby Football Club.

The 1950s were a difficult period for the club, with so many key players being selected to play for their county that results suffered. In 1950 Bristol dropped the fixture against Clifton from a Saturday to a less attractive midweek match.

The 1950s saw a Clifton player gain an international cap for the first time since 1887. Many players have played for their country before or after playing for Clifton, but John David Currie, who was also at Oxford University, was capped to play against Wales in 1956 whilst an active club player. He played eight times in all for England whilst at Clifton, but moved to Harlequins when he completed his degree.

The Clifton 1st XV of 1960-61. (L-R) Back Row: R.J. Bradford, D.F. Saunders, R.A.M. Whyte, S. Richards, M. Wallington, J.G.S. Young, M. McClaren, J. Parrott, T. Garrett. Seated: M. Skelton, G. Jones (Vice-Captain), Col. G.S. Castle (President), M.J. Moss (Captain), R. Blake. On the ground: W. Painter, I. French, A. Lewis.

1962 was the year that Clifton started its almost annual overseas tours with trips to France in 1962, Italy in 1963, and Spain in 1964.

On the first tour Colin McFadyean scored two tries on his debut against the French 1st Division Club Stade Marmande of Bordeaux, Clifton winning 16-11.

The Clifton and Marmande teams that played on 22nd April 1962. Colin McFadyean is standing third from the left.

This tour was notable for the boisterous behaviour of the players. This started when the team coach arrived at the hotel in Bordeaux; the occupants found that it couldn't park outside because the road was narrow and there were two cars standing in front of it. Everyone got off the coach, picked up the two cars and moved them bodily. Two of the party then took it into their heads to visit every pub in the area. They arrived later at a civic reception, given by the Mayor of Bordeaux, in no fit condition for social niceties - indeed one of the pair passed out. The next day during the match the second of the culprits, sporting a huge hangover, asked the Clifton captain Mike Moss in which direction he was supposed to be playing. Later on that day, at another evening reception, the same player felt unwell halfway through a speech and had to retire to the public gardens in front of the Town Hall.

The Clifton 1st XV of 1962-63. (L-R) Back Row: P. Rowe, G. Watson, D. Cook, P. Duggan, C. Tatham, R. Blake. Middle Row: R. Clifton, I. Lindsay, J. Budd, M. Wallington, V. Leadbetter, J. Munro, R. Bradford. Front Row: J. Parrott, R. Rossiter, G. Jones, M. Moss (Captain), I. French, D. Saunders. P. Murray

The year continued in boisterous vein. On 18th December 1962 the *Bristol Evening Post* reported allegations concerning an incident at the Clifton Rugby Club annual ball the previous evening. It was alleged that a firework was thrown at the group 'The Raindrops' while it was performing 'The Locomotion'. According to the report, *their leader Mr Leonard Beadle claimed "it was a disgusting exhibition of hooliganism". "We were told the dance would be noisy", said Mr. Beadle. "We did not mind this. Neither did we mind the bread rolls being thrown, but we do seriously object to china being thrown. One of the group was hit on the shoulder by a plate, just below the neck, but fortunately he was only bruised. Jackie Lee, our 24 year old girl singer was greatly distressed by our reception. She was hit in the face by a cream bun." The Raindrops, currently appearing at a Bristol club claim their act was due to last 30 minutes, but they abandoned it after only ten, when the alleged the firework was thrown.*

Club spokesman Louis Eskell who was at the Victoria Rooms, said "the whole thing is a gross exaggeration. I don't know what Mr. Beadle is talking about. Of course, bread rolls were thrown. They always are, it's traditional, as all rugby followers know. But there was no crockery thrown, and I certainly did not see the Raindrops' girl singer hit on the face with a cream puff. There were no cream puffs included in the supper menu."

Clifton skipper Mike Moss said "We all thought it was a great success. They were well received in the usual spirit of rugby club dances."

The Evening Post reporter continued: *from where I was sitting at the dance, I did not see anything hit or go anywhere near the close harmony group. A couple of plates were sent curling-fashion across the dance floor, but did not rise above the floor or go within 30ft of the cabaret stage. It was certainly one of the quietest, good-natured rugby club dances I have attended. There were no cream puffs or pies available as missiles.*

The Raindrops were an up-and-coming band at the time, and their original line-up in 1958 featured Vince Hill. The group, who at one time appeared on televisions 'New Faces', obtained a two year regular feature on BBC Radio's 'Parade Of The Pops' during which they would sing the pop songs of the day. The other members of the group were Beadle, his wife Jackie (Lee) and future successful songwriter Johnny Worth (a.k.a. Les Vandyke). Jackie Lee had a future career as a soloist and reached the chart on a couple of occasions - her best known work was 'White Horses' by 'Jacky'. As well as her career as a member of the Raindrops she recorded as 'Jacky', 'Jackie Lee' and 'Jackie Lee & The Raindrops'.

As a consequence Bristol University banned Clifton RFC from using the Victoria Rooms again. As far as we are aware that ban still exists.

In 1964 Clifton appointed Dickie Rossiter as the club's first Chairman; until that year it had been part of the captain's role. Dickie had captained Clifton during the previous season. He played cricket for Gloucestershire 2nd XV and the Royal Navy and would later become the President of Gloucestershire County Cricket Club.

The Clifton 1st XV of 1964-65. (L-R) Back Row: Cautley Tatum, Malcolm Wallington, Peter Niven, Roger Bradford, Dick Fogden, John Budd. Seated: David Saunders, Mike Moss, Graham Jones (Captain), Dickie Rossiter, Mario Polledri. On the ground: Chris King, Jim Marshall, Bill Painter, David Horne.

In 1969 Clifton appointed its first official coach, Elwyn Price. He would later teach rugby at St. Brendan's and work for Bristol as the Colts Coach and a talent scout. Through the ranks at St. Brendan's Grammar School he coached Peter Johnson, Mike Rafter, Nigel Pomphrey, Pete Polledri and Mark Regan. He then moved to Colston's School and helped Andy Robinson coach the side that won the Daily Mail u-18s Cup.

Elwyn Price was born on 5th July 1927 and was educated at Loughborough University. He played football for Barnet and had a trial with the Welsh Amateur national team, but decided to turn his attention to rugby.

During his 34 seasons of coaching rugby, Elwyn Price had produced more than 20 schoolboy and colt internationals. Four went on to become full internationals. The highlight of his coaching career came during the 1977-78 season when, uniquely, he had players in all four England teams of the day. Mike Rafter appeared in the full national side, Peter Polledri and Nigel Pomphrey played for the under-23s, Mark Schiefler, who later played for Canada, for the under-19s and Paul Jeffery for the under-16s.

Elwyn Price who died on the 11th October 1996 in Bristol.

For the 1971-72 season the RFU acceded to club pressure without fully accepting leagues, and introduced the Knock-Out Cup. A limited amount of commercialism was also accepted, with an agency employed to sell perimeter advertising at Twickenham in 1973 and the Knock-Out Cup sponsored by cigarette company John Player from 1975.

1972-1973 was the Centenary of the club. The season started with a combined Clifton/Bristol team beating Newport 15-9 on 5th September 1972.

A Centenary Dinner was held at the Grand Hotel, Bristol on 15th September 1972, the same venue as for the Jubilee Dinner held in 1922. The dinner was attended by F.M. Arkle, L.J. and M.D. Corbett, Lt.-Colonel V.F. Eberle, Lt.-Colonel C.J. Gardiner (First Rhodes Scholar at Oxford), V. Leadbetter (ex-Clifton RFC and England), A.T. Voyce (Gloucester and England) and P.D. Young (ex-Clifton RFC and England Captain). Unfortunately C.A.L. Richards (Clifton RFC and Oxford University), S.B. Richards (Clifton RFC and England) and John Rickman were three of 25 who couldn't make it.

Clifton RFC XV 1972/73. (L-R) Back Row: John Poole (Touch Judge), Andy Pesynski, Gary Rogers, Chris Jenkins, Pat Donovan, David Rogers, Steve Gregory, Alex Hay. Seated: Keith Lowe, Mario Polledri, Grant Watson, Graham Mansfield, Simon Luxmore. On the ground: Phil Hepburn, John Cannon, Martin Hinchliffe (Ballboy), Mike Wagstaff, Ken Nelson. This photograph was taken before the Centenary match against Blackheath on 7th April 1973.

The season finished with a tour of the Bahamas and West Indies.

Rugby union's commitment to amateurism was increasingly out of line with other major sports. Cricket abolished the distinction between amateurism and professionalism in 1963, tennis went open in 1968 and football followed cricket's example in 1974. The increase in games and the demands on players made professionalism inevitable.

Clifton RFC 1st XV 1975/76 at Eastfield Road for the last season. (L-R) Back Row: N. Ellis, C. Morley, R. Osborn, R. Miller, N. Williams, P. Nash, S. Eaves, K. Lowe. Seated: F. Thomas, P. Johnson, S. Luxmore, D. Rogers, J. Cannon, P. Donovan, G. Watson, I. Elvin.

In 1976 Clifton moved to a new ground at Cribbs Causeway, which immediately went into the Guinness Book of Records as having the tallest rugby posts in the world. An incredible 66ft 6ins high, they involved the use of 860ft of steel tubing used in triple thickness.

Jack Rowell moved to Lucas Ingredients in Kingswood as an accountant. He started coaching at Clifton in 1977 and moved to Bath in 1978-79. He took with him from Clifton the forwards Simon Luxmore and Nick Williams. Between 1978 and 1994 Rowell coached Bath during their golden era, winning eight John Player/Pilkington Cups and five League Championships. He left Bath in 1995 to take over from Geoff Cooke as England coach, announcing that England would give up the forward-dominated, risk-free strategies that had won so many Five Nations titles in the past, instead adopting a 'running rugby' style. Rowell's England won twenty-one of their twenty-nine matches, including the 1995 World Cup quarter-final against Australia. In percentage terms of games won, Rowell is England's most successful rugby union coach. In 1998 he became a non-executive director on the board of Bristol when millionaire businessman Malcolm Pearce saved the club from extinction. In September 2000 he became Managing Director and in 2002 returned to Bath as Director of Rugby.

The Clifton Juniors started life on 16th October 1977. Four club members initiated the first session on a very wet Sunday morning in the long grass of the 1st XV goal area at Cribbs Causeway. Six small boys turned up for the first week, a good coaching ratio, and 16 came in the second week but were still not allowed onto the main pitches. The parents soon took an active interest on and off the pitch

The four club members involved were three teachers, club captain Ian Elvin, John Cannon and Roger Opie as well as Steve Rowlands who was keen to input some Welsh creativity into the sessions.

Clifton wins the first Bass South West Merit Table in 1979-80

The Clifton 1st XV 1980-81. (L-R) Back Row: Pete Robb, Dave Trew, Huw Davies, Andy Rendle, Jon Masters, Marcus Aniol, Peter Brown, John Jeffrey , Alistair Watson, ?, John Cannon. Seated: Des Morgan, Steve Peters, Martin Dart, Jim Jamison, Peter Johnson, Paul Pearce, Mark Wilcox. On the ground: Tony Sandham, Kevin Rafter, Alistair Hitchin, Neil Morgan, Stuart Cooke, Dave Norman, Nick Penny

It is the 1987 Atlanta – Bahamas Tour Programme that reminds us of the story which became part of Michael Green's 'Even Coarser Rugby' book:-

Two whole teams were involved in one unfortunate experience. The famous Bristol club, Clifton, were playing a 2nd XV game with Trowbridge and both sides lined up for a minute's silence before the game in respect to the dead, only to find out they were paying their last respects to someone's cat. The animal belonged to John Hickey, usually 1st XV full-back, who had been irritated at the lack of sympathy shown by team-mates at the death of the pet, so he decided to get his own back and told the referee that a valued member of Clifton had died and could they have a minute's silence before the game. Afterwards he tried to collect money for a wreath, but no one would contribute.

Alan Morley joined Clifton as Head Coach in 1990 along with Peter Polledri and started a golden period for Clifton. Alan was still at Colston's School when he played for Bristol United. He joined Bristol in 1968 and started as a centre, but was moved to the wing by the Bristol coach because "you don't like passing". This move was a revelation as Morley could swerve while running at top speed. He was watched by Wales as he qualified for the country through a Welsh mother. He opted for England and was selected for their tour of South Africa. He has played for the British Lions, Barbarians and Gloucestershire on 73 occasions and scored a try on his debut for England against South Africa. Amazingly he only received seven England caps. Peter Polledri played for Bristol, Gloucestershire and England U-23, who he captained.

In the 1993-1994 season Clifton was unbeaten, and most unusually there were very few injuries so the same team took to the field for most of the season. The main players used were: Full backs - Mark Beresford and Adrian Freeman, Wings - Trevor Davis and John Phillips (top try scorer in the league), Centres - Kerry Lock and Pete Naivalurua, Fly Half - Simon Hogg, Scrum half - Paul Jeffrey, Props - Andrew Ellis Fisher, Paul Cox and Andrew Heywood (ex Weston), Hooker - Lee Ashford, Second Rows - Chris Blake and Tim Edbrooke, Back Row - Peter Polledri, Wayne Hone and Mark Wyatt. Clifton won the Courage Division 4 Championship but unfortunately the club was relegated the following season.

The 1993-1994 Courage Division 4 Champions. (L-R) Back Row: Mike Anderton (Vice President), Sheridan Smith (Team Sec.), Mike Skinner (Team Manager), Derek Farley (Vice President), Simon Swales, Andy Heywood, Mark Wyatt, Chris Blake, Andy Fisher, Peter Naivalura, Grant Watson (President), Fred Cannon (Vice President), Norman Golding (Chairman), Bob Miller (Assistant Coach), Brian Jordan (Fixtures Sec). Seated: Charles Newth, Paul Cox, Paul Jeffrey, Wayne Hone (Captain), Kerry Lock, Richard John, Mark Beresford, Peter Polledri (Coach). On the ground: Phil Cue (Assistant Coach), John Phillips, Trevor Davies, Mike Cotton, Simon Hogg.

An International Rugby Board report of 1995 recognized the breaches of amateurism where players, although not paid cash, received cars and numerous other perks. Players around the world were also increasingly being enticed to play rugby league. Rugby union was the last major team sport not to have turned professional at the highest level. On 26th August 1995 the International Rugby Board declared rugby union an "open game" and the Heineken Cup started the following season.

English rugby was to struggle for six years with infighting. The three main parties, the Rugby Football Union, the club owners and players, seemed to be constantly in dispute.

In August 1995 the Rugby Football Union tried to regain some measure of control by announcing a one year moratorium on professional rugby in England, but a succession of wealthy businessmen starting emerging to invest in clubs – Nick Wray at Saracens, Sir John Hall at Newcastle and Tom Walkinshaw at Gloucester.

Sixty players were being lured away by the World Rugby Championship, a Kerry Packer style series being planned behind the Rugby Football Union's back. The World Rugby Championship fell apart when the South Africans, the current world champions, ripped up their provisional agreements and accepted the terms of their Union. The English players opted to sign with their clubs. Chaos was averted for a short time. Professionalism was here to stay.

The many smaller unions across the globe have struggled (both financially and in playing terms) to compete with the major nations since the start of the open era. In England, whilst some teams flourished in the professional era, others such as Richmond, Wakefield, Orrell, Waterloo and London Scottish found the going much tougher and have either folded or dropped down the leagues.

Clifton 1st V 1998-99. (L-R) Back Row: Gozie Ezulike, Mark Harraway, Andy Collins, Eddie Smith, Stuart Roberts, Alex Adams, Adam Barnes, Nick Cooper, Andy Blackmore, Ralph Knibbs (Captain), Peter Polledri (Director of Coaching). Front Row: Justin Morris, Duncan Jeffrey, Barnaby Kent, Andy Stephens, Tony Hussey, Rhys Oakley, Mark Wyatt, Nick Lloyd, Mark Lloyd, Jason Packer.

After England won the World Cup on 22nd November 2003, rugby clubs across the country saw an increase in people wanting to watch and play the game. The mini and junior sections at Clifton, in particular, saw a large increase in members.

After losing the ownership of the Memorial Ground in 1998 Bristol moved their headquarters and training facilities to Clifton's Cribbs Causeway Ground.

Clifton 1st team squad 2005-2006. (L-R) Back Row: Leo Costello, Iain Johnston, Daniel Moussa, Sam Kent, Luke Harris, Bobby Blake, Ryan Cox, Mike Kempton, Eddie Smith, Carl Broaders, Ollie Sills, Dave Healy. Front Row: Tom Gawman, Greg Shortman, Chad Steetskamp, Andy le Bell, Tom Lambert, Paul Morgan, John Barnes, Rob Viol

The 2008-09 season was one of the most memorable in the club's history with the club promoted as champions of South West 1. In fact the team succeeded in this without even completing their fixtures; the away game against Bracknell, and last fixture of the season, was cancelled. Bournemouth conceded second place to Bracknell after agreeing that Clifton would not beat Bracknell by the 140 or so points required to dent Bracknell's points difference sufficiently for Bournemouth to claim the second place from them.

In that season Clifton also made its first Twickenham appearance, losing the Intermediate Cup Final to Hartpury College 31-41 on 18th April 2009. A few weeks later the Combination Cup Final was won 45-21 against St. Mary's Old Boys at the Memorial Stadium on 6th May.

The Clifton squad at Twickenham on the 18th April 2009. (L-R) Back Row: Charlotte Walker, Wayne Cochran, Sam Wilkes, Rob White, David Butler, Vince Murrell, Darren Barry, Paul Reid, Sam Kent, Chris Rowlands, Leo Glass, Fielies Coetsee, Barnaby Kent, Mike Young. Middle Row: Alistair Allison, Ollie Sills, Andy le Bell, Graham Hardy, Daniel Frost, John Barnes, Steve Leonard, Rob Viol, Phil Schmidt. Bottom Row: John Levis, Andy Raines, Henry Mace, David Rees.

Clifton RATS

The Clifton RATS were born in 1982 out of the old Extra A XV at Clifton Rugby Club. The side had been captained by Ingram Lovelock who was giving up because selection took place on a Monday, and by Friday all the players had been moved up the sides to fill the gaps. Steve Gundry was then asked to take it on and he agreed to do this only if the team could be taken out of the club selection process. It was pointed out to Gundry that this would make the team similar to an invitation side known as the RATS, so the name was adopted. Before this time John Cannon and Peter Martin ran occasional games for retired players, who were also known as the RATS.

It is claimed that the name RATS is an acronym of Rebels Against Time and Senility – older members dedicated to playing the game at a reasonable level without the difficult bits such as selection and training. The idea was to give an opportunity for rugby players over the age of 35, who had stopped playing at the highest level and wished to prolong their rugby career for a few more years. The very first game John organized was against Cardiff Vets at home under floodlights, but unfortunately the game did not last very long as a balloon collided with a power cable and all electricity at the club was lost. However in true rugby tradition Cardiff returned the following Wednesday and the match was completed. Fixtures were initially sparse, but eventually the committee agreed that the RATS could take over the Extra A fixtures and there were regular games most Saturdays after that. The reputation for skilful rugby, albeit at a slower pace, was soon recognised and an influx of players who would hitherto have retired joined the club's ranks. These included ex-Bristol players such as John Watson, John Carr, John Lane and Peter Stiff as well as ex-Clifton stars such as Pete Johnson and Jon Masters. On one occasion Gareth Evans of Cardiff, Wales and the British Lions guested for the team against Avon & Somerset Police.

The Clifton RATS started regular weekly fixtures in 1982-83 under Steve Gundry. There was a weekend trip to Paris, which was very memorable. Captaincy then went to Tony Brooke in 1984 and to Richard Pettinger in 1985. As the side evolved, more and more people joined and the success grew. Regular touring started in 1985 with a trip to play army teams in Berlin: out on Friday, two games on Saturday and Sunday, returning on Monday evening after a long lunch in KaDeWe, a department store in Berlin rather like Harrods food hall. The new tourists could not understand why they would go to a department store for our last day. Once greeted with the magnificent selection of lobster and scallops they soon shut up. This put paid to the rumour that good seafood only comes from the coast.

In 1989 Richard Pettinger took over as captain of the Clifton RATS and organised tours to Berlin on a regular basis as well as to Paris; however, when John Hickey embarked on his RATS career he and Richard decided that they should tour much further afield and in the space of 12 years the whole of the world was covered, North and South America, Africa, Russia, China and Australasia. These tours included the winning of two World Veterans Tournaments in Ottawa in 1992 and San Francisco in 1995, where their opponents in the final were Richmond Heavies. There were some strong opponents on some of these tours, particularly in South Africa where the RATS were unbeaten and in Argentina where they narrowly lost to the Pumas who fielded a number of ex-internationals. Richard and John's organisational skills allowed for extra-curricular activities, which included private cabaret in Las Vegas, white water rafting in Zimbabwe, sailing in South Africa and skiing in Canada.

The Clifton RATS on tour in Berlin in front of the Olympic Stadium in 1991. (L-R) Back Row: Alf Troughton, Mike Nangreave, Tony Godfrey, Selwyn Lloyd, Mike Crook, Charles Faye, George Wysocki, Nick Hornsby, Mark Wilcox, Tony Brooke. Front Row Dave Sables, Paul Stevens, Dave Crews, Richard Pettinger, Nick Baker, John Hickey, Jon Masters.

The Clifton RATS toured South Africa in 1996 and won all four games against very good opposition including Villagers and Hamiltons, South Africa's two oldest clubs. Ed Morrison went with them and refereed all the games. In the preceding year he had refereed the World Cup Final and met Nelson Mandela. Ed was something of a celebrity in South Africa, much to his amazement. This was a pivotal trip for him, some time before professional refereeing was instigated. Ed had given up his job to officiate at the World Cup and was still out of work one year on. The RATS managed to get him sponsored and took him with them, a very wise move. In their final match against Villagers they had two South African international referees running the line, just so they could say they had refereed with Ed.

Special mention should go to A-Gas, the RATS principal sponsor. Yearly dinners were organised to raise money to assist the RATS who may have been 'between jobs' to come on tour. This in fact enabled Ed Morrison to do so and to carry out a speaking engagement to A-Gas major customers in South Africa. Jon Masters joined A-Gas during these years and is now Managing Director. The residue from these dinners was given to St Peters Hospice.

The Clifton RATS on tour in South Africa, in front of Table Mountain in 1996. (L-R) Back Row: Steve Hucker, Pete Polledri, Pete Smith, Geoff Crane, Charles Faye, Mark Wyatt, Robert Parr-Head, Steve Wyatt, Simon Beech. Row 2: Mark Wilcox, Mike Crook, Dick Owsley, John Stewart, Dave Sables, Nick Baker, Ed Morrison, Austin Shepherd. Row 3: Doug Stewart, Steve Gundry, Jon Masters, John Watson, John Carr, Kyl Hamilton (The Ghurkha), Pete Stiff, Jake Haskell. Front Row: Jon Reynolds (The Doc), Tony Godfrey, Roger Hill, John Hickey, Richard Pettinger (Captain), John Raine (Chairman), Ingram Lovelock. Missing from photo but on tour: Mark Nutbeen, Andy Rendle, Dave Rae, Dave Crews.

Clifton RATS organised a dinner for the club's 125th anniversary in 1997. The theme was Five Nations with speakers from them all. RATS Captain, Richard Pettinger recalls

Willie John McBride, Chris Rea and Neville Walsh represented Ireland, Scotland and Wales, with Paul (Tapper) Thompson (ex-CRFC) filling the England spot. This presented the dilemma of where to find a Frenchman so he was invented under the name of Pierre L'Embrouille, the 'legendary French flanker from Toulouse'. He was in fact a school teacher from Kent, speaking a little French. L'Embrouille is French for mix up or muddle up. One of the most amusing sights was watching Dickie Rossiter greeting him in pidgin French and trying to make him welcome, remembering all his caps for France.

The RATS toured Argentina and Uruguay during May 1998. Even though it had been 16 years since the Falklands conflict, there were still some worries about the reception they would receive. Richard Pettinger recalls:

When we toured Argentina, which was not long after the Falklands conflict, we met and were looked after by an Argentinean player called Ricardo Bellver. He did a fine job of hosting us and any concerns we had post-Falklands were soon swept away by the genuine warmth of our reception. His opening comments were "So nice to see you down here so soon after the troubles, well....why wouldn't you come, you won after all". This broke the ice superbly! When we toured Chile the following year Ricardo flew over and joined in as a player and tourist. In the Prince of Wales Club in Santiago I had to give a speech at a dinner following the game, Ricardo of course was with us and at the time relationships between Chile and Argentina were not good to say the least. General Pinochet and Margaret Thatcher had formed a strong friendship and British planes took off from Chile to attack Argentinean targets. At the dinner I was seated next to an English-speaking Chilean architect. I was picking his brains as to what I could say in my speech. I noticed when we arrived at the club that there was a tree in the grounds that had been planted by Margaret Thatcher. This tree did not look in great health, and I suggested that I may make a comparison between the tree and Margaret Thatcher. I was told in no uncertain terms that this would not go down well as Lady Thatcher was a personal friend of the General, and so for that matter was everyone else in the room. It transpired that we were seated with the power brokers who ran Chile! Ricardo had asked me earlier if he might say a few words, so after my speech (delivered in restrained fashion) Ricardo stood to speak. He delivered a most moving speech describing past friendships and latterly hostility between their two countries. After his speech he received a standing ovation from the Chileans, a wonderful moment I will never forget. Ricardo remains a true friend to this day.

Clifton RATS played their last game on 23rd April 2005. The Evening Post reported: *Clifton's world famous Rats team hang up their boots for the final time after facing St Brendan's Old Boys at Cribbs Causeway tomorrow (4pm).*

Recalling the supposed expansion of the acronym, fly-half John Hickey surmised that

The rebellion seems to be over, and time and senility have finally won. The bumps and bruises are finally becoming too much for the likes of Pettinger and Hickey, who are now all nearing or over 50, to bear.

There hasn't been a game this season when I haven't finished with a small injury but there is also the problem of regularly getting a side together, said former Northern and Gosforth prop Pettinger, *Rugby is declining. It is becoming more difficult to get players*

to turn out every week. One of our guys, Daryl Hickey, is playing for the Clifton first team at the moment. He is playing for Clifton against Penryn at 2.30pm and then will play the first 15 minutes of our game. But a lot of guys in their early 30s are packing up now. We can cope in the scrum and can hold our own against many first-team packs. The problem is running.

John Hickey added:

You are expecting a lot of guys to take our places but they all retired ten years ago. When we go it has always been blokes. We have never taken the wives. The wives did say to us 'you can go on tour. We don't mind but you can only go for one week'. They thought we were going to Cornwall or Bournemouth but we went for long weekends to Canada! In a one-week tour of Australia we went to Sydney, Perth, the Great Barrier Reef and then back home. There hasn't been a particular place we have not been able to go because it's too far away. We just jump on a plane and go. We said from the outset: let's go to places where rugby teams haven't been before.

The Clifton RATS before their final game. (L-R) Back Row: George Wysocki, Tony Brooke, Nick Baker, Peter Brown, John Hickey, Mark Wyatt, Doug Stewart, John Carr, Pete Stiff, Mark Wilcox, Dave Rae, Jon Mastes, Kevin Rafter, Front row: Frazer Halliday, Paul Lander, Simon Beech, John Lane, Richard Pettinger, Dave Crews, Paul Stevens, Nick Leader,

The RATS produced lavish programmes with pen pictures for each player as well as photographs from the previous tour.

Pettinger said:

The pinnacle for me was going to Cape Town and winning all four of our games out there. Willie John McBride's British Lions and Clifton RATS are the only teams not to lose in South Africa. We have also played in Argentina and the match was refereed by Pablo Deluca. They enjoyed the game so much they quickly arranged for us to play a second match against the Pumas' veterans' side.

Clifton Ladies

Clifton Ladies started in 1985 after a one-off charity match against Weston Hornets. The game was advertised as Hornet Honeys v Clifton Suspenders in aid of the Guide Dogs for the Blind Appeal, and its success was largely down to the efforts of Martyn Boot and Hannah Penry. Playing in that match were Martyn's wife Jill and Tina Cumberlidge, who has for a number of years coached at Clifton. Hannah's husband was coaching one of the junior sides at Clifton; Martyn Boot was captain of the Bandits and volunteered to help coach along with Paul "Josh" Josham, who was the Colts captain. The St Brendan's teacher Elwyn Price also encouraged three or four of his 6th form girls to join the squad. Clifton won by one try to nil, scored by Sue Bloor in her one and only appearance.

The glory years for Clifton Ladies were between 2001 and 2004: they won the Premiership League in 2004, Cup in 2002 and were League Runners-up in 2001 and 2003.

In their final season as Clifton Ladies six players gained international honours for Wales and five for England, who took the Six Nations Grand Slam. In the regional competition six more Clifton squad members represented the South West team that reached the national final.

In their time the Clifton Ladies produced 36 internationals. For England there were 15 - Sarah Wenn, Karen Henderson, Pip Spivey, Val Blackett, Monica Lewinska, Katy Storie, Jo Poore. Suzie Appleby, Sophie Hemming, Georgia Stevens, Kim Oliver, Nolli Waterman, Alexandra Pilkington, Fiona Britten and Heather Fisher. For Wales there were 18 - Elaine Skiffington, Marie Louise Bowen, Helen Calhane, Kate Eaves, Fran Margerison, Pip Evans, Jackie Morgan, Dawn Mason, April Dent, Cath Bufton, Nadge Griffiths, Jo O'Mahoney, Liza Burgess, Mel Berry, Jamie Kift, Claire Flowers, Naomi Thomas and Non Evans. There was also Dutch international Beatrice Terpstra, Irish international Orla Lacey and French international Nadia Nougaret.

Clifton Ladies in 2006-2007. This was taken at the last match of the season when they won promotion back into the Premiership. (L-R) Back Row: Nolli Waterman, Emma Baldwin, Kim Oliver, Georgia Stevens, Heather Fisher, Heidi Thompson, Suzie Appleby, Kathryn Tulley, Monica Lewinska, Clare Turner, Sophie Hemming, Mair Harding, Alexandra Pilkington, Megan Jones. Front Row: Claire Flowers, Letitia Delaney, Jamie Kift, Toya Chapman, Rhiannon Parker, Emma Liddle.

In 2008 Clifton Ladies became part of the Bristol Rugby set-up and changed their name to Bristol Ladies. They still play their home matches at Clifton's Cribbs Causeway ground.

Present Day

Today, Clifton RFC is one of the largest clubs in England's West Country, running four senior men's teams and all mini and junior age groups from under-sevens to under-19s.

For the 2009-2010 season Clifton strengthened the 1st XV team with former Bristol captain Matt Salter, as a player and coach. He also coaches at the Bristol Academy.

The league structure for 2009-2010 was changed by the RFU. Clifton play at Level 4: National Two North & South with a total of 16 clubs in the division, increased from 14, which replaces National Three North & South. This means:

- 30 matches per season in each league
- Champions promoted from each league, and the bottom three teams in each league relegated at the end of season 2009/10
- Promotion play-off for clubs finishing second in each league
- The two champions meet in a National Final

The 1st XV and Wanderers squad taken on 17th September 2009. (L-R) Top Row - Evan Sawyer, Greg Setherton, Dan Venn, Nick Gerrish, Darren Barry, Ben Glynne, Richard Walker, Barnabus Purbrook,

Adam Jones, Steve Leonard, David Rees. Middle Row - Charlotte Walker, Lee Watkins, Steve White, Paul Reid, Rob White, Ali Alison, Gareth Price, Paul Morgan, Tom Prince, Will Pomphrey, Barnaby Kent, Vince Murrell, Phil Schmidt, Dave Cook, Andy le Bell, Leo Glass, Norman Golding, Andy Petts, Mark Nichols. Bottom Row - Jack Martin, Sam Smee, Sam Wilkes, Sam Kent, Fielies Coetsee, John Levis, Darren Lloyd, John Barnes, Mark Regan, Matt Salter, Henry Mace, Dean Taylor, Harrison Tovey. Absent - Andy Raines, Rob Viol, Ollie Sacco, Pierre Clarke, Barnaby Nelson, Gareth Mason, Mako Vunipola

The Wanderers play in the West of England Merit table and are part of the First Team squad. The Wanderers and First Team train together, and a strong fixture list ensures that for those who do not make the first team there are nevertheless plenty of competitive games.

The Clifton Bandits taken on 3rd October 2009 at Cotham Park. (L-R) Back Row: Ben Sharpington, Nick Smith, Spencer Halliday, Chris Nussey, Tom Dickie, Charlton Charles, Jamie Lopez, Pete Milmine, Adam Golding, Ali Roberts, Frazer Halliday, Felix Ellis, Mike Auty. Front Row: Sam Parker, Jon Maycock, Marc Kendall, Joe Marsden (c), Mike Wilcox, Andy Bates, Roger Carver, Chris Ruell.

The Bandits play in the Evening Post 2nd XV Merit table and are coached by Mark Nichols. They are made up of a combination of youth and experience and train on the same days as the First Team squad.

Clifton Nomads 2008-2009 merit table 3rd XV winners. (L-R) Back Row:Will Handley, Alex Dunbar, Steve White, Chris Reull, Ross Borthwick, Jirx Singh. Middle Row: Trevor Davis, Rupert, Tim Gomm, Andy Rendle, Matt Alexander, Antony Demison, Tim Frost, Rob Churcher. Front Row: Andy Stephens, Gary Boyland, Scott McGrath, Jamie Farrell (Vice-Captain), Aftab Hamid (Captain), John Carr, Chris Ball.

The Nomads play in the Bristol Combination 3rd XV Merit Table. Although they do not train, they are a very skilful group made up of many ex-first team players and some ex-Bristol players. A number of the world-famous RATS also turn out for them from time to time.

Clifton Juniors have constituted for a number of years the flagship of the club. There are over 300 players spread across twelve age-groups. The standards and achievements are high.

Some of the players who started in the Junior section now perform in Premiership rugby and represent their country. Some of the players who have gone through the junior ranks at Clifton are:

Ross Blake - Cambridge University and London Irish (formerly Bristol and Bath) and Scotland u-21.
Alex Brown - Gloucester (formerly Pontypool, Bath and Bristol) and England.
Joe Ewens - Weston-super-Mare (formerly Rotherham, Bristol, Bath, Bedford and Gloucester) and England u-21.
Duncan Hayward - London Scottish (formerly London Welsh and Bristol) and England u-21.

Ollie Kohn – Harlequins (formerly Plymouth and Bristol).
Sean Marsden - Exeter (formerly Bristol, Exeter, Neath and Glasgow) and England u-21.
Rhys Oakley - Leeds Carnegie (formerly Gwent and Bristol) and Wales.
Jonathan Pritchard - (formerly Bath, Bristol, Newport and Rotherham) and Wales A.
John P O'Reilly - Esher (formerly Leicester, Worcester and Leeds Tykes)

Clifton Juniors (u15s and 16s) taken on 13th September 2009. Photograph by Kayna Clarke.

Clifton Juniors (u13s and u14s) taken on 13th September 2009. Photograph by Kayna Clarke.

Clifton Minis (u10s, u11s and u12s) taken on 13th September 2009. Photograph by Kayna Clarke.

Clifton Minis (u7s, u8s and u9s) taken on 13th September 2009. Photograph by Kayna Clarke.

The **Executive Committee** at the club for the 2009-2010 season:

President - Norman Golding
Joint Chairmen - Andy Sayner & Steve White
Honorary Secretary - Roger Bealing
Honorary Treasurer - Keith Bonham MBE, DL
Club Captain - Sam Kent
Marketing / Finance - Mike Anderton
Fixtures Secretary - Ben Jordan
Marketing - Peter Gibbons
Marketing / Communications - Adam Brooks
Licensee - Martyn Boot
Projects Consultant - Rob Davies
Director of Rugby - Darren Lloyd

Team Coaches
Head Coach - John Barnes
Forwards Coach - Mark Regan
Assistant Coach - Fielies Coetsee
Player Coach - Matt Salter
Wanderers Coach/Manager - Mark Nichols
Team Manager and Fitness - Andy Petts
Club Physiotherapist - Lee Watkins

Team Captains
1st XV - John Levis
Wanderers XV - Paul Morgan
Senior Players' Group - Sam Kent, John Levis, Henry Mace, Rob Viol, Vince Murrell

Bandits XV Captain - Joe Marsden
Bandits Vice-Captain - Spencer Halliday
Nomads XV Captain - Aftaab Hamid
Nomads Vice-Captain - Jamie Farrell
Youth Development Officer - Mark Nichols

Clifton Junior Section
Coaching Co-ordinator - Andy Sayner
Membership Secretary - Henrietta Gibbs
Hon. Treasurer - Mike Anderton
Club Shop Manager - Nicky Anderson
Fixture Secretary - Mark Baker
Child Protection Officer - Rosie Heald
Clifton Tournament Co-ordinator - Steve Carpenter

At the start of the 2009-2010 season Brian Jordan became President of the Gloucestershire Rugby Football Union. He joined a list of several Clifton men who have held this important position.

The annual match between Clifton College and the club ended in the 1960s for health and safety reasons. The last 1st XV match was on 29th September 1962, but the Wanderers carried on for a number of years. However Clifton College still provides many players to the Clifton Rugby Football Club at all levels.

Famous Players

Picking out a selection of famous players inevitably involves a subjective approach, so the authors would like first of all to acknowledge the valuable contribution of all the club's members since its foundation. A fuller and ever-growing list of prominent individuals can be found on the Clifton RFC History website www.cliftonrfchistory.co.uk

Born on 5th November 1854 at Prestbury in Gloucestershire, **Charles Strachan** was educated at Cheltenham College from 1866 to 1871. His father Richard Ellison Strachan and uncle, James Fuller Eberle were amongst the founders of Clifton RFC in 1872. Charles was club captain during its first five years from 1872 to 1877, and his brother Walter was a fellow team-member.

He died in 1931 at his home, Towerleaze, in Sneyd Park facing the Downs. In 1934 the house became a health hydro owned by T.J. and D.B. Elliott. It began with 45 bedrooms, and a new wing was added in 1950. A single room cost between 17 and 21 guineas a week and a double room between 18 and 23 guineas. It was closed in the 1970s and demolished to make way for flats bearing the same name.

James Arthur Bush was born on 28th July 1850 in Cawnpore (now Kanpur) in the Indian state of Uttar Pradesh. His father was a major in the British Army. When the family returned to England, James attended Clifton College from 1863 to 1868. He excelled at cricket and rugby and in June 1870 he appeared for Gloucestershire CCC in their first match against Surrey on Durdham Down in Bristol. He continued to appear for the county as wicket-keeper until July 1890.

James Bush initially played rugby for Blackheath because at the time when he won his first cap (1872) England selections were made only from clubs affiliated to the Rugby Football Union. As the RFU had only been in existence for one year, very few clubs were affiliated; this of course proved to be a problem for many players. It was the RFU's way of forcing the clubs to become affiliated and to standardise the rules, and meant that in the early days of internationals all the players selected were attached to London clubs. Bush played five times for Blackheath and joined Clifton RFC when the club was founded, seven months later. He went on to gain four further caps for England, the last on 6th May 1876 in the last 20-a-side rugby international.

James Bush played rugby for Clifton until 1877 and then turned to association football as a goalkeeper for Clifton Association FC.

He became a close friend of W.G. Grace and was best man at his wedding on 9th October 1873 at St.Mathias Church in West Brompton, London. He took part in the 1873 MCC tour of Australia which also served as W.G's honeymoon.

James Bush took over the family business in 1905 with his brother George de Lisle Bush. The family had run a warehousing company since 1700 and the building was known as Bush Warehouse. The company was inherited by James's son, Reginald Arthur Bush, in 1926 and was known as J&R Bush until it ceased trading in the 1960s. The building is now more famous as the home of The Arnolfini, a leading centre for contemporary arts.

He died on 21st September 1924 in Clevedon, near Bristol, and is buried at Canford Cemetery.

Born on 14th November 1850 at Shoreham-by-Sea, Sussex, **William Octavius Moberly** was the son of the Reverend C.E. Moberly, an assistant master at Rugby School. William was educated at Rugby School, where he was a member of the rugby XV and cricket XI in 1868-69. He became captain of Oxford University RFC in 1872 and his one international cap for England was gained on 5th February 1872. On November 7th 1869, upon the foundation of their club, OURFC had set out rules amongst which Rule 2 stated "that the Captain always be a Rugbeian". Rugby School provided captains for the university team from 1869 until 1933.

Moberly, like James Bush, was hamstrung by the RFU's affiliation policy. OURFC was not affiliated, so he joined Ravenscourt Park although he never actually played for the club.

He joined Clifton RFC in 1876, having joined the teaching staff at Clifton College in 1874.

Moberly played cricket on 64 occasions for Gloucestershire between 1870 and 1887 and also represented Worcestershire and Leicestershire. He usually played as a batsman but could also turn his hand to wicket-keeping if his team-mate James Bush was unavailable.

On 30th July 1884 Moberly married Emma Florence, the sister of fellow Clifton RFC player and Gloucestershire cricketer, Edmund Judkin Taylor (Clifton College 1864-1867). The couple were married by the Bishop of Exeter, assisted by the headmaster of Clifton College as chaplain.

William Moberly died on 2nd February 1914 at Polurrian, Mullion in Cornwall after retiring from Clifton College in 1913.

Walter Fairbanks was born on 13th April 1852 in Chatham, Kent, the son of Reverend J.H. Fairbanks. He was educated at Clifton College from 1869 to 1871 and at Clare College Cambridge where he was a Rugby Blue in 1873 and 1874. He became an Assistant Master at Clifton College in 1875 and remained there until 1896, joining Clifton RFC in his first year there. He played cricket three times for Cambridge University, although he was not awarded his 'Blue', and 24 times for Gloucestershire.

In 1891 Fairbanks was a founding member of the Bristol & Clifton Golf Club. He won the Moncrieffe Cup in 1891 and 1893-1895, and the Broke Cup in 1895. He was club captain from 1891 to 1896.

Fairbanks moved to Denver, Colorado in 1898 and spent his winters in southern California honing his golf game. Even though he was nearing 50 at the time of his first Denver Country Club club championship in 1899, he won the title a total of ten times. He also won the Colorado State Match Play title in four consecutive years from 1902 to 1905. In addition to his Colorado victories, Fairbanks was a three-time Southern California Golf Association Champion, a Florida State Champion and won the first Pacific Coast Championship. On a national level he reached the rank of 16 at the 1899 United States Amateur tournament and qualified again for the match play field at the 1901 tournament. His finest golfing achievement occurred in 1913 when he won the US Senior Golf Association Championship at the Apawamis Club in Rye, New York. Fairbanks, whose picture hangs in the hallway to the men's grille at Denver Country Club, was known as "40-holes Fairbanks", a nickname he acquired as a result of his first round win at the U.S. Amateur tournament in 1899, when he prevailed following play-off holes in his match against J.F. Curtis: "1-up" after "40 holes". Walter Fairbanks was a director of the D.C.C from 1903 to 1906 and oversaw the construction of the club's course at its current location during that time. He remained a member of a club until his death on 25th August 1924 in Guildford, Surrey at the home of his sister, Edith Smith. His former home at 1435 Vine Street, Denver, is still known today as Grove-Fairbanks House and is listed on the National Register of Historic Places in the USA.

Robert Edwin Bush was born on 11th October 1855, the brother of James Arthur and John Ernest Bush. He was educated at Clifton College from 1865 to 1875, joined Clifton RFC in 1873 and played both rugby and cricket for Gloucestershire.

On 12th March 1878 at the age of 22 he arrived in Freemantle. After exploring Western Australia he spent more than 30 years running a sheep station on the Gascoyne River, where he renamed part of his land Upper and Lower Clifton Down. From 1890 to 1893 he was a member of Western Australia's first Legislative Council.

In 1904 he returned to England and in 1907, by then aged fifty-two, married Margery Scott. There were five children from the marriage.

Robert Bush and his wife Margery

Robert and Margery converted their home, Bishop's Knoll in Stoke Bishop, to a wartime hospital of 100 beds (for Australian soldiers) at their own expense. The hospital received its first patients on 13th September 1914 and was the only privately-owned hospital in the country to receive wounded soldiers directly from the front.

Above: Bishop's Knoll in 1917

He became Chairman of Gloucestershire County Cricket Club and Sherriff of Bristol (in 1911). He was present at the unveiling of the Clifton Rugby War Memorial on 21st November 1931 and died at Bishop's Knoll on 29th December 1939.

Edmund Judkin Taylor was born on 30th December 1853 in Stoke Bishop, Bristol, the son of Thomas, a merchant and goldsmith.

He played cricket for Gloucestershire between 1876 and 1886, 14 times at either Clifton or Cheltenham College's ground, although the majority of his 24 appearances were made in 1876 and 1877 and his career was punctuated by gaps. He played twice for the county against Australia, in 1882 and 1884.

His sister, Emma Florence married the Clifton RFC and England player William Octavius Moberly on July 30th 1884 at Frenchay Church.

Edmund Taylor was a solicitor and the Town Clerk of Bristol. On 14th February 1891, at the Imperial Hotel Clifton, E.J. Taylor was a founding member of Bristol & Clifton Golf Club and was appointed its first secretary. He died on 28th December 1936.

The oldest known photograph of a Rugby School XX, 1871. (L-R) Back Row: A.S. Forbes, C.W. Crosse, A.K. Purvis, E.A. Brownfield, M.W. Wooten, C.H. Hinton, F.G. Boggs, E.R. Dalton, J.D. Anderson, E.H. Nash. Seated: A.D. Bulpett, D.A. Ogilvie, W. Lewthwaite, W.H. Bolton, E.J. Taylor, J.M. Finnerty, A.H. Young. On the ground: R.J. Bealey, J.A. Howell, S.H. Lomax.

Born on 18th March 1857, **John Day Miller** was the son of John, a solicitor, and was educated at Clifton College from 1865 to 1874. He joined Clifton RFC when he left school and served the club as captain for three seasons from 1877 to 1880 as well as becoming the first captain of Gloucestershire (a Cliftonian captained the Gloucestershire side from 1878 to 1889). He played for The South in the 1875 England Trial at Whalley Range, Manchester.

John Miller represented the Western Counties from 1880 and Clifton from 1883 until 1886 on the Rugby Union Committee.

He became a solicitor, partnering his father. The John Miller & Son company was taken over in 1904 by Meade-King & Sons which continued operating separately until 1910, at which point the merger was formalised with Isaac Cooke & Sons joining to form 'Meade-King, Cooke, Wansey and John Miller'. In 1920 the name was changed again to 'Meade-King & Co'. The company is based at Queen Square in Bristol.

John Day Miller died on 14th October 1925 at his home, Freshford Villa on Richmond Hill in Clifton.

Michael Martyn Curtis was born on 17th November 1853 in Bristol, the son of the accountant John Curtis of Bristol. He was educated at Malvern College, played for the 1869 Clifton club and was one of the new club's founding signatories in 1872.

With John Miller, he played for The South in the 1875 England trial at Whalley Range, Manchester. He appears in the 1874-75 1st XV photograph, and the 1909 and 1922 'History of Clifton Rugby Club' books state that he played for England in 1876-77. The club history published in 1972 claims that he played for Wales that same season; this is an error as there is no record of this elsewhere and Wales did not field an international team until 1881.

He is recorded as being an inmate in the Brislington House Asylum in the 1891 census, suffering from mania. He lived for over 30 more years, however, and died on 23rd November 1924, aged 71.

The son of the Reverend George Butterworth, vicar of Deerhurst from 1856 to1893, **Alexander Kaye Butterworth** was born on 4th December 1854 at Henbury Court, Bristol. His mother was Frances Maria Kaye, youngest daughter of Dr. John Kaye, Bishop successively of Bristol and Lincoln. Alexander was educated at Marlborough College from 1868 to 1874 and was captain of Marlborough Nomads. Both he and his brother George joined Clifton RFC in 1874. Alexander also played for The South in the 1875 England Trial at Whalley Range, Manchester and is another to appear in the 1874-75 1st XV photograph.

His great-grandfather was Joseph Butterworth, MP for Coventry in 1812 and Dover in 1820, who worked with William Willberforce for the abolition of slavery.

Alexander was a scholar of the Inner Temple in 1878 and Bachelor of Laws of London University. He became a solicitor in 1884 and worked in the Solicitors Department of the Great Western Railway. Later he moved to the North Eastern Railway, working there as a solicitor from 1891 and as general manager from 1906 until 1921. He somehow found time to serve as Clerk of the Peace for Bedfordshire in 1890, and was knighted in 1914.

Sir Alexander's son was George Sainton Kaye Butterworth, the composer who was killed at the Battle of the Somme in 1916.

His long life ended at his home in Frognal Gardens, Hampstead on 23rd January 1946 and he was buried at Hampstead Parish Church.

Reginald Wynn Rucker was born on 27th December 1854 in Clapham, Surrey, attended Clifton College from 1868-1874 and was Head of School from May 1874. He then went to Brasenose College, Oxford and was a rugby Blue in 1874 (20-a-side) and 1876 (15-a-side), in between times missing the 1875 Varsity match owing to an accident. He joined Clifton RFC in 1873-74.

He became Joint Manager of the British Metal Corporation, formed at the end of the Great War as a state-sponsored organisation to conduct the development of the nonferrous-metals industry.

The Oxford University XV of 1876 (L-R) Back Row: J.H. Moubray, C.C. Atkinson, M. Macmillan, H. Brembridge, C. Phillips. Middle Row: J. James, J. Forman, R.W. Rucker, R.B. Gaisford. Front Row: F.W. Champneys, J.H. Bainbrigge, T.W. Wall, F.H. Lee, W.H. Cornish, A.C. Sim.

Reginald Wynn Rucker died of pneumonia on 14th May 1924 in London and is buried at Putney Vale Cemetery.

Edward Innes Pocock was born on 3rd December 1855 at 5 Worcester Terrace, Clifton and was educated at Clifton College from 1872 to 1875. He began playing for Clifton RFC in 1873, and his three brothers Herbert, Reginald and Walter also played for the club.

After moving to Edinburgh and joining Edinburgh Wanderers he played twice for Scotland in 1877, for which the Scottish Rugby Union needed special permission from the RFU. There are good accounts of his first international, but in the second he had such a bad game that he was moved from the backs to the forwards.

The Scotland XV that played Ireland in Belfast on 19th February 1877. Image courtesy of the SRU. (L-R) Back Row: D. Lang (Paisley), H.H. Johnston (Edinburgh University). Middle Row: J.R.H. Gordon (Edinburgh Academicals), J. Junor (Glasgow Academicals), J.R. Reid (Edinburgh Wanderers), J.H.S. Graham (Edinburgh Academicals), C. Villars (Edinburgh Wanderers). Seated: D.H. Watson (Glasgow Academicals), M. Cross (Glasgow Academicals), R.W. Irvine [Captain] (Edinburgh Academicals), R.C. MacKenzie (Glasgow Academicals). On the ground: S.H. Smith (Glasgow Academicals), E.I. Pocock (Edinburgh Wanderers), H.M. Napier (West of Scotland).

On 18th April 1890 Captain Edward Pocock was recruited by Cecil John Rhodes to be part of C Troop of the Pioneer Column, organised by Rhodes and his British South Africa Company that year and used in his efforts to annex the territory of Mashonaland, later part of Southern Rhodesia and now Zimbabwe. The column consisted of a Pioneer Corps of 180 men, accompanied by a paramilitary police force (later christened the British South Africa Police) of 300 men.

On 16th August 1890 Pocock captained one of the teams participating in the first ever cricket match held in Zimbabwe, staged at Providential Pass near Fort Victoria (now known as Masvingo).

The Pioneer Corps was officially disbanded on 1st October 1890 and each member was granted land on which to farm, with mining concessions. Some of the men sold their farm right for £100 and their claim right for the same sum. By 1899 over 15.7 million acres had been granted, with only some four million left for the native Ndebele.

Pocock was appointed Gwelo District Mines Inspector in February 1896. He admitted he knew very little about mining. In one of his letters he wrote that the Chief Inspector of Mines had been coming to his district, so in order to avoid having his knowledge tested he had mounted his horse and left the area until the Chief Inspector returned to Salisbury. In another letter to his mother, he mentioned that he had had a promotion and, as a result, had been given an ox cart and span of oxen, the equivalent of today's company car. He was appointed Mining Commissioner for the Lomagundi District in November 1897 but resigned from the Civil Service in 1901 and joined United Excelsior Mines Ltd. to take charge of the Alliance Mine in Abercorn District, 68 miles south of Salisbury. He continued to live on the property after mining operations ceased in June 1903.

Edward Pocock died of pneumonia on 14th January 1905 in Salisbury Hospital, aged 49. He is buried in the Pioneer Cemetery in Salisbury (now Harare).

Born on 26th September 1858 in Chipping Sodbury, Gloucestershire, **Graeme Vassall Cox** was the cousin of the England rugby captain Harry Vassall. Educated at Clifton College from 1868 - 1876 and then at Trinity College, Oxford, he gained his Blue in 1878. He joined Clifton RFC the following season and also played rugby for Gloucestershire and Somerset.

Cox became an Assistant Master at Manchester Grammar School and in April 1911 Warden at the University Settlement, Manchester at Ancoats Hall on Every Street. The aim of university settlements was for men and women from universities to live amongst the poor and to reduce some of the inequalities of life. In May 1913 ill-health forced him to relinquish some of his duties and he eventually resigned.

He joined up in 1914 and served as a private with the 2me Régiment Étranger de l'Armée Française in France. Graeme Cox died on October 14th 1927 in Aberdovey, Wales aged 69.

Arthur James Budd was born on 14th October 1853 in Bristol. His father was Dr. William Budd (1811-1880), originally a country doctor from Devon who moved to Bristol in the 1840s and is now acknowledged as being instrumental in the discovery of the cause of typhoid fever.

Arthur attended Clifton College from 1864 to 1872 and Pembroke College, Cambridge from 1872 to 1877. He joined Clifton RFC in 1872, moved to Ravenscourt Park in 1876 and played for Edinburgh Wanderers in 1877-78 before joining Blackheath, where he won his five England caps.

Arthur Budd's final season for Blackheath was in 1888-1889. That same season he became President of the RFU after serving for two seasons as Vice-President. He remains the only person to become President of the RFU while still playing the game. He became one of the most controversial figures in rugby history because of his opposition to payments to players, which marked the start of events leading to the Northern Union and the formation of the Rugby League.

Arthur Budd left for Johannesburg, South Africa in 1893 but returned to London sometime before 1st November 1894 when he attended an RFU meeting at the Craven Hotel, Charing Cross. It was reported in the Liverpool Mercury on 18th August 1899 that he had been found in Fetter Lane, London in an unconscious condition on the pavement. He was taken to in St. Bartholomew's Hospital where he died on 27th August 1899 from cirrhosis of the liver, chronic pneumonia and neuritis.

The England team that played Scotland on 19th March 1881 - Arthur Budd's last England cap. Image courtesy of the World Rugby Museum, Twickenham. (L-R) Back Row: H.C. Rowley (Manchester), H. Vassall (Oxford University), A. Budd (Blackheath), G.W. Burton (Blackheath), C.H. Coates (Leeds), H. Fowler (Walthamstow), A.N. Hornby (Manchester). Middle Row (L-R): R. Hunt (Manchester), E.T. Gurdon (Richmond), C. Gurdon (Richmond), C.W.L. Fernandez (Leeds), C. Phillips (Birkenhead Park), W.W.

Hewitt (Queen's House), L. Stokes [captain] (Blackheath). On the ground: F.T. Wright (Edinburgh Academicals), emergency substitute for H.H.Taylor (Blackheath) who missed the train.

William John Penny was born on 15th November 1856 in Kingsbury Episcopi just south of Langport, Somerset. He worked at Kings College Hospital with Joseph Lister and played for United Hospitals and (for a few months in the 1879-80 season) Blackheath before taking up a position at Bristol General Hospital and joining Clifton in 1883.

Blackheath 1st XV 1878-79 (L-R) Back Row: A. Budd, F.S. Ireland, A.S. Marsden, Aub. Spurling, G. Stokes, H.C. Harrison, P. Brunskill, N. Smith. Seated: W.H. White, W.J. Penny, H.D. Bateson, L. Stokes, G.W. Burton, A. Poland, G. Budd. On the ground: O. Richardson, G. Spurling, A.H. Jackson, R. Cuff, A.R. Layman.

The above photograph also includes Arthur (see previous entry) and his brother George Turnavine Budd.

William Penny scored on his debut for England versus Ireland on 11th March 1878, the first full-back to score for England. He died in December 1904 near Mombasa, in British East Africa.

John Ernest Bush was born on 31st December 1859 in Brislington, Bristol, the brother of James Arthur and Robert Edwin Bush. He was educated at Clifton College from 1870 to 1877.

He was commissioned, from the Militia, as a Second Lieutenant in the 106th Bombay Light Infantry in 1880, fought in Egypt with the 2nd Battalion DLI at the Battle of Ginnis in 1885 and served in the Boer War in 1902 as Garrison Adjutant at Orange River.

He was given command of 2nd Durham Light Infantry from 1906 to 1910 and was made a Brigadier General in 1914. Bush commanded the York and Durham (150th) Brigade during the 2nd Battle of Ypres in 1915 until January 1916, was awarded the Order of the Bath in 1916 and retired from the army in 1917.

He died on 28th October 1943 and his obituary, which appeared in 'The Times' of November 1st 1943, included the following:

Brigadier-General John Ernest Bush, C.B., late Durham Light Infantry, died at Berkhamsted on Thursday.
The son of the late Major Robert Bush, 96th Regiment, he was educated at Clifton and joined the army in 1880. He played Rugby football for Gloucestershire and for England against Ireland, 1880-1881.

There is some uncertainty surrounding his supposed international appearance, but it seems likeliest that it simply didn't happen. The 1947 'Clifton College Register' states that JE Bush played rugby for Ireland in 1881. One player selected for England to play Ireland on 30th January 1880 apparently succumbed to sea-sickness on the voyage to Dublin and was replaced by Ernest Woodhead of Dublin University (who thus gained his one and only England cap); there is no evidence that this was Bush.

James Alfred Bevan was born on 15th April 1858 at St. Kilda in Victoria, Australia. He was the son of James Bevan and Elizabeth Fly, who tragically died on the SS London in 1866 when he was seven years old. He went to live with his uncle in Grosmont, Monmouthshire and was educated at Hereford Cathedral School and St. Johns College, Cambridge. He gained rugby blues in 1877 and 1880 and played for Clifton in the 1878-1879 season. He became the first captain of Wales in 1881.

Whilst Bevan was working for Sibly & Dickinson, solicitors in Bristol, he met Annie Woodall at Great Dinham Farm in Monmouthshire on the occasion of a shooting party. The Woodall family was apparently very religious and James was told that, if he wanted to marry Annie, he would have to give up smoking, drinking and hunting. This he did, to the extent that he became very involved in the church, gave up his legal studies and went to theological college in London, living in Hampstead. Annie apart, the catalyst for his conversion was an evangelist meeting in Bristol held by a William Clarke, who was also a well known athlete. Bevan would later name one of his sons

William Clarke. Bevan and Annie had eleven children in all, and of their seven sons six entered the church.

Bevan was resident at St. Paul's Vicarage, Leytonstone in 1938, where he died on 3rd February of prostate cancer. He was buried in Hampstead Cemetery with his wife and two of their daughters.

James Bevan and his family in August 1907. (L-R) Back Row: William Clarke, Dorothea, John, Edith, Eric. Seated: Hubert, Annie Susan (Winifred on knee), James Alfred, Ernest Guy. On the ground: Kenneth, Geoff.

Born on 4th October 1856 in Bath, **Herbert George Fuller** attended Christ's College, Finchley. He became captain of Bath aged only 19 in 1875-76, a post he held for two seasons before going to Peterhouse, Cambridge on 2nd October 1878. He became a rugby blue on a record six occasions, which subsequently led the university to create a limit of no more than four blues per person. He joined Clifton RFC in 1879-80 and captained Somerset from 1882-1884, winning six caps for England between 1882 and 1886 and finding time to serve as President of CURFC in 1885. His bald pate was so conspicuous in scrums and rucks that he is said to have invented the scrum cap.

Cambridge University XV of 1883 with Herbert George Fuller winning his record 6th Blue. (L-R) Back Row: G.B. Guthrie, W.P. Richardson, R. Threlfall, J. Lees, B.C. Burton, E.W. Chillcott. Middle Row: E.B. Brutton, H.G. Fuller. Front Row: E.A. Douglas, H.F. Ransome, C.J.B. Milne, C.J.B. Marriott, W.B. Salmon, G.L. Colbourne, C.H. Sample.

Herbert Fuller died of a cerebral tumour on 2nd January 1896 in Streatham, London, aged only 39, and is buried at Lansdown Cemetery, Bath.

Charles Cyril Bradford was born in Clyffe Pypard, Wiltshire on 9th June 1865. He attended Clifton College from 1880 to 1884 and Brasenose College Oxford where he gained a rugby blue in 1887. He joined Clifton RFC in 1889.

Bradford took up a teaching career and was an assistant master at Harrow from 1889 to 1890. He moved on to Bingley in Yorkshire where he taught classics and modern languages. Later he taught at JH Wilkinson's School in Clifton and by the turn of the century was at a school near Wallingford in Oxfordshire. He played cricket for Oxfordshire (and was captain from 1897-1901) and became an Oxfordshire Justice of the Peace.

Oxford University XV of 1887. (L-R) Back Row: W. Rashleigh, J.B. Sayer, W.G. Wilson, R.O.B. Lane, C.C. Bradford, R.J.N. Fleming. Seated: L.R. Paterson, J.D. Boswell, R.C.M. Kitto, H.H. Castens. On the ground: J.M. Glubb, D.W. Evans, E.P. Simpson. Absent: R.D.Budworth

He was Receiver of the Dowager Duchess of Somerset's Broad Town Charity from 1904 until 1921, and left teaching to become a solicitor from 1905 to 1913 in Swindon (Messrs Bradford & Co.). By 1912 he was living at The Quarry House, Swindon. He died at The Rookery, Adderbury near Banbury on 21st June 1945.

Herbert Lavington Evans, also known as Harry Loft Evans, was born on 14th December 1859 in Clifton. He attended preparatory school in Reigate and then Clifton College from 1875 to 1877, and then he moved on to Edinburgh University to study medicine, eventually qualifying as a surgeon in 1888. He practised for many years in Bradfield, Berkshire.

Herbert Evans played for Scotland against Ireland on 21st February 1885, but the match was abandoned after 30 minutes because of heavy rain with Scotland leading by one try to nil. For more than 100 years this fixture remained erased from the record books, with only the replayed fixture officially recognised. The original match was eventually recognised by both unions and given retrospective test status in both

Ireland and Scotland. Evans played in the replay on 7th March 1885 at Raeburn Place in Edinburgh. He joined Clifton in 1879, played intermittently whilst at university but more regularly when he returned from Edinburgh.

The Scotland team that beat Ireland in Edinburgh on 7th March 1885. A crowd of 8,000 watched this match in clear but cold weather. Image courtesy of the SRU. (L-R) Back Row: J.Gordon Mitchell (West of Scotland), Dr.J. Dod (Watsonians), T.W. Irvine (Edinburgh Academicals), H.L. Evans (Edinburgh University). Middle Row: P.H. Don Wauchops (Fettesian Lorettonians), G. Maitland (Edinburgh Institution FP), J.P. Veitch (Royal High School FP), T. Ainslie (Edinburgh Institution FP). Seated: W.A. Peterkin (Edinburgh University), J.B. Brown (Glasgow Academicals), W.E. MacLagan [Captain] (Edinburgh Academicals), A.R. Don Wauchope (Fettesian Lorettonians), J. Jamieson (West of Scotland), J.G. Tait (Edinburgh Academicals). Front: C. Reid (Edinburgh Academicals).

Herbert Lavington Evans died of pneumonia on 9th April 1925 near Goring, Oxon.

Hiatt Cowles Baker was born on the 30th June 1863 in Bristol. His father, William Mills Baker, went from rags to riches after he and his brother Thomas came to Bristol to seek their fortune in the 1840s; their father, a farmer near Bridgwater, had been forced into bankruptcy. They joined the firm of Culverwell Son & Co., wholesale and retail drapers operating from premises in Wine Street and Bridge Street. The 1851 census describes William as a servant, working as a Linen Drapers Assistant and living at 5 Castle Street within the precincts of Bristol Castle with 17 others. By 1860 the two brothers had become partners and, a few years later, the company name was changed to Ramsdale, Baker & Baker.

Hiatt Baker joined Clifton in 1883 and was captain from 1886 until 1889. His one England appearance, away to Wales on 8th January 1887, was played in appalling conditions on a bitterly cold afternoon with snow and hail adding to the difficulties. A severe frost had rendered the main Stradey Park unplayable, and eventually the match was staged on the adjoining cricket ground where 8,000 spectators huddled together around the makeshift touchlines. The ground was too hard for any heroics, particularly for a forward. Rowland Hill of the RFU refereed because the Scottish official had become snow-bound en route to Llanelli. The England side on this day featured eight new caps.

That his England career stopped as soon as it started was mainly because England played no international matches during the next two seasons as a result of the dispute with the other home nations over the establishment of the IRB. By the time England resumed international matches, Hiatt Baker had retired.

He worked as Managing Director of his family clothing and drapery business; by now Ramsdale had been seen off and the company had become Baker, Baker & Co. He was pro-chancellor of Bristol University from 1929 to 1934, having been a founding member of the university council in 1909 and remaining a member until 1934. He received an honorary LLD degree from the university in 1931 and many years later he gave his name to the Hiatt Baker hall of residence, opened in 1965.

Hiatt Baker died on 19th September 1934 at his home Oaklands in Almondsbury. He is buried at the church of St Mary the Virgin, Lower Almondsbury, next to his son Harold Owen Baker who died in 1905 at the age of four months.

Richard Thomas Dutton Budworth was born on 17th October 1867 at Greensted, Essex and was educated at Brecon College and Magdalen College, Oxford. His father was Philip John Budworth, a magistrate and unsuccessful parliamentary candidate for the Borough of Sandwich in 1840.

Richard Budworth was an Oxford University blue in three consecutive years from 1887. He was capped three times for England in 1890 and 1891 while playing for Blackheath, later joining Clifton RFC in 1897. Budworth's first match for England was also his country's first following the international dispute.

One of the original members of the Barbarians Club, Budworth was a clergyman ordained in 1902. He taught at Lancing College, Clifton College (1898 until 1907), and was appointed headmaster at Durham School in 1907. He became Canon at Durham Cathedral and retired in 1932.

The England team that played Wales on 15th February 1890 in Dewsbury. Image courtesy of the World Rugby Museum, Twickenham. (L-R) Back Row: F. Evershed (Burton), J.H. Dewhurst (Richmond), P.F. Hancock (Blackheath), R.D. Budworth (Blackheath), F.W. Lowrie (Batley), W.G. Mitchell (Richmond). Seated: J.L. Hickson (Bradford), A. Robinson (Blackheath), A.E. Stoddart [Captain] (Blackheath), J. Valentine (Swinton), J.F. Wright (Bradford). On the ground: S.M.J. Woods (Cambridge University), J.H. Rodgers (Moseley), F.H. Fox (Wellington), P.H. Morrison (Cambridge University).

Budworth spent his last days as vicar of Horspath, a village on the outskirts of Oxford, and died in London on 7th December 1937 whilst visiting for the Varsity match.

George Heinrich Frederick Cookson was born in Frome in 1870. His mother, née Brutzer, came from Baden-Württemberg; she and her husband William Edgar Cookson, a retired captain R.N., lived with their two sons and three daughters on Clifton Wood Road.

George was educated at Clifton College between 1881 and 1889 and then at Lincoln College, Oxford. He occasionally played for Clifton in 1892 and 1893, including an appearance in the Bristol fixture on 21st January 1893. He also played for

Gloucestershire and had a trial for England in 1892. He played for Oxford University in the varsity matches of 1891 and 1892; in the latter match he captained the team when C.D. Baker was unable to play owing to a damaged breastbone. The match was drawn 0-0 in torrential rain.

Above: the Oxford University XV of 1892. (L-R) Back Row: A. Latter, W.B. Stewart, A.H. Grant, J.A. Smith, A.C. Elwes, A.H. Colville. Seated: F.O. Poole, G.M. Carey, G.H.F. Cookson, C.D. Baker, J. Conway-Rees, W.H. Wakefield, L. Mortimer. On the ground: W.P. Donaldson, L.C. Humfrey, H.M. Taberer.

He embarked on a career in education and was an assistant master at Fettes College, Edinburgh. He also had spells at Tewfikieh Training College, Cairo and at the Royal Naval College, Dartmouth where he taught the Prince of Wales. He was appointed H.M. Inspector of Schools in January 1912 and in his spare time served as editor of 'English – the magazine of the English Association' and of 'English Poetry For Primary Schools' as well as writing poetry.

During the Great War he was a captain in the Duke of Cornwall's Light Infantry. He was in the Labour Corps in France and Belgium and in 1918 a captain at RAF Kingsworth Airship Station.

George Cookson died aged 78 on 24th September 1949 in Surrey.

Edwin Field was born on 16th December 1871 in Hampstead, the son of the prominent artist Walter Field (1837-1901), and educated at Clifton College from 1882 until 1891 and at Trinity College, Cambridge from 1891 to 1894, where he gained three rugby blues from 1892-4 and a Cricket Blue in 1894. He started playing for Clifton RFC in 1883. He appeared twice for England in 1893 whilst with the Middlesex Wanderers club, and three times for the Barbarians in 1893 and 1894. He finished his rugby career at Richmond. Another all-round sportsman, Field also played cricket for Berkshire in 1895 and for Middlesex from 1904 to 1906.

The England team that played Wales on 7th January 1893. Image courtesy of the World Rugby Museum, Twickenham. (L-R) Back Row: E. Field (Middlesex Wanderers and Cambridge University), W.E. Bromet (Richmond), F.H.R. Alderson (Hartlepool Rovers), S.M.J. Woods (Wellington), F. Evershed (Blackheath), F.C. Lohden (Blackheath), J.H. Greenwell (Rockcliff). Seated (L-R): T. Broadley (Bingley), P. Maud (Blackheath), R.F.C. de Winton (Blackheath), A.E. Stoddart [Captain] (Blackheath), J. Toothill (Bradford), R.E. Lockwood (Heckmondwike), H. Marshall (Blackheath), H. Bradshaw Bramley).

Edwin Field's debut for England was the first Wales-England encounter to take place at Cardiff. There was some doubt as to whether the game would take place as the south of Britain was engulfed by a severe frost. Cardiff groundsmen had used braziers and 18 tons of coal to soften the pitch throughout the night. The plan half succeeded: the pitch was like a chequers board with alternating squares - muddy where the braziers had been and icy where they hadn't. The match went ahead watched by a crowd of 20,000, a record for a Welsh international at the time. The majority of the spectators left the ground believing that the result was a 14-14 draw, but two days beforehand the IRB had met and decreed that all goals should be worth three points, and tries two. Unfortunately there had been little publicity about the change, which turned the result in the favour of Wales who subsequently won the Triple Crown for the first time.

Edwin Field worked as a solicitor in London and died on 9th January 1947 in Bromley Cottage Hospital. The cremation service took place at St. Mary's, Plaistow, Bromley.

Charles Alexander Hooper was born on 6th June 1869 in Eastington, Gloucestershire. He was educated at Clifton College from 1880 to 1888, where he was head of school, and then at Cambridge University where he won his rugby blue in 1890. He also played for Gloucestershire and the Barbarians and won three caps for England in 1894, at which time he was playing for Middlesex Wanderers; when that club folded he joined Richmond.

The England team that beat Wales 24-3 on 6th January 1894. Image courtesy of the World Rugby Museum, Twickenham. (L-R) Back Row: E.W. Taylor (Rockcliff), Charles Hooper (Middlesex Wanderers), C.M. Wells (Cambridge University & Harlequins), W.E. Tucker (Blackheath), J. Hall (North Durham), J.F. Byre (Moseley), A. Allport (Blackheath). Seated: T. Broadley (Bingley), H. Bradshaw (Bramley), J. Toothill (Bradford), R.E. Lockwood [Captain] (Heckmondwike), H. Speed (Castleford), Frank Soane (Bath). On the ground: F. Firth (Halifax), S. Morfitt (West Hartlepool)

Charles Hooper appeared in the first two matches that Clifton played against Bristol in 1889 and in the first match played on Buffalo Bill's Field.

He worked as a solicitor from 1894-1914 until emigrating to Hong Kong in 1914, where he served in the Hong Kong Special Police Force during the Great War. He died on the September 16th 1950 at the Ethorpe Hotel, Gerrards Cross, aged 81.

William Henry Trenley Birch was born in 1869 in Fort Beaufort in the Eastern Cape of South Africa. He captained Clifton in 1891-92 and later Gloucestershire. He moved to Bristol Rugby Club in 1892, returned to Clifton a few seasons later and had two trials for England in 1894-95.

W.H. Birch as he appeared in the book 'Famous Footballers' in 1896.

The book 'Famous Footballers', published in 1896, describes him as follows:

Rugby Football in the West of England has had few more energetic exponents than the Captain of Gloucestershire XV, W.H.Birch. Born in South Africa, he went to school at Bath College, so that his early training as a Footballer was also in the West Country. At one time he was Captain of the Clifton F.C., and for six years he has been quite one of the foremost figures in Rugby Football in Gloucestershire. He has played continuously since 1891, and last season acted as Captain of the team. He also played during the winter of 1894-95 for the Western Counties, as well as for London and the Western Counties against the Universities, two of the International trials. Standing just over 6ft. and weighing little over 13 stone, he is a strong scrummager, using his weight to the best advantage. In addition he is a resolute tackler, while his foot work is of the most brilliant description.

He died in Chertsey on 2nd May 1925 aged 56 and was cremated at Woking Crematorium four days later.

William John Lias was born on 13th March 1868 in Kensington, the son of the clergyman and author John James Lias. He was educated at Haileybury School, Hertfordshire and Jesus College, Cambridge from 1886, gaining a B.A. in 1889 and an M.A. in 1898. He was editor of the Cambridge Review in 1890-1.

The Jesus College, Cambridge rugby XV 1889-90. (L-R) Back Row John Stanley Manford, Charlton James Blackwell Monypenny, Bernard Wild, William John Lias, Arnold Beetham Williams, Robert James Younger, Edwin Vidal Palmer. Middle: William Irvine Rowell, Seated: Gregor MacGregor. Samuel Moses James Woods, Percy Holden Illingworth (Captain), Percy Temple Williams, Cecil Edwin Fitch. On the ground: William Martyn Scott, Charles William Chamberlayne Ingles, James Smith.

He began a career in education and was headmaster of the Downs School, Clifton from 1893 until 1898. During the three years when Clifton RFC was based at Buffalo Bill's Field (1893-6) he was club captain, and led his side in the historic match against Bristol on 23rd September 1893.

His career later took a change of direction; he was called to the Bar, Lincoln's Inn, on 1st May 1901 and practised in Liverpool. He served in the Great War (Captain, Lancashire Fusiliers and Royal Engineers) and was mentioned in despatches.

In 1910 he contested the seat of West Derby Division of Liverpool as a Liberal and came second to the Unionist candidate.

He was Professor of International Law at Sheffield University from 1924-9, and a county court judge in Sheffield from 1922 to 1930 and in Plymouth from 1930 to 1940. William Lias died on 20th July 1941 in Torquay.

On 6th April 1945 his eldest son, Able Seaman David John Lias, was killed on board the Aircraft Carrier HMS Slinger, which was supporting the US-led assault on Okinawa. He was only 19 years old.

William Wyamar Vaughan was born on 25th February 1865 in Hampstead, London, the younger son of Henry Halford Vaughan (1811–1885), regius professor of modern history at Oxford, and his wife, Adeline Maria (1837–1881), daughter of John Jackson MD of the East India Company's service and the leading English physician in Calcutta. He was grandson of the judge Sir John Vaughan (1769–1839), great-nephew of the physician Sir Henry Halford, and first cousin through his mother of the historian and Liberal politician H.A.L. Fisher and of Admiral Sir William Wordsworth Fisher who commanded a battleship at the Battle of Jutland. He was educated at Rugby School and at New College, Oxford (1884–8), where he gained a second in classical moderations followed by a degree in *literae humaniores* at the University of Paris.

In 1898 he married Margaret (Madge) Symmonds (born 1869), daughter of John Addington Symonds (1840-1893); they had two sons and a daughter, Janet Vaughan the physiologist. Margaret died in 1925, but not before she had had an affair with Vaughan's cousin Virginia Woolf. In 1929 Vaughan re-married to Elizabeth Geldard, daughter of John Geldard of Settle, at Rathmell Church, Yorkshire.

Vaughan taught at Clifton College from 1890 to 1904 before being appointed Headmaster of Giggleswick School, the first permanent Headmaster not in holy orders. He became Headmaster of Wellington College in 1910 and of Rugby School in 1921. He retired in July 1931.

Vaughan joined Clifton RFC in 1890-91 and played in several notable matches, including the first match at the Fishponds ground in 1892 versus Taunton and the second match at Buffalo Bill's Field against Bath in 1893.

He was president of the Modern Languages Association in 1915, of the Incorporated Association of Headmasters in 1916, of the Science Masters Association in 1919, and of the educational section of the British Association in 1925. After his retirement his services were in ever greater demand on educational bodies; in 1932 he presided over the International Congress of Secondary Teachers and in 1935 he became chairman of the Central Council for School Broadcasting. He also served on the consultative committee of the Board of Education (1920–26), on the government committee for considering the place of science in education, on the Teachers' Registration Council (1928–32), and visited the Gold Coast (now Ghana) as a member of the advisory committee on education in the colonies.

During his attendance of the Indian Science Congress in December 1937, he fell and broke his leg on an excursion to the Taj Mahal. This resulted in amputation of his leg and he died two months later on 4th February 1938 in the Thomason Hospital, Agra.

Frederick Charles Belson was born on 13th February 1874 in Ramsgate, Kent and educated at Clifton College from 1886 until 1889. He joined Clifton RFC in 1891, transferred to Bath in 1894 and also played for Bristol, Newport and Abergavenny.

In 1899 he was invited to join a Great Britain touring team to Australia, known then as the Anglo-Australian Touring Team and not dubbed the British Lions until 1924. A second leg to New Zealand was cancelled. The Australian tour started on 14th June with a match against Central Southern Union and finished on 12th August when the team beat Australia 13-0.

Belson was one of 16 county players of a squad of 22. He worked for The National Provincial Bank and approached his manager to explain that he had been invited to join the tour to Australia, and could he please have six months' leave of absence? He was told that he was free to go, but that he should not expect his job to be waiting for him on his return.

He played in the first of the four tests against Australia on the 24th June 1899 at the Sydney Cricket Ground, which Australia won 13-3 in front of 28,000 people. He also played against Central Southern Union (won 11-3), New South Wales (won 4-3), and Toowoomba (won 19-5). It was reported in the Bath Chronicle on 24th September 1899 that he had obtained an appointment in Sydney, and would not finish the tour with the team. He never did represent his country.

Still in the southern hemisphere, he was commissioned captain in Thorneycroft's Mounted Infantry during the Boer War. The brigade was involved in the Battle of Spion Kop on 23rd-24th January 1900.

At some point he emigrated to Canada, but returned to England to fight in the Great War with the Army Service Corps. His two sons were born in England in 1916 and

1917, but three years after the war he left the country again with his family for British Columbia.

Frederick Belson died on 10th August 1952 in Portsmouth.

William Gilbert Grace Jnr. was born on 6th July 1874 in West Brompton, Kensington, the son of perhaps the most famous cricketer of them all. He was educated at Clifton College from 1887 to 1893 and at Pembroke College, Cambridge, where he played cricket for Cambridge University - twice a cricket blue in 1895 and 1896 - and subsequently for Gloucestershire and London County.

W.G. Jr. was a quiet man. He did not get on well with his father, but it could not have been easy to be the son of the most celebrated cricketer of the time, and he could never live up to his father's high expectations. W.G. took a great interest in his eldest son's sporting progress and would use his influence to better it. A notable Bristol athlete, J.W.S.Toms recalled:

'W.G.' was very keen for his son, young 'W.G', to win the Public Schools' quarter-mile championship and asked me to help in the preparation. The training was on the County Ground and very drastic it was too. 'W.G.', believing in stamina, would make me run 350 to 400 yards all out. Then he would yell until the finish, 'Come on, lazybones!'

To W.G.'s disappointment, his son was second to a new record time for the event.

W.G. also overdid the pressure when it came to cricket. When his son was not picked for the University's match against the MCC at Fenner's, W.G. picked him for the MCC instead. Father and son opened the batting for the MCC only for W.G. junior to suffer the humiliation of a duck. W.G. himself went on to score 139. To rub salt into the young man's wounds, exactly the same thing happened in the return match at Lord's; he was dismissed without scoring and his father scored 196.

However, to his father's pride and delight, he managed to get his blue the following year and performed creditably in the match, opening the innings and making 40 and 28. Unfortunately in his final year and second varsity match he made a pair against Oxford. As he trudged back to the Lord's pavilion after his second dismissal, his mother and sister, Bessie, who had made the journey from Bristol to watch him, sat in silence, tears streaming down their faces.

He didn't play much first-class cricket after that. It is said that he chose a position at Oundle School because of those offered to him it was the furthest away from his father.

He was not renowned for his rugby prowess but nevertheless represented Northamptonshire and East Midlands. He was a guest player for Clifton in the first rugby match played on Buffalo Bill's Field against Bristol in 1893.

From 1897 until 1903 he was an assistant master at Oundle, and during the last two years of his life he occupied a similar position at the Royal Naval College, Osborne.

He died suddenly on 2nd March 1905 at East Cowes, Isle of Wight after an operation for appendicitis, and was buried at Elmers End Road Cemetery. His father was buried next to him ten years later.

In August 1898 the captain of Clifton RFC, Gerald Harry Beloe, proposed as a playing member **Gilbert Laird Osbourne Jessop**, at the time in his third year at Cambridge University where he captained the cricket team. Gilbert was born on 19th May 1874 in Cheltenham, the eleventh child of a doctor. He was already good enough to be named Wisden Cricketer of the Year in 1898 and played for Gloucestershire from 1894 to 1914, for Cambridge University from 1896 to 1899, for the MCC from 1896 until 1914 and for London County from 1900 to 1902. An all-round sportsman, he was also a good footballer and rugby player.

His first match for Gloucestershire was against Lancashire at Old Trafford, and the Gloucestershire side included W.G. and E.M. Grace. Jessop was one of the most exciting cricket players of his era. His great innings included one of 286 in less than three hours, another of 157 runs in an hour against the West Indian team of 1900, and famously the century that won the Oval Test of 1902. Going in to bat with England 48/5, he made 104 out of 139 in 75 minutes, taking England to an improbable victory.

Originally a fast bowler, he strained his back when over-bowled in his first Test match in 1899, and afterwards was less effective. As a fielder, the power and accuracy of his returns from cover combined with fleetness of foot made him the undisputed master of that position prior to the First World War. Named after W.G. Grace, he eventually followed him as captain of Gloucestershire, and later became club secretary. Originally a school teacher, Jessop married an Australian whom he met on the boat returning from the 1901-2 tour (his son later played for Hampshire). When war broke out in 1914 he joined up, but was so badly injured in an accident in 1916 that he was unable to work again until 1924. He then became secretary to the Edgware Golf Club. When the club was sold in 1936, he went to live with his son at St. George's Vicarage, Dorchester, and died on 11th May 1955 at Fordington, Dorset.

George Strachan John Fuller Eberle was born on 14th October 1881, the son of club founder James Fuller Eberle. George was educated at Clifton College from 1892 to 1900 and at Trinity College, Oxford. He joined Clifton RFC in 1900 and was an Oxford rugby blue in 1901 and 1902; in the latter match he scored a try.

The Oxford University XV of 1901. (L-R) Back Row: V.H. Cartright, G.S.J.F. Eberle, N. Kennedy, W.B. Odgers, D.D. Dobson. Seated: S.H. Osbourne, E.J. Walton, J.E. Crabbie, F. Kershaw, R.C. Grellet, J. Strand-Jones. On the ground: A.J. Swanzy, H.F. Terry, J.E. Raphael.

After university he joined Bristol RFC. He played in all the England trials of 1901/2 and 1902/3 but severely damaged a cartilage in the final trial in 1903. He was elected captain of Bristol, but again damaged the cartilage in the third match of the season, against Bridgwater on 26rd September 1903 and never played again. After his injury he helped with the coaching at Clifton.

As captain of the Clifton College Cadet Corps he mounted a guard of honour on the occasion of Queen Victoria's last visit to Bristol. During the First World War he was a Territorial Officer (Lt.-Colonel.) with the 2nd Battalion of the Royal Gloucestershire Royal Engineer Volunteers and was mobilised in 1916. His two brothers also played for Clifton RFC.

He became a solicitor in Bristol and retired in 1958. George Eberle died on 30th May 1968 on the Leigh Woods Golf Course. He was a large man and had become very deaf. Whether true or not, it has passed into folklore that he was walking to the first tee with his three rather younger, regular, golfing partners when one of them asked “Who’s going to have to play with George today?” Unbeknown to his companions, George was wearing his hearing aid. Determined that he was not going to lose, he put all his strength into his first drive and fell dead on the spot.

Christopher William Wordsworth was born on 7th October 1879, a great-grandson of the poet William Wordsworth. He was educated at the Loretto School near Edinburgh and at Queen's College, Oxford where he won a blue for rugby in 1901 and for hockey in 1902 and 1903. He played in the North vs. South international trials and also represented Westmorland at cricket. He joined Clifton RFC in 1906 having become a member of the teaching staff at Clifton College.

The Oxford University XV of 1902. (L-R) Back Row: C.D. Fisher, W.B. Odgers, G.S.J.F. Eberle, C.W. Wordsworth, R.O. Hutchison, A.D. Sloane, G.V. Kyrke. Seated: A.J. Swanzy, V.H. Cartright, R.C. Grellet, S.H. Osbourne, J.E. Raphael. On the ground: A.D. Stoop, J.R.P. Sandford, A.M.P. Lyle

From 1912 to 1916 Wordsworth was rector of Halesowen, West Midlands, returning thence to his alma mater Loretto Junior School where he was master-in-charge until 1932. He spent most of the rest of his working life in Suffolk, firstly as vicar of Assington (1933-5) and then of Coddenham and Hemingstone (1935-42), serving concurrently as Dean at Claydon (1939-42). From 1945 until 1949, when he retired, he was rector at Broughton Poggs with Filkins in west Oxfordshire.

Wordsworth married Ella Thompson and they had two sons and two daughters between 1911 and 1917. He died in Kent on 11th July 1965.

Edward Watkins Baker was born on 30th June 1878. He was educated at Clifton College from 1890 to 1896, spent two years at Winchester College and then studied at Edinburgh University from 1898, where he played rugby and cricket. He also played rugby for Bristol, Harlequins, Edinburgh Wanderers, Blackheath and Gloucestershire. He was one of seven brothers who played rugby for Clifton and is the only serving Clifton player to have appeared for the Barbarians.

The Barbarians side that played Devonport Albion on 5th April 1904. (L-R) Back Row: E. de Lissa, C.G. Robson, R.S. Wix, A. Brown, A.R. Thompson, E.M. Harrison (Guy's Hospital), N.W. Godfrey (Moseley), F.H. Palmer (Richmond), G. Fraser, T.A. Gibson. Seated: E.C. Galloway (Marlborough Nomads), F.M. Stout (Gloucester), B.C. Hartley [Captain] (Blackheath), W.L.Y. Rogers (Blackheath), D.R. Bedell-Sivright (West of Scotland). On the ground: G.V. Kyrke (Marlborough Nomads), F.C. Hulme (Birkenhead Park), S.F. Cropper (Blackheath), P. Hutchison (Birkenhead Park), E. Watkins Baker (Clifton).

Edward Watkins Baker emigrated to Vancouver, British Columbia in 1907 and played for British Columbia against an Australian Maori side that year at Brockton Oval in Stanley Park, Vancouver. It was his first and last game in British Columbia colours.

In 1924 he moved to the North Shore and was instrumental in forming North Shore All Blacks in 1930. The club merged with West Vancouver Barbarians in 1969 to become Capilano Rugby Club.

Although a qualified doctor in England, he was not allowed to practise in Canada without re-sitting his medical exams, so he became a game warden in West Vancouver. Edward Watkins Baker died on 12th January 1967 aged 88.

Edward Watkins Baker, aged 78, showing his Gloucestershire cap to Vancouver Rugby President Bob Spray prior to the British Columbia match vs. Barbarians on May 4th 1957 at the Empire Stadium in Vancouver. The Barbarians won 19-6.

Worthington Wynn Hoskin was born on 8th May 1885 in Steynsburg, South Africa, and was educated at St. Andrews College, Grahamstown. His father had come from England to teach at Bishops College in Cape Town, but on the voyage south he had met J.B. Robinson, the Kimberley mining magnate, on the ship and went instead to work for him on his farms in the Steynsburg area.

Worthington Hoskin was a Rhodes Scholar at Oxford University and a four-time rugby blue between 1904 and 1907. He captained Oxford in his last year there.

The 1907 Oxford University XV. (L-R) Back Row: Henry Edmunds Latham, Lawrence Cave Bencowe, Arthur Howard, Stephanus Nicholas Cronje, Hugh Martin, Francis Nathaniel Tarr. Seated: Noel Willoughby Milton, Henry Holland ('Jumbo') Vassall, Harold Augustus Hodges, Worthington Wynn Hoskin (Captain), Randolph Stonehewer Wix, David B. Davies, Geoffrey Dorling ('Khaki') Roberts. On the ground: George Cunningham, Rupert Henry Williamson.

His first match for Clifton was during the 1904-05 season against Bridgwater. Hoskin appeared for the Barbarians and also played for Blackheath, Northampton and Gloucestershire. He was also a fine cricketer and played five matches for Gloucestershire. He worked as a private tutor in England from 1908 to 1912 but left to return to his home country and become housemaster at his old school, St. Andrew's College, where he rose to become Vice-Principal from 1925 until 1939. He was the First XV rugby coach from 1913 onwards.

Hoskin retired at the end of 1939 and moved to Salisbury in Rhodesia. He ended his days in George on South Africa's Western Cape and died on 4th March 1956.

Charles James Gardner was born on 7th December 1883 and like Hoskin was educated at St.Andrew's College, Grahamstown. He was one of the first Rhodes Scholars and an Oxford rugby blue in 1904 and 1905.

The 1905 Oxford University XV. (L-R) Back Row: H.A. Hodges, A.A. Hoadley, I. Parker, J.V. Nesbit, N.F. Howe-Brown, C.J. Gardner. Seated: A.A. Lawrie, W.W. Hoskin, B. Cozens-Hardy, P. Munro, A.M.P. Lyle, R.S. Wix, D. Davies. On the ground: N.W. Milton, N.T. White.

Their lives in England continued in parallel, Gardner's first Clifton match was also the Bridgwater fixture in the 1904-5 season.

The Oxford University and South Africa sides that played in 1906. Clifton's Worthington Wynn Hoskin, seated fourth left, next to South African captain Paul Roos, and Charles Gardner seated second right. This was the first Springbok side to tour England. The Oxford University side included seven South Africans.

Gardner became a lawyer in 1907 and fought in the Great War; he was a lieutenant, acting captain, and adjutant, R.F.A. He served in France in 1917 and in Italy from 1917 to 1919. He was awarded the M.C. on 3rd June 1919 and was mentioned in despatches from Italy.

He became a K.C. in 1927 and enjoyed a distinguished legal career back in his native South Africa which culminated in his appointment as Judge President of the Local District Supreme Court from 1949 to 1953. He died on 3rd July 1963 in Grahamstown.

Above: Judge Charles James Gardner

John Lloyd Mathias was born in 1878 in Cardigan, Wales. He played for Clifton in 1910-11 following a distinguished career at Bristol, where he made nearly 200 appearances and was captain between 1901 and 1903. He also played 28 times for Gloucestershire and gained four caps for England in the 1904-05 season. He died on 21st November 1940.

Victor Fuller Eberle was born on 28th June 1887 in Bristol, a son of one of the founders of Clifton Rugby Club, James Fuller Eberle. He was educated at Clifton College from 1899 to 1905 and at Trinity College, Oxford from 1905 to 1908 where he was awarded an M.A. in English Literature.

He joined Clifton RFC in 1905 and was captain from 1911-13. His two brothers George and Ellison also played for Clifton.

He was Managing Director of Henry Pritchard & Co. Ltd., a director of several other companies and a member of the council of Clifton College from 1927.

The 1906-1907 Trinity College, Oxford rugby XV. (L-R) Back Row: J.L. Waggett, R.C. Wingfield, H.V. Hunt, V.F. Eberle. Middle Row: D.T. Monteath, F.E. Steinth, N. Thirkel-White, W.W. Hoskin, H.A. Hodges. Seated: C.J. Gardner, H.E. Latham, B. Cozens-Hardy, R.M. Oliphant. On the ground: W.K. Flemmer, R.M. Chadwick, R.H. Williamson, T. Entwistle.

This 1906-7 Trinity College team included four Rhodes Scholars from St. Andrews College: Hoskin, Gardner, Flemmer and Williamson. Victor Fuller Eberle was unfortunate to miss out on a blue because of injury.

Eberle's distinguished service in the Great War culminated in the award of the Military Cross. Beginning the war as a subaltern in No. 2 Field Company, 48th South Midland Royal Engineers (a division of Territorials), he fought, or mostly dug, his way with his team of sappers up and down the Western Front and as far afield as Italy. He rose to the rank of Lieutenant-Colonel and was largely responsible for the development of a fearsome explosive device called the 'Bangalore Torpedo'. He was involved in early battles around Ypres and Loos, and fought at the Somme in 1916 and Passchendaele in 1917. His experiences are recorded in his book 'My Sapper Venture' (Pitman, 1973) and are remarkable for the matter-of-fact account of extraordinary events.

Victor Fuller Eberle died on 14th August 1974 at Southmead Hospital, after a short illness.

Frank Manning Arkle was born in 1894 in Birkenhead, Cheshire. His father was William Baillie Arkle, a shipping agent. After the First World War he played for Birkenhead Park and a few games for Bristol. In 1920 he joined Clifton RFC on a permanent basis; by the end of the season he was vice-captain of the 1st XV and was made captain the following season. He became Club President from 1935 until 1950 and Sheriff of Bristol in 1949.

On 24th March 1965 Arkle retired from the board of Directors of Imperial Tobacco, where he had been Chairman for ten years from 1936 to 1946. He died in 1974.

Geoffrey Neame Loriston Clarke was born about 1900 in Clifton, the son of Charles Loriston-Clarke, a solicitor. He was educated at Pembroke College, Cambridge and played rugby for the university without gaining a blue. He also played for the United Services and for Hampshire.

A career sailor, he was appointed lieutenant in 1920 and was commander of HMS Southdown in the North Atlantic from February 1941 to January 1942. He was awarded the C.B.E. in 1944.

His daughter is the equestrian Jennifer Loriston Clarke (born 1943), who competed at four Olympic Games between 1972 and 1988.

Wilfrid Fletcher Gaisford was born on 6th April 1902 in Keynsham and educated at Bristol Grammar School. He joined Clifton RFC in 1921 and went on to play for St. Bartholomew's Hospital and Richmond.

He was Professor of Child Health and Paediatrics and the Director of the Department of Child Health at Manchester University. In April 1940 he was elected Fellow of the Royal College of Physicians and in December 1967 became Professor Emeritus at Manchester University. He died in March 1988 in Cornwall.

Bevan Stanishaw ('Bunny') Chantrill was born on 11th February 1897 in Bristol and educated at Bristol Grammar School, where an entry in the 1912 BGS Chronicle described his tackling as weak and needing improvement.

He played rugby for Clifton before the First World War and for half a season afterwards. He then played for Richmond, Weston-super-Mare and for Bristol where he gained all his England caps in the 1924 Grand Slam winning side. His BGS critic would have been gratified to know he tackled so hard that the local press described the opposition as being 'Chantrilled'.

The England team that played Wales on 19th February 1924 - Bunny Chantrill's debut. Image courtesy of the World Rugby Museum, Twickenham. (L-R) Back Row: H.C. Catcheside (Percy Park), B.S. Chantrill (Bristol), H.P. Jacob (Oxford University), R. Cove-Smith (O.M.Ts), A.F. Blakiston (Liverpool), H.M. Locke (Birkenhead Park), A.W. Angus [referee, Scotland). Seated: G.S. Conway (Rugby), R. Edwards (Newport), A.T. Voyce (Gloucester), W.W. Wakefield [captain] (Leicester), E. Myers (Bradford), L.J. Corbett (Bristol), W.G.E. Luddington (Devonport Services). On the ground: A. Robson (Northern), A.T. Young (Cambridge University).

Injury prevented him from gaining more caps. In 1926 he joined Rosslyn Park before heading to South Africa in 1929, where he prospected for gold. Whilst there he played for Natal, before returning to Bristol in 1931. Shortly afterwards, however, he emigrated to South Africa for good and fought in the South African Airforce during the Second World War.

Bunny Chantrill died in South Africa in 1988. He was once quoted as saying "I love tackling more than anything else in rugby. What a glorious feeling it is".

Edward Turk Benson was born on 20th November 1907 at Tredegarville, Cardiff. He was educated at Blundell's School and Merton College, Oxford, where he gained a rugby blue in 1928 and cricket blues in 1928 and 1929 as wicket-keeper. He played in a trial match for the England rugby team, played cricket for the Gentlemen versus Players in 1929 and for Gloucestershire. He toured New Zealand in 1929 with A.H.A. Gilligan's team, but played no test matches.

Benson served in the Second World War as a colonel in the Royal Artillery and spent some time in India. Around 1950 he joined the Prudential Assurance Company in South Africa and rose to become its branch manager in Cape Town. He retired in 1966 on grounds of ill health. Edward Benson died on 11th September 1967 in Newlands, Cape Town.

Charles Anthony Langdon Richards, born on 18th April 1911, was educated at Clifton College from 1921 until 1929 (where his father was a music teacher from 1919 to 1930) and then at Oxford University where he gained a rugby blue in 1932. He appeared in a North versus South England trial and was selected as a reserve for the 1934 England v Ireland match. He was in the Gloucestershire side that won the County Championship at Boscombe on February 3rd 1934, beating Hampshire 10-9.

Charles Richards from the Oxford University
1930 squad that toured France

Richards joined the Colonial Civil Service and was posted to Uganda in 1934; later he returned to the country and served as Commissioner for Community Development in 1953-54 and Minister of Local Government 1960-1. He retired from the service just before Ugandan independence and by 1968 was working in the Engineering Department of the Swindon Borough Council. He died in August 1996 in Swindon, Wiltshire, aged 85.

Maurice John Daly was born in 1915. He played for Old Haberdashers RFC from 1932 to 1937 and then joined Harlequins. The Second World War interrupted his career but he returned to Harlequins afterwards. Clifton RFC records around this time are sketchy, but it seems likely that he made his appearances for the club either immediately before or during the war, when matches were arranged mainly against service sides.

The Ireland side that played England on 12th Feb 1938 at Lansdowne Road, Dublin. Image courtesy of the Irish Rugby Union. (L-R) Back Row: Dr H. Emerson (Pres IRFU), M.J. Daly (Harlequins), L. McMahon (Blackrock College), J.W.S. Irwin (NIFC), J. Megaw (Richmond & Instonians), R.B. Mayne (Queens University), A.H. Bailey (UC Dublin), D.B. O'Loughlin (UC Cork). Seated: P. Crowe (Blackrock College), E.

Ryan (Dolphin), G.J. Morgan [Captain] (Clontarf), S. Walker (Instonians), C.R.A, Graves (Wanderers), R. Alexander (NIFC). On the ground: G.E. Cromey (Queens University), V.J. Lyttle (Belfast Collegians & Bedford).

He played once for Ireland in 1938, scored a try and was never selected again. England won the match 36-14 and Ireland finished with the wooden spoon. At half-time England was winning 23-0 but Ireland staged something of a recovery; Daly scored Ireland's fourth try towards the end of the match.

He captained Middlesex in the 1946-47 season and Harlequins in the Middlesex Sevens in 1947-48, losing in the final to Wasps 14-5.

Daly emigrated to Australia in 1972, and until 1989 he farmed a Sussex cattle stud at Balnarring near his home at Mount Eliza, Victoria. He died there on 3rd November 1994, survived by two sons, two daughters and his wife.

John Arthur Gregory was born on 22nd June 1923 at Sea Mills, Bristol and educated at St. Andrew's College, Dublin and Rydal School. He was banned from playing rugby union for a year, having played rugby league for Huddersfield in 1947.

Jack Gregory comes out for his first match for Blackheath versus Guy's Hospital. This was his first match after leaving Clifton and he scored a try after only two minutes.

He was All-Ireland 100 yards and 220 yards champion from 1947 to 1949 and a silver medallist in the 4x100m relay team at the 1948 Olympics in London. The medals were briefly upgraded to gold when the American team was disqualified, but on appeal the winners were reinstated. He also appeared for the Great Britain relay team in the 1952 Helsinki Olympics where the team came 4th. He raced for the Dublin athletic club Crusaders.

Gregory joined Clifton from the Dublin club Wanderers but quickly moved to Blackheath where he won his only England cap. In 1949 he joined Bristol where he became captain in 1952. He appeared twice for the Barbarians and scored a try against the East Midlands.

He retired in 1954 and died on 15th December 2003 at Laurel Court Residential Home, Nailsea near Bristol.

Born on 24th August 1927 in Wales, **Glyn Davies** was first selected to play for Wales in the two Victory Internationals of 1946 whilst still attending Pontypridd Grammar School. He went on to win eleven caps for his country. He was a mercurial outside half, a beautiful runner with a devastating sidestep and nicknamed "El Supremo" by his adoring fans. He won three rugby blues at Oxford, for the last of which in 1950 he was captain. He played for Clifton RFC in the 1950s and also had spells with Pontypridd, Bristol, Newport and Glamorgan Wanderers. Glyn Davies died on 7th November 1976 in Bristol.

Peter Dalton Young was born on 9th November 1927 in Bristol and educated at Clifton College from 1937 to 1945. He won a Cambridge blue in 1949, later captained Gloucestershire and played nine times for England, on the last two occasions as captain. He scored one try for England against Scotland on 20th March 1954.

After school he started his club career with Clifton RFC, but when he met his future wife in Dublin he stayed there and joined Dublin Wanderers. Young was called up to the England team after captaining The Rest, who beat England 8-6 in the final Trial at Twickenham on 2nd January 1954. His selection as England captain when based in Ireland caused fierce criticism. Undaunted, he led England to the Triple Crown.

In 1955 he married Ann the daughter of T.V. Murphy, whose family set up and owned the Irish Independent newspaper group. They had a son and two daughters.

The 1949 Cambridge University XV. (L-R) Back Row: B.M. Jones, G.A.B. Covell, G.P. Vaughan, P.D. Young, J.M. Jenkins, H. Wills. Seated: R.C.C. Thomas, R.V. Thompson, Glyn Davies (Hon Sec.) A.F. Dorwood (Captain), A.M. James, J.V. Smith, J.M. Williams. On the ground: I.S. Gloag, J.C. Davies.

Young later made his career in the shipping industry, working for Palgrave Murphy, of which he became joint managing director. He then founded Galway Ferries, which ran the MV Galway to the Aran Islands.

Young's principal interest was in horses. This led to him becoming chairman of the Irish Pony Club, where he was largely responsible for turning it into a national organisation; its membership grew significantly during his ten years as chairman.

Young also set up and ran the Dublin Indoor International Horse Show, and from 1992 to 1996 was chef d'équipe of the Irish three-day eventing team. He founded, launched and was first chairman of the Golden Saddle Award scholarship scheme, which has successfully fostered the younger generation of equestrian talent within Ireland.

In 1990 the Irish President, Mary Robinson, awarded him the Equestrian Federation of Ireland badge of honour for his services to the Irish equestrian world. Peter Young died on 23rd May 2002.

Victor H. Leadbetter was born in Kettering on 14th February 1930. He was a Cambridge blue in 1951 and won two caps for England. He joined Clifton at the start of the 1961-62 season and was still playing and coaching at the club in 1966. He played five times for the Barbarians during the Easter tours of Wales in 1954 and 1955; his first Barbarians match took place only six days after his England debut when England beat Scotland to win the Calcutta Cup.

The England team that lost against France 3-11 on 10th April 1954 at Stade Colombes in Paris. This team had won the Triple Crown three weeks previously. (L-R) Back Row: Ivor David [Referee, Wales], John Kendall-Carpenter (Bath), Alec Lewis (Bath), Dyson Stayt 'Tug' Wilson (Harlequins), Christopher Elliot Winn (Rosslyn Park), Peter Dalton Young (Dublin Wanderers), Nigel Gibbs (Harlequins), Victor H. Leadbetter (Edinburgh Wanderers), John Edward Woodward (Wasps), James Patrick Quinn (New Brighton). Front Row: John Edward Williams (Old Millhillians), Eric Evans (Sale), Donald Louis 'Sandy' Sanders (Harlequins), Robert Victor Stirling (Wasps), Martin Regan (Liverpool), Jeffrey Butterfield (Northampton).

He is now retired after running the construction company, Leadbetter Construction, based in Avonmouth, Bristol.

Robert Kenneth Gillespie MacEwen was born on 25th February 1928 in Oxford and was educated at Clifton College, Bristol Grammar School and Cambridge University. He was twice a rugby blue at Cambridge, in 1953 and 1954. He played 13 times for Scotland, six times for the Barbarians whilst at Cambridge University and later for London Scottish and Gloucestershire. He started his club rugby career at Clifton and ended it playing for Lansdowne in Dublin.

The Scotland side that played France on 9th January 1954 - Robert MacEwen's debut. © Yerbury Photography, image courtesy of Scottish Rugby Union Library. (L-R) Back Row: H.F. McLeod (Hawick), R.K.G. MacEwen (Cambridge University), E.A.J. Ferguson (Oxford University), E.J.S. Michie (Aberdeen University), J.C. Marshall (London Scottish), A. Robson (Hawick), Ivor David (Wales Referee). Front Row: J.H. Henderson (Richmond), J.S. Swan (London Scottish), A.D. Cameron (Hillhead High School F.P.), P.W. Kininmouth (Richmond), J.N.G. Davidson [Captain] (Edinburgh University), T.P.L. McGlasham (Royal High School F.P.), D. Cameron (Glasgow High School F.P.), T.G. Weatherstone (Stewart's College F.P.), A.K. Fulton (Dollar Academicals).

John David Currie was born 3rd May 1932 in Clifton and began playing for Clifton RFC whilst still at Bristol Grammar School in the 2nd half of the 1950-51 season. After school he studied at Wadham College, Oxford where he gained four rugby blues. A noted cricketer, he played nine times for Oxford University (in 1956 and 1957) and one match for Somerset in 1953 against Leicestershire, scoring 4 and 13. In 1959 he played in three 2nd XI matches for Gloucestershire.

John Currie is the most capped England international to have played for Clifton. He gained his first eight caps whilst attached to Clifton RFC and Oxford University, the next 14 whilst at Harlequins, and his last three after joining Bristol in 1961. He was an England selector from 1986 to 1988 and Harlequins chairman from 1980 to 1988.

The Oxford University XV of 1954. (L-R) Back Row: Mr Ivor David (Referee), R. Leslie, M.J.K. Smith, R.A. Plumridge, J.D. Currie, V.W. Jones, J.S. Abbott, P.W. Watson, W.M. Butcher, Mr A.W. Ramsey (Touch Judge). Seated: J.P. Fellows-Smith, R.C.P. Allaway, P.G. Johnstone, (Captain), J.C. Baggaley, P.G.D. Robbins. On the ground: S. Coles, W. Lawrence.

When asked by a reporter why he had been inactive in some of the line-outs in front of the West Stand during an England trial, he answered: "I only jump on the other side of the field. Then the selectors can see the number on my jersey when I go up".

John Currie died on 8th December 1990 in a Leicester hospital after he fell ill en route to Loughborough to pick up his son David from university. In 1991 David Currie would become an Oxford blue like his father.

Benjamin Tuttiett was born in Bristol in 1925 and captained Clifton RFC from 1952 to 1954. He played for Somerset from 1948, or the South West Counties against South Africa and in an England trial. He created a valuable half-back partnership with Michael Corbett, the son of Bristol and England legend Len Corbett, for both Clifton and Somerset.

The Somerset team that lost the County Championship semi-final to Lancashire in 1952. (L-R) Back Row: F.W. Williams (Committee), Arthur House (Hon. Treas.), L.W. Bisgrove (Hon.Sec.), B.C. Barber (Committee), H.L. Bradford (Committee). Middle Row: A.O. Lewis, R.T. Moule (Bristol), I.W. Macey (Wellington), K.C. Smith (Bristol), J.T. Dingle (Bath). A.M. Bain, K.R. Griffin, J.A. Teakle, D. Wilson (Committee). Front Row: J.A. Scott (Bristol), D. Coles (Weston), J. Sainsbury (Weston-super-Mare), H.R. Bastable (Bridgwater), M.D. Corbett [Captain] (Bristol), R.G.B. Quick (Vice President), B.A. Tuttiett (Clifton), J.A. Holt (Bristol).

Tuttiett inspired Clifton to an 8-5 win over Bristol at the Memorial Ground on 31st March 1954. In all he won 38 caps for Somerset and captained his county.

David Cecil Mills was born on 23rd April 1937 in Camborne, Cornwall. He was educated at Clifton College from 1951 to 1956 and won a Cambridge blue in 1958. He also played rugby for Cornwall and cricket for Gloucestershire.

The 1958 Cambridge University XV. (L-R) Back Row: D.C. Mills, D.R.J. Bird, V.S.J. Harding, D.G. Perry, J.J. Rainforth, M.R. Wade. Seated: H.J. Davies, K.R.F. Bearne, S.R. Smith, G. Windsor Lewis (Captain), D.A. MacSweeney, K.J.F. Scotland, P.R. Mills. On the ground: G.H. Waddell, M.T. Weston.

Stephen Brookhouse Richards was born on 28th August 1941 in West Kirby and educated at Clifton College from 1949 to 1959. He started his club rugby at Clifton before going to Oxford University in 1959 where he was in the 1962 Oxford team that lost to Cambridge. He won nine caps for England from 1965 to 1967. His last game for England is more memorable as the debut for Wales of an 18 year old Keith Jarrett. The Newport player had only left Monmouth School a couple of months earlier and found himself selected in the unaccustomed position of full-back. He kicked seven of eight penalties and scored a 50-yard solo try. At the time this equalled the Welsh International record for most points (19) scored in a match.

The England side that played Wales on 15th April 1967. (L-R) Back Row: D.H. Easby (Touch-Judge), R.D. Hearn, D.M. Rollitt, J. Barton, D.E.J. Watt, M.J. Coulman, S.B. Richards, D.J.C. McMahon (Scotland)(Referee). Seated: R. Webb, D.P. Rodgers, P.E. Judd (Captain), R.W. Hosen, C.W. McFadyean. On the ground: K.F. Savage, R.D.A. Pickering, R.B. Taylor, J. Finlan.

Steve Richards played for Richmond and Middlesex before moving to Sheffield and playing for Sheffield RUFC and Yorkshire.

Colin William McFadyean was born on 11th March 1943 in Plymouth and educated at Bristol Grammar School. He made his debut for Clifton against the French 1st Division club Stade Marmande of Bordeaux while on a tour of France in 1962, and scored two tries in a 16-11 win.

Colin McFadyean was captain of the 1965 Loughborough College team that lost the final of the Middlesex Sevens to London Scottish 15-8. He won eleven caps for England, the last two as captain. His caps were won in succession while a club player at Moseley. He scored a drop goal against Scotland on 19th March 1966, and tries against Ireland on 11th February 1967, a brace against Scotland on 18th March 1967 and another in his first match as captain against Wales on 20th January 1968.

He toured with the British Lions in 1966 to Australia, New Zealand and Canada. A disappointing tour saw four tests lost to the All Blacks, the highlight of the tour being the 31-0 win against Australia in Brisbane on 4th June.

The England team that played Wales on 20th January 1968, Colin McFadyean's first match as England captain. (L-R) Back Row: D.W. Brown (touch judge), B.W. Redwood (Bristol), B. Keen (Newcastle University), D.H. Prout (Northampton), R.H. Lloyd (Harlequins), B.R. West (Northampton), M.J. Parsons (Northampton), D.J. Gay (Bath), R.B. Hiller (Harlequins), M.J. Coulman, D.P. d'Arcy (referee). Seated: P.J. Bell (Blackheath), J.F. Finlan (Moseley), C.W. McFadyean [captain] (Moseley), J.V. Pullin (Bristol), P.J. Larter (Northampton), K.F. Savage (Northampton).

In 1991 he became head coach at Bristol and then Cleve, until sidelined by a knee replacement in 2000. In 2001 McFadyean was Deputy Head of Ilminster Avenue Primary School in Bristol.

Robert Hoskins Lloyd was born on 3rd March 1943 in Plymouth but moved to Glasgow when he was two years old. He joined Clifton whilst a pupil at Cheltenham College. His father played rugby for Weston-super-Mare and his brother, Steve, represented Cambridge University and Cheltenham. Robert won five caps in 1967 and 1968 for England and scored two tries against the All Blacks on his debut. He also made two appearances for the Barbarians in 1967, the first being against the All Blacks six weeks after his England debut when he again scored a try.

Lloyd spent most of his rugby career at Harlequins and featured in the club's Middlesex Sevens winning side in 1967. He also played for Surrey and in the teams that won the 1967 and 1971 County Championships. He captained Harlequins in 1971.

The England team that played Scotland on 16th March 1968, Bob Lloyd's last appearance for England. (L-R) Back Row: D.P. d'Arcy [Referee, Ireland], T.J. Brooke, P.J. Bell, DJ. Gay, M.J. Parsons, B.R. West, P.J. Larter. Seated: K.F. Savage, R.E. Webb, J.V. Pullin, M.P. Weston (Captain), M.J. Coulman, R.H. Lloyd, B. Keen. On the ground: R.D.A. Pickering, R.B. Hiller.

Bob Lloyd graduated from Hatfield Polytechnic in 1969 with a degree in Civil Engineering. He moved to Hong Kong in 1973, worked for the Highways Department and later joined the Chun Wo Construction and Engineering Company in July 2004 as a Business Development Director. He has since retired.

John A. Cannon made his debut for Clifton in 1966 and was captain during the 1971-72 season. He played for Gloucestershire 19 times, including two Championship Finals, and was the 101st Clifton player to play for Gloucestershire. He also played for the Western Counties against the All Blacks in 1974.

John Cannon from the 1980 Clifton USA Tour Programme

John Cannon retired in 2006 after 19 years as Headmaster of Redwick and Northwick School, Pilning in Bristol, but is still a school governor.

Peter Johnson was educated at St. Brendan's, Bristol and Exeter University and played for England Schools. He joined Clifton RFC in the 1972-73 season and, apart from a short period with Bristol in 1974-5 where he played ten games, he stayed until 1980-81. He played for the South & South West Counties team that beat Australia at Bath on 27th October 1973, and had a trial for England on 15th December 1973 at Bristol.

Peter Johnson from the 1980 Clifton USA Tour Programme

He became Director of Rugby at Penzance & Newlyn RFC, now Cornish Pirates, and then Academy Manager at Bristol Rugby until May 2006. He has written several books on rugby and is now Director of Rugby at Bristol University.

Rather better known as a cricketer and the senior partner of the only father and son duo to have both won the Ashes, **Brian Christopher Broad** was born on 29th September 1957 in Knowle and educated at Colston's Collegiate School. He joined Clifton RFC in 1980, having previously played for Bristol United. He was already playing cricket for Gloucestershire and decided in 1983 to leave rugby behind him and to concentrate on the summer game.

He left Gloucestershire in 1984 and joined Nottinghamshire, complaining that his former county's lack of ambition had held him back. His move was rewarded by selection for England, with spectacular results against the weak Australian team of 1986-87 when Broad equalled Jack Hobbs and Wally Hammond by scoring centuries in three successive Ashes tests. He scored a further 139 in the inconclusive Sydney bicentenary test a year later, but smashed the stumps down after being bowled; after he showed dissent having been adjudged LBW in the first innings of the 1989 Lord's test against Australia, he was dropped, ostensibly for loss of form, but the England management was becoming increasingly tough after the free-for-all of the Ian Botham era, and petulance was out of fashion. To give the selectors their due, Broad had scored just 153 runs in his last eight innings.

Later he returned to Gloucestershire and then joined the BBC TV commentary team before it was disbanded. He retired at the end of the 1994 season with a hip injury. In 2003 he became an ICC Test Official, acting as match referee for Test matches and one-day internationals. He oversaw the first match of the World Cricket Tsunami Appeal and served as match referee for the World Cup Super Eights game between the West Indies and Australia. Broad was the match referee when the convoy carrying the Sri Lankan cricket team was attacked by terrorists during the second test in Lahore, Pakistan in 2009.

His son Stuart plays cricket for Nottinghamshire and England.

Andrew Christopher Thomas was born on 1st June 1958 in Bristol and educated at Colston's Collegiate School and Keble College, Oxford University. He won a rugby blue in 1979 and later joined Bristol. For several years he was a coach at Clifton RFC.

Above: Andy Thomas

Gareth Lloyd Evans was born on 2nd November 1952 in Newport. He played for the Newport High School Old Boys club and Cross Keys prior to joining Newport in 1975. On his debut at Welford Rd on February 8th of that year he scored the winning try against Leicester in a game won 10-6 by Newport. He was Newport captain in 1979/80 and won three caps for Wales in 1977 and 1978. Evans was selected for the British Lions tour of New Zealand, forcing him to stand down from Newport's winning cup final team of 1977. He later joined Cardiff and then moved to Clifton in February 1983. He became Newport coach with Nev Johnson in the club's successful promotion year from the 1st Division in 1990/1.

Gareth Evans became a senior manager of the National Farmers' Union of Wales.

Alan Sharp was born on 7th October 1968. He was educated at St. Brendan's College, Bristol and qualified to play for Scotland through a grandmother born in Brechin. He joined Clifton from Bristol in November 1990 but returned to his former club for the 1992/93 season. He represented England Schools and England B but also the Scotland u-19 and u-21 teams. Having played through pain during a Scotland trial in 1992-93, he was selected to play against Ireland in 1993 but was diagnosed with a fractured leg on the eve of the match. He began his international career with Scotland the following season, but it was regularly interrupted by injuries which led to him missing the 1995 World Cup. He left Bristol at the end of the 1995/96 season and joined Coventry, returning once more to help Bristol to promotion from the second division in 1998-99.

He retired at the end of the 1999-2000 season and subsequently became landlord of The Bear and Rugged Staff public house on Southmead Road in Bristol.

The Scotland side that played England on 5th February 1994, Alan Sharp's debut. © Yerbury Photography, image courtesy of Scottish Rugby Union Library. (L-R) Back Row: K D McKenzie [replacement] (Stirling County), A G J Watt [replacement] (Glasgow HS/Kelvinside), I C Jardine [replacement] (Stirling County), I R Smith [replacement] (Gloucester), D A Stark [replacement] (Boroughmuir), B W Redpath [replacement] (Melrose). Middle Row: D R Davies [Touch Judge] (Wales), L McLachlan [Referee] (New Zealand), S Hastings (Watsonians), P Walton (Northampton), D S Munro (Glasgow HS/Kelvinside), A I Reed (Bath), G W Weir (Melrose), R I Wainwright (Edinburgh Academicals), K S Milne (Heriots FP), A G Stanger (Hawick), C Thomas [Touch Judge' Wales]. Front Row: K M Logan (Stirling County), G Armstrong (Jed Forest), A P Burnell (London Scottish), A G Hastings [Captain] (Watsonians), A V Sharp (Bristol), G P J Townsend (Gala), D S Wyllie (Stewart's Melville FP)

Paul D. Johnstone was born on 16th October 1970 in Bulawayo, Zimbabwe and swam for Zimbabwe in the All African Games at the age of 17. He played six rugby internationals for his country. When he moved to the UK he joined Clifton RFC, then moved on to London Scottish and later Bristol. After retirement he was a coach at Dings Crusaders in Bristol.

Peter Polledri was born in Bristol to Italian parents on 10th June 1957. Educated at St. Brendan's College and coached by Elwyn Price who later became Clifton RFC's first coach, he played for Bristol and Gloucestershire and captained England Students to victories against the Argentina and Italy national teams. He captained England u-23s but was never selected for a full international.

In the mid 1980s he played for an Italian XV and was encouraged to move to Italy with the prospect of playing for the country, but (although tempted) he decided to stay in Bristol where he had just started a business. He played 474 first team games for Bristol, a total surpassed only by Dave Watt and Alan Morley. He joined Clifton in June 1990 and became a coach for the club until moving to St. Mary's Old Boys in 2001.

Simon Hogg was born on 27th October 1960 and educated at Bristol Grammar School and Exeter University. He played for England Students, England u-23s, Devon, Gloucestershire and the South West. He joined Bristol United just after leaving school but then moved to Bristol, playing over 200 games for the club, including three Cup Finals, and scoring over 1,000 points. He joined Clifton, with other former Bristol players, in 1992.

He became a teacher at Taunton School teaching mathematics, coaching rugby and taking charge of cricket.

Andy Blackmore was born on 1st November 1965 and played for Bristol, Gloucestershire, Barbarians and England B. He did play for the full England team in 1993 against Canada during a tour of North America, but no caps were awarded for these matches.

He joined Coventry in 1995 and then returned to Bristol to play for Clifton. Andy Blackmore is now employed by the RFU as Rugby Development Officer for the South West.

Dean Dewdney was born on 5th November 1974 in Bindure, Zimbabwe and came to England to take up a short term teaching contract at Clifton College in 1995. He played for Clifton for a few months but was soon invited to join Bristol. In 2001 he joined Neath for a short period and moved to Cardiff Blues in August 2002.

His first appearance for the Barbarians was in the Mobbs Memorial match against the East Midlands, played at Bedford's Goldington Road ground on 15th March 2006. The fixture was inaugurated on 10th February 1921 in honour of Lt.-Colonel Edgar Mobbs, a former captain of the East Midlands, Barbarians and England, who had fallen at Passchendaele at the age of 35. He had also been a committee member of the Barbarian Football Club and the Rugby Football Union. The annual match is staged at either Northampton or Bedford, with the East Midlands Rugby Union providing the opposition.

Dean Dewdney retired from professional rugby with Cardiff in April 2006 because of injury. He made 58 appearances for Cardiff, scoring 18 tries, and represented Zimbabwe on three occasions.

Ralph Knibbs was born on 3rd August 1964 and educated at Whitefield Comprehensive School and Brunel College, Bristol. He played for Bristol Schools and appeared in an England schools trial. He joined Bristol and scored a try with his first touch of the ball on his debut against Pontypridd in March 1982.

He turned down a chance to tour South Africa with England in 1984, making a stand against apartheid. Over the next few seasons he trained with both the England B and full England squads, but he continually missed out on international selection. In 1997 he joined Coventry and became coach, but moved on to Clifton as captain in 1998, retiring from the game in 2001.

James Maxwell Michael Averis was born on 28th May 1974 in Bristol. He was educated at Bristol Cathedral School and Portsmouth University, and also represented Oxford University where he won rugby (at fly-half) and cricket blues whilst studying as a postgraduate on a Major Stanley's scholarship.

James Averis. Image courtesy OURFC.

He played for Clifton RFC as a teenager and was a member of the team that won the u-17s Gloucestershire County Cup in 1990-1. He also played rugby for Bristol but eventually settled for a full-time career playing cricket for Gloucestershire. He left Gloucestershire CCC in 2006 to concentrate on a Law degree.

David Llewellyn Rees was born on 15th October 1974 in Kingston-upon-Thames, Surrey. He went to school in Gosforth before moving to the Royal Grammar School in Newcastle. He went on to study graphic design and advertising at Manchester Metropolitan University.

David Rees.

An all round sportsman, he became a Northumberland schools sprint champion and county tennis player, and was nationally ranked in junior table tennis. He represented Northumberland at rugby in the 1995 CIS County Cup Final against Warwickshire and played football for Newcastle Boys.

Whilst at university he played for Sale, appearing 44 times for the Cheshire club and winning eleven England caps.

Rees played in the 1999 World Cup and moved to Bristol in the same year. He was selected for the England squad to tour Argentina in 2002. In 2003 he transferred to Leeds Tykes after Bristol's relegation, and in 2006 moved to Newbury R.F.C. In the 2008-2009 season he joined Clifton RFC.

Adam Reuben was born on 25th March 1972 in Leeds and played for Clifton whilst a medical student at Bristol University. He played for Bristol University from 1992-97 and won three caps for England Students, as well as Oxford rugby blues whilst a postgraduate student in 1997 and 1998. He also represented Cardiff, Cheltenham and Taunton.

Adam Reuben. Image courtesy OURFC.

Adam Reuben gave up rugby to concentrate on his work at The Royal Devon & Exeter Hospital.

Andrew Stanley Collins was educated at King Edward's, Bath and Swansea University before embarking on a postgraduate MPhil in Social Anthropology at Oxford University. He has represented Somerset, the South-West and England at u-18, u-19 and u-21 levels. He has also played for England Students and his previous clubs were Bath, Bristol (while at Bristol University) and Ponypridd. After playing for Clifton he then moved on to Worcester and Pertemp Bees.

Andy Collins. Image courtesy OURFC.

He gained Oxford University rugby blues as a prop forward in 1998 and 1999.

Rhys Oakley was born on 16th September 1980 in Plymouth and attended Marlwood School in Bristol. He started playing rugby at Thornbury but moved to Clifton and played through the junior teams to the 1st XV. He joined Bristol in 2002 and won the man of the match award when Bristol beat Montferrand 24-19 on 19th October 2002; Montferrand had 12 internationals in their team and were pre-tournament favourites. Bristol was relegated at the end of that season.

In September 2003 Oakley joined Newport Gwent Dragons. He played for the England u-21 team but was also eligible through his grandparents to play for Wales and won two caps in 2003 in warm-up matches for the World Cup. He appeared again for Wales in the 2006 Commonwealth Games in Melbourne as part of the squad which won the Rugby Sevens Plate competition. He joined Leeds Carnegie at the start of the 2006-2007 season.

Rhys Oakley. Image courtesy of Leeds Carnegie RFC.

Alex Brown was born on 17th May 1979 in Bristol, the son of former Clifton captain Peter Brown. He was educated at Colston's School in Bristol and was part of its award-winning rugby team of the 1990s. He is the first Clifton player to have gone though the junior ranks from u-7 to 1st XV and then play for England.

From the 6th November 1984 issue of the *Bristol Evening Post*, Clifton's Peter Brown and his five year old son Alex.

Following spells with Bath and Pontypool he joined Bristol, where he won the first Under-21 Zurich Premiership. When Bristol was relegated in 2003 he joined Gloucester.

He won his first England cap on 11th June 2006 against Australia in Sydney.

Alex Brown. Image courtesy of Gloucester RFC. Photo by Martin Bennett.

Oliver Sacco was born on 26th February 1983 and educated at St. Brendan's Sixth Form College in Bristol. He has, so far, won 26 caps for Malta over a seven year period, scoring 45 points.

Ollie Sacco (Centre) lines up for Malta against Netherlands on 25th April 2009 at Valletta in a qualifying round for the 2011 Rugby World Cup.

Ross Blake was born on 29th December 1979 in Glasgow. He was educated at Bristol Grammar School and Hughes Hall, Cambridge University. After playing for Clifton in the junior section he returned and joined the 1st XV in 2005-2006. He also played for Bristol and Bath.

He won blues for Cambridge at scrum-half in 2006 and 2007 and captained the 2007 team to a 22-16 victory over Oxford in front of 34,500 people.

He joined London Irish on a short-term contract in March 2008.

Ross Blake captain of the 2007 Cambridge University team, seated centre. James Lumby is in the middle row 4th from the left. Image courtesy CURFC.

James Lumby was born on 3rd September 1985 and educated at Caldicott School, Bristol University and Hughes Hall, Cambridge University. James played a few games for Clifton at No. 8 while at Bristol University. He has also played for Bristol and Bedford. He scored Cambridge's final try in the 2007 varsity match.

Matt Salter was born on the 2nd December 1976 in Greenwich, London. He was educated at St. Dunstans College, Lewisham, London. He originally played rugby league for London Broncos in 1999 but switched codes and briefly played for West

Hartlepool before joining Bristol in 2000. He left Bristol in 2003 after they were relegated and joined Leeds Tykes. He rejoined Bristol in 2004-05 and became captain for four seasons in a row. In 2009 he left Bristol to coach at the Bristol Academy and joined Clifton as a player/coach.

Matt Salter

Famous Matches

England v Scotland: 5th February 1872, The Oval, London

The England team that played Scotland on 5th February 1872. Image courtesy of the World Rugby Museum, Twickenham. (L-R) Back Row: J.A. Body (Gipsies), F.I. Currey (Marlborough Nomads), S. Finney (R.I.E. College), H. Freeman (Marlborough Nomads), F.W. Mills (Marlborough Nomads), A.St.G. Hamersley (Marlborough Nomads), F.W. Isherwood (Ravenscourt Park), A.G. Guillemard (West Kent), W.W. Pinching (Guys Hospital), P. Wilkinson (Law Club), J.E.H. Mackinlay (St. George's Hospital), F. Luscombe (Gipsies), C.W. Sherrard (Royal Engineers). Front Row: F.B.G. D'Aguilar (Royal Engineers/Bath), J.A. Bush (Blackheath), F. Stokes (Blackheath), T. Batson (Blackheath), J.E. Bentley (Gipsies), W.O. Moberly (Ravenscourt Park). Absent: D.L.P. Turner (Richmond).

This second international rugby fixture provided England with revenge for the previous year's reverse, north of the border, in the inaugural international between the countries. This time England won by a goal, drop goal and two tries to one drop goal.

Clifton RFC's formation still lay seven months in the future, and two of the club's most famous players, James Bush and William Moberly, were attached to London clubs for reasons of RFU affiliation referred to elsewhere in this book (note the complete absence of players from Northern clubs in the photograph).

Oxford v Cambridge: 10th February 1872, The Parks, Oxford.

This first 'varsity match' saw Oxford captained by William Moberly, just five days after his participation in the victory over Scotland. This was a 20-a-side match - 16 of the Oxford side had been at Rugby School and the other four at Marlborough College. Oxford had prepared for the match by pitting 20 Old Rugbeians against 20 from other schools in a trial match.

Cambridge had to leave behind their captain, E. Winnington Ingram, who was detained by important studies. I.C. Lambert was hastily elected captain instead.

Oxford wore dark blue for the match and Cambridge pink; their light-blue shirts were adopted later. Oxford used 14 forwards, three half-backs and three backs. Cambridge played with 15 forwards, three half-backs and two backs. For this match there was no referee, and disputes were decided by agreement of the captains.

Although three tries were scored in this match, no goals were kicked and so under prevailing rules the game was drawn.

Moberly resigned the captaincy in October 1872, although he did continue as Honorary Secretary.

Clifton v Sydney College: 1872, Coldharbour Lane

The first match played by Clifton RFC, sometime late in 1872, was against Sydney College, Bath at Coldharbour Lane. Playing 20 a-side (16 forwards, two half backs and two goal keepers), there were no referees and the laws of the game decreed that "the captains of the respective sides shall be the sole arbiters of all disputes". Clifton won by one goal, three tries and two touches to nil. The book 'Fifty Years with the Clifton Rugby Football Club" lists that first team as *Backs: Charles Strachan, David Henry Walsh; Halves: George A. Newall, Osbourne Henry Channer, Alexander Stewart Ward Young. Forwards: C.E.Atkinson, Patrick Duncan Jnr., Michael Martyn Curtis, William J. G. Lovell, Edwards, William F. Bence-Jones, Thomas Alexander Verner, Frank Evans, Alfred Charles Henderson Borrett, Claude Chamberlain.* Oddly there are only 15 players listed for a 20-a-side match. George A. Newall scored the new club's first try.

Since 1916, the site of Sydney College, Bath has housed the Holburne Museum of Art and belongs to Bath University. It displays the treasures collected by Sir William Holburne and is situated at the end of Great Pulteney Street.

Scotland v England: 3rd March 1873, Hamilton Crescent Glasgow

By now free of his Blackheath shackles, James Bush's second England cap was also the first won by a current Clifton RFC player, less than six months into the club's existence.

The England team that played Scotland on 3rd March 1873; image courtesy of the World Rugby Museum, Twickenham. (L-R) Back Row: E.C. Cheston (Law Club), J.E.H. Mackinlay (St.George's Hospital), M.W. Marshall (Blackheath), H. Freeman (Marlborough Nomads), W.R.B. Fletcher (Marlborough Nomads), S. Morse (Law Club), C.H. Rickards (Gipsies), C.W. Boyle (Oxford University), E.R. Still (Ravenscourt Park), C.H.R. Vanderspar (Richmond). Seated: J.E.H. Mackinlay (St. George's Hospital), D.P. Turner (Richmond), F. Stokes [Captain] (Blackheath), F. Luscombe (Gipsies), J.A. Bush (Clifton RFC), F.W. Mills (Marlborough Nomads). On the ground: H. Marsh (R.I.E. College), J.A. Body (Gipsies), S. Finney (R.I.E. College), Hon. H.A. Lawrence (Richmond).

A crowd of 5,000 watched a game that was played at the home of the West of Scotland club. Melting snow and incessant rain turned the game into a morass. Before the match the England captain Frederick Stokes arranged for a cobbler to alter the soles of the England players' boots to counter the wet, muddy conditions. Unfortunately the boots of two England players, Freeman and Boyle, were not returned and they had to play in "dress-boots".

The game ended with neither side scoring, so the rivalry stood at a win, a loss and a draw for both countries after three internationals, with the official formation of the Scottish Rugby Union still to take place.

Clifton College v Clifton RFC: 12th December 1874, Clifton College

This was the first club versus college match. The scoring rules were still to be changed, so the match was drawn despite the club scoring a try. A match report appeared in 'The Cliftonian' magazine, Vol. IV, and gives a typical Victorian account of a rugby match:

THE COLLEGE v. THE CLIFTON CLUB
This match was played on Saturday, Dec. 12th, on Bigside. The strangers mustered, as we had expected, a strong and heavy team forward, with fair men behind the scrimmage. Dakyns won the toss and chose the bottom goal, the strangers kicked off, and for some while the ball remained on the lower side, about half way down the ground. As the ground was exceedingly greasy the work forward was very hard; the strangers, notwithstanding their weight and good play forward, could not drive back the School much, and what was lost was soon recovered by the good play of our half-backs. Deacon helped the strangers greatly by the powers of running. After some while he made a run which carried play across the other side of the ground and considerably nearer the School goal, from there it was brought back again by a very fine run and drop of Pocock's, and then a good drop goal into touch brought the ball into the strangers' quarters; but no advantage was gained as the School was again driven back to the middle of the ground. After this the strangers played up and drove the School slowly down the ground, and finally they were compelled to touch the ball down in self defence; and again, immediately after the drop out, they were compelled to do so a second time. Soon after this, owing to some mistake or misunderstanding, the ball was thrown far out of touch, and Deacon getting the ball had a fair start and run in between the posts; the try by J.A.Bush was a failure, being well charged by Trevor.

For some while after changing ends the strangers kept the ball up near our goal, but by the good play of the forwards, and of Heath, half-back, the ball was slowly driven down the hill, and for the rest of the day the School had considerably the best of it, penning their adversaries and keeping their goal in continual danger. On one occasion Pocock very nearly finished a good run by landing the ball behind the line, but was unfortunately collared just too soon. The School however were prevented from gaining any decisive advantage until "no-side[4]" was called. During this period Butterworth helped the strangers by two fine runs, while Strachan and Deacon were exceedingly useful throughout. E.J.Taylor played well back, and proved himself a most difficult man to pass. For the strangers the most conspicuous forward, and almost universal good

[4] The old term for the end of a game of rugby.

play, were the two Pauls, the two Curtis, and Bush. For the school Miller played as well as usual whole-back[5], taking one or two enormous drops; Maw also played fairly whole-back, displaying great coolness; Pocock, Block, and Heath all played exceedingly well half-back; while among the forwards, Fowler, the two Trevors, and Burt were very conspicuous. The match was, as we have seen, drawn slightly in favour of the Club. Reviewing it as a whole our twenty, although not playing so brilliantly as against Oxford, played exceedingly well, and fortune certainly helped the Club to win their one advantage. For the rest we only wish that there had been a quarter of an hour's longer play.

We add a list of the twenties. Clifton Club: A.H. Allen, A.J. Taylor (whole-back), F. Allen, E.J. Taylor (three-quarter-back), C. Strachan (captain), E.A. Deacon, A.K. Butterworth (half-back), W.M. Bird, J.G. Budd, J.A. Bush, J. Curtis, M.M. Curtis, J.H. Dunn, F. Morris, W.S. Paul, A.C.St. Paul, E. Phillips, W. Strachan, J.G. Thomson, W.R. Webb. The College: J.D. Miller, A.W. Leach, W. Maw (whole-back), E.I. Pocock, A. Block, A.H. Heath (half-back), G. Dakyns, W. Trevor, H. Fowler, C. Slater, A.S. Trevor, R.E. Bush, J. Haig, H.P. Burt, J. Sharp, H. Grylls, J. Hood, H. Marsh, H. Meuricoffee, (aeg., H.R. King, R. Turner, R. Baker, E.L. Maisey, J. Bryant.).

The Clifton College captain, George Doherty Dakyns, was the son of Thomas Henry Dakyns. The Clifton College players J.D. Miller, E.I. Pocock and R.E. Bush would become regular players for the club and are covered in the Famous Players chapter.

This match became an annual event, usually played at the beginning of the season.

England v Scotland: 6th March 1876, The Oval, London

This was the last 20-a-side international, and James Bush's last appearance for England. The game became 15-a-side on February 5th 1877.

4,000 spectators saw a fast, exciting game won by England by one goal and one try to nil.

[5] An old term for a Full-back.

The England team that played Scotland on 6th March 1876 at the Oval. Image courtesy of the World Rugby Museum. (L-R) Back Row: F.H. Lee (Oxford University), H.J. Graham (Wimbledon Hornets), W.H. Hunt (Preston Grasshoppers), A.W. Pearson (Blackheath), R. Walker (Manchester), W.C. Hutchinson (R.I.E. College). Middle Row: A.H. Heath (Oxford University), F.R. Adams (Richmond), E. Kewley (Liverpool), W.E. Collins (St.George's Hospital), L. Stokes (Blackheath), M.W. Marshall (Blackheath). Front Row: E.C. Cheston (Richmond), R.H. Birkett (Clapham Rovers), T.S. Tetley (Bradford), F. Luscombe [Captain] (Gipsies), J.A. Bush (Clifton), W.C.W. Rawlinson (Blackheath). On the ground: W. Greg (Manchester), G.R. Turner (St.George's Hospital).

South Wales v Clifton: 12th January 1878, Newport

Clifton drew this match, with each side scoring one goal and one touch. This South Wales side was the forerunner of the first Welsh national team of 1881. Appearing for South Wales on this occasion was James Alfred Bevan, who would join Clifton the following season and become the first captain of Wales on 19th February 1881.

Somerset v Gloucestershire: 2nd January 1879, Weston-super-Mare.

Another first – this time the first county match played by Gloucestershire, drawn with one try apiece. There were six Clifton players in the Gloucestershire side including the captain John Day Miller.

The *Bristol Mercury* commented:

FOOTBALL.-Gloucestershire v Somersetshire. This match, the first county match played by Gloucestershire came off on Thursday at Weston-super-Mare, in the presence of numerous spectators. The game was evenly contested from first to last, and was very fast, considering that the ground was covered by snow some two inches deep. Willmot won the toss and kicked off, the ball being well returned was kept unpleasantly close to the Somersetshire goal, until they were obliged to touch down. After this the Somerset team compelled Gloucester to touch down, and no other advantage was gained by either side until after half time, when the Somerset backs passed the ball, and the close quarters in which it was kept made the game look dangerous for Gloucester. It was, however, touched down by Patterson, fortunately too near the touchline to enable Willmot to place a goal. The next point of importance was a touch gained by Gloucestershire, but all their efforts to gain a try were unavailing. An enjoyable game finally resulted in an even draw, both sides having scored one try and two touches. The play of both teams throughout was very good, the home team perhaps having the advantage forward and the visitors behind the scrimmage. Patterson, Foord, Lysaght, and Baker forward and Fuller behind played best for Somerset; and for Gloucestershire Hirst, Lamb, Cartwright, Winterbotham, and Evans showed to the most advantage. The Gloucestershire team were hospitably entertained at dinner by the Somerset men after the match. The sides were :- Gloucester- J.D.Miller (Clifton) (Captain), and H.J.Berry (Gloucester), backs; H.L.Evans (Clifton), H.M.Hamilton (Stroud), and R.Gribble (Clifton), three-quarter backs; J.F.Brown (Gloucester), and G.G.Pruen (Cheltenham), half backs; J.E.Bush (Clifton), G.M.Cartwright (Stroud), J.H.Dunn (Clifton), J.C.Gilmore (Clifton), C.Hirst (Rockleaze), S.J.Lamb (Cheltenham), P.R.Pakenham (Cheltenham), forwards. Somerset- F.Johnston (Wellington), and C.N.Cornish (Taunton), backs; F.G.F.Thompson (Bridgwater), and S.Marten (Weston), three-quarter backs; J.G.E.Willmot (Weston) (Captain), H.G.Miller (Bath), half backs; A.Foord (Wells), A.Lysaght (Bath), H.Patterson (Weston), G.H.Sparkes (Wellington), C.Baker (Wellington), E.C.Heming (Yeovil), E.Barham (Bridgwater), A.Elsworth (Wells), A.A.Michell (Bridgwater), forwards.

Scotland v England: 10th March 1879, Raeburn Place Edinburgh

In 1879 this annual fixture took on an extra dimension with the introduction of the award of the Calcutta Cup to the winners. The name came from the Calcutta rugby club, which upon its dissolution, had its funds (in silver rupees) melted down, made into the handsome trophy and presented to the RFU on condition that it be competed for annually.

The England team that played Scotland on 10th March 1879. Image courtesy of the World Rugby Museum. (L-R) Back Row: H. Huth (Huddersfield), R. Walker (Manchester), L. Stokes (Blackheath), F.R. Adams (Richmond), S. Neame (Old Cheltonians), G. Harrison (Hull), N.F. McLeod (R.I.E. College), H.C. Rowley (Manchester), H.H. Taylor (St.George's Hospital). Seated: W.J. Penny (United Hospitals/Kings College Hospital), A. Budd (Blackheath), G.W. Burton (Blackheath), H.H. Springman (Liverpool), F.D. Fowler (Manchester). On the ground: W.A.D. Evanson (Richmond), G.F. Vernon [Reserve] (Blackheath).

In the England side were former Clifton player Arthur Budd and future Clifton player William John Penny. The game was drawn, although a converted try for England against a drop goal for Scotland would soon have given a very different result.

Newport v Clifton: 10th January 1880, Newport

The previous season's fixture on 22nd February 1879 had seen, according to the *Star of Gwent*, an outbreak of hooliganism. The winter of 1878-79 was one of the worst on record; snow still lay heavily on the ground. Newport won by a goal and a try with no reply from the visitors. *"Roughs and cultured mingling together pelted with snowballs old and young alike; Magistrates sober and staid; policemen officious and bumptious; the Clifton boys stalwart and muscular; children young and tender; all fell in for a share of the uncouth and unpleasant treatment. Snowballing may be invigorating and to some a pleasing pastime but those unfortunate to be on the receiving end cannot be said to view it with much favour. The Magistrates and policemen in question did not admire the play, while the Clifton lads did not consider it a kindly welcome to Newport."*

The match went ahead nonetheless, and this time Clifton beat Newport by a goal and four touches to nil. Ward scored the try for Clifton, which was converted by the captain John Miller. Clifton again beat Newport at home a month later, and this double win over Newport would not be repeated by any other club in the county until Bristol managed the feat in 1913-14. Clifton finished the season unbeaten after 14 games and did not once concede a try.

This match followed Blackheath's win against Newport on 20th November 1879, which had ended Newport's unbeaten record and invincible reputation.

England v Wales: 19th February 1881, Blackheath

This game was as notable for the chaotic organisation of the Welsh side as for the result. It was Wales's first international and organised before the Welsh RFU was formed. There had been an attempt to arrange a trial match at Swansea in December 1880, but it did not take place and further attempts to stage the event were disrupted by bad weather. It certainly did not help, either, that the (English) RFU insisted that the match be played on 19th February; this was the day that Swansea was due to play Llanelli at Neath in a semi-final cup-tie, thus depriving Wales of several top players. Eventually the main force behind the Welsh side, Richard Mullock, selected the team himself. The team had never played together before, and one player, Major Richard Summers, was selected for Wales on the strength of his performances a couple of years earlier for his school, Cheltenham College, in matches against Cardiff and Newport. No formal invitations to play were sent out to the Welsh XV. Two of those expected to appear did not arrive for the match, so bystanders, university undergraduates with tenuous Welsh links but who had travelled to London to see the match, had to be co-opted to play for Wales. It was also unhelpful that the changing rooms were located in a local pub, The Princess of Wales, which remains there to this day. Both teams had to walk the half mile across the common to play the match. Rumour has it that the Welsh team needed some Dutch courage before the match and had over-estimated how much 'courage' was advisable.

The game was a farce. The Welsh were hopelessly outplayed and under modern scoring values lost 82-0. Harry Vassall scored a hat-trick of tries on this, his debut for England. It was recorded that that the England captain Lennard Stokes threw a colossal pass to Hunt, giving him an easy try, but the umpires ordered that in their opinion a long pass was 'not football'.

The RFU was not impressed by the course of events and the fixture was dropped the following season.

The first Welsh team of 1881 that lost heavily to England at Blackheath. Ten of these players, including Bevan, never played for Wales again. (L-R) Back Row: W.D. Phillips (Cardiff), G. Harding (Newport), R. Mullock (Newport), F. Purdon (Newport), G. Darbishire (Bangor), E. Treharne (Pontypridd), R.G.D. Williams (Abercamlais). Seated: T.A. Rees (Oxford University & Llandovery), E. Peake (Oxford University & Chepstow), J.A. Bevan [Captain] (Cambridge University & Grosmont), B.E. Girling (Cardiff), B.B. Mann (Cardiff). On the ground: L. Watkins (Oxford University & Llandaff), C.H. Newman (Cambridge University & Newport), E.J. Lewis (Cambridge University & Llandovery), R.H.B. Summers (Haverfordwest).

Clifton v Cardiff: 30th October 1881, Coldharbour Lane

A close game was expected by a large crowd but Clifton easily beat Cardiff by three goals, four tries and eight touches to one touch. Jack Nichols scored five tries in this game and would later score another five tries against Weston-super-Mare that same season. He was in the running for an England trial - and possibly an international cap - when an injury against Taunton in October 1882 ended his rugby career.

Clifton had another good season, losing only two games out of twelve and conceding only one goal.

Gloucestershire v New Zealand Natives: 2nd February 1889, Gloucester Spa

Two Clifton players appeared in this Gloucestershire team: Edward Leonard and Hiatt Cowles Baker, club captain who also captained the county team on this occasion. 8,000 people watched the match at The Spa in Gloucester. The New Zealand Natives won 4-1 through a goal (E. McCausland) and two tries (both by P. Keogh) to a try scored by Gloucestershire's R. Grist. Gloucestershire player S.A. Ball had a try disallowed, and Hiatt Cowles Baker missed two kicks at goal. A strong Gloucestershire side came closer to winning than the final score might suggest.

The *Western Daily Press* on 4th February 1889 reported:
THE MAORIS v GLOUCESTERSHIRE - This long-anticipated match was played at the Spa, Gloucester, on Saturday. The weather was favourable, and there were about 8,000 spectators present.

The teams were Gloucester: A.F.Hughes, back; G.W.Coates, T.Bagwell, C.E.Brain, R.Grist, three-quarter backs; S.A.Ball, W.George, half-backs; T.Collings, R.C.Jenkins, C.J.Whitcombe, H.C.Baker, E.Leonard, R.Edwards, J.Faulkener and H.V.Page, forwards. Maoris: W.Warbrick, back; McCausland, W. Wynyard, and F.Warbrick, three-quarter backs; Ihimaira, D.Gage, P.Keogh, half-backs; Ellison, G.Wynyard, H.Lee, Taiaroa, Maynard, Williams, Anderson and Rene, forwards.

The Maoris kicked off, and Brown sent the ball dead in touch outside the centre flag. Eventually packed scrimmages followed, and the Maoris' heeling out well, carried the play their opponents' quarters. Page dribbled to beyond the half-way flag, but Leonard being offside gave the Maoris a "free[6]". Nothing came of the kick, and Hughes returned into touch near the Maoris' 25 flag.

Shortly afterwards the home county claimed a free kick, and a possible easy chance of scoring was lost to them by not following up. Play continued in the Maoris' quarters until some fine passing transferred hostilities to the Gloucestershire territory, where a claim for hand ball was successfully made for the visitors, and Brown, mulling the return, almost let them in. The home team, however, gradually worked out, but the Maoris again and again pressed the attack, and Hughes averted danger by kicking out. Evenly-packed scrummages followed, and the home backs indulged in some spirited passing, from which an easy chance of scoring was lost to them by a forward ball. The Maoris made repeated efforts to score after this, but the defence offered most subborn, and Gloucester gradually worked out to the centre, where a round of grand passes by the Maoris was loudly applauded.

The match was now being fought out on the home goal line, but by an almost superhuman effort Gloucester successfully averted danger, to the relief of the spectators. Subsequently Gloucester invaded the Maori ground, and Ball got over the

---

[6] Free kick

line amidst load cheers, but to the dismay of the spectators the leather[7] was ordered back, and a scrummage was formed in front of the goal. Afterwards the Maoris gained some ground by a free kick, and "Smiler" made repeated efforts to score but was always repulsed. After the break up of the scrummage Keogh got the ball, and made a powerful run over the line and scored. The place by McCausland was a failure, and nothing further of importance happened to half-time.

After changing over, renewed vigour was infused into the play, and Keogh, again getting possession, in fine style won another try, which McCausland converted into the premier point. After this reverse the home men, heartily cheered by the spectators, played magnificently, and once Grist was awarded a free near the centre line, and Baker took the place, the ball falling just inside the cross-bar. Coates, George, Bagwell, and Page put in some sterling work, but the defence was too stubborn to be broken through, and the ball travelled up and down the field with great rapidity, neither side being able to claim advantage, after some passing by the home team, Coates handled the leather to Grist who galloped over the line and registered a try amid immense cheering, Baker took the place but failed to improve it.

The remainder, of the game was remarkable for the fine play shown by the home county, but they were unable to equal the score of their opponents, the result being that the Maoris were winners by a goal, a try, and one minor to a try.

Clifton v Bristol: 23rd March 1889, Leach's Field

This was the second fixture organised between the sides after the first, arranged at Bristol's ground, was cancelled because of a waterlogged pitch. After Carlton and Redland Park amalgamated in 1888 to form Bristol, this was dubbed the match to decide the leading rugby team in Bristol. Against the odds, it was Bristol that took the crown.

An account of the match appeared in the Western Daily Press on 25th March 1889:

CLIFTON CLUB v BRISTOL –
In fine weather and in the presence of a goodly number of spectators, chiefly partisans of the latter team, the two clubs met on Saturday for the first time this season. Hiatt Baker won the toss, and chose to play with the wind. Clifton kept the game for some time on the Bristol goal line until the latter worked it into the centre and Bryan, after a good sprint got past the Clifton back and scored a try amid considerable cheering, which was redoubled when the same player converted it into a goal. Baker restarted with a splendid kick, and Bristol touched down. This was followed by some hard play in the latter's territory, Edwards and Fred Budgett doing some good service for their side.

[7] An old term for a rugby ball

Cruickshank now put in a good run. Hill neutralised, and Bristol again touched down. Hard forward play from both sides then prevailed until half-time.

Resuming play again, Clifton were forced quickly to touch down. Soon after this Luffman got possession and succeeded in getting over the line. Bryan made a very good attempt at goal. Haskins and Prout next put in some good runs, and Frank Budgett, intercepting a pass, took the ball to the half-way flag; Bryan returned it, and Clifton touched down. Frank Budgett and Bryan now played well for their respective sides, Lowther and Bryan rendering material assistance with some good kicking. The Bristol forwards now brought off some good forward play. Graham replied with a good run, but failed to reach the line, and Haskins dribbled back to Clifton territory, where play was carried on for some time Clifton eventually touching down. Prout put in another good run for his side, and Leonard was also conspicuous.

After several free kicks and a lot more forward play the whistle sounded for "No side," Bristol being left winners by one goal, one try, and six minors to three minors. Of the winners, behind the scrimmage Cruikshank played an admirable game, and Bryan and Prout were likewise very useful. All the forwards on both sides played well; for Bristol, Lockey, Brown and Lambert were most noticeable; for Clifton, Edwards, Leonard and Salisbury. Of the Clifton backs, Frank Budgett the three-quarter played best, though he foolishly attempted to drop a goal when he could have run in easily. Hooper and Hill were useful, but the former lost many opportunities of passing, and the latter had very few chances, but played well.

Teams:- Bristol- J.E.Aldridge, back; Bryan, Lowther, T.A.Prout, and Haskins, three-quarter backs; R.D.Cruikshank and F.Hill, half backs; A.Gee, S.W.Brown, R.Bryan, Lambert, P.Lockey, Winter, W.Thompson, and Luffman forwards.

Clifton- E.F.Woodgate, back; E.E.Hill, C.A.Hooper, H.Brook, and F.Budgett, three-quarter backs; G.Graham and F.B.Budgett, half backs; H.C.Baker. E.Leonard, R.Edwards, E.P.Press, A.Salisbury, W.Garnett, M.M.Baker, and W.H.Birch, forwards; referee Mr.A.E.Master.

Hartlepool Rovers v Barbarians: 27th December 1890, Hartlepool

The first match played by the Barbarians included in the team's ranks Richard Budworth, who joined Clifton some seven years later. The Barbarians were founded by William Percy Carpmael of Blackheath, who had the idea late in the evening of 9th April 1890 in Leuchter's Restaurant, Bradford. At the time there were very few touring teams, and Carpmael's idea was to create a team that would tour the provinces at holiday times, and which would include not only English players but also guests from the other home countries. The first tour, lasting four days, was to have been against Hartlepool Rovers, Bradford and Swinton; the last game was cancelled owing to frost.

The Barbarians won this first match 9-4.

In the beginning the team played against clubs, mostly in the North and in Wales. It was not until 1948 that the Barbarians started playing international sides.

Clifton v Bristol: 23rd September 1893, Buffalo Bill's Field

Clifton's new pitch at Buffalo Bill's Field in Horfield was christened by another fixture against Bristol. Anticipating a large crowd, Clifton hired five policemen and four stewards. The club had strengthened its team with Hooper, who had played in the first fixture between the clubs in 1889, Field and Grace, W.G's eldest son. Bristol had gained three players from Clifton a year before: Birch, Hunt and Ford. This was the eighth fixture between the clubs; previously Clifton had won two, Bristol five, and one had been drawn. This time Bristol won 11-0 to extend the supremacy over Clifton.

The following account of the match appeared in the *Bristol Times & Mirror* on 25th September 1893:

Nearly 4,000 persons assembled upon the new ground of the Clifton Club, at Horfield, on Saturday afternoon when a match was played between the home team and the Bristol Club. The weather threatened rain all afternoon, but fortunately the downpour kept off. A chill east wind was blowing, and this made the cold enough for any winter pastime. Both sides were well represented although Bristol were without Turner and Wilcocks, whose places on the three-quarter line were taken by Chard and Thomas; and Clifton had secured powerful assistance in C.A.Hooper and Field. The game was started by Clifton, for whom Belson kicked off. The ball was charged down, and some tough scrummaging followed upon the half-way line. This was broken by Lias getting the ball smartly out to Hooper, who was marked before he could get clear. Hooper made his mark a moment or two later, and Thompson relieved with a long kick, which found touch. Grace then started a fine running dribble, which led the Clifton forwards well into the Bristol 25. Pearce worked out with a dodgy little run, but Lias handed out of the pack to Hooper, and pretty passing amongst the three-quarters again bought the visitors' goal into jeopardy. Stronger play by the Bristol three-quarters slowly forced the game over the half-way line, where Field got possession, and put in a brilliant run, which was only just checked by Mackay a few yards from goal. Fenner speedily following up a long kick by Lockyer, secured the ball, and reached the 25 flag of his opponents line. In the scrum, the ball was again handed to him, and after a useful spurt he passed to Jarman, enabling him to score a try, which Ashford could not convert. The kick out was charged down, and after this the first notable event was smart play between Jarman, Ford, Pearce and Thompson. Ashford started off well from the half-way line, but was pulled down by Cooper. Stiff, close work followed, and Ashford, receiving the leather, threw all his weight upon his leg to start off quickly, and the ligature of the knee, unable to bear the strain, gave way. He lay upon the ground for a few moments, and was carried off, to be sent home in a cab. A delay of some five minutes was thus caused. Lockyer went back in place of Ashford, and Thompson moved into the centre. Clifton were first to assume the aggressive, but Fenner turned the tables with a fine run, and Lockyer lost a good opening through bad passing. Half time was called with the score - Bristol, one try; Clifton, nil. When play was resumed Hooper and Field played in the centre, with Rogerson and Davies on the wings. The game was fairly even and a bit dull at the outset, and then the Bristol forwards made their weight felt, and soon reached the Clifton 25. Hunt spoiled the work by kicking right behind. Scrummaging followed the kick out, and the ball coming out the Bristol side, Pearce quickly gave to Fenner, and he raced along close to the touch line, scoring near the corner. Thompson was successful with a difficult goal kick. Clifton had their innings after this, and Hooper and Field gained a lot of ground by their combination play. The home forwards beat the city men altogether in the loose, and rushed up the right wing, carrying the ball over the goal line, and were prevented from scoring by Lockyer touching down. When play was re-started Lias initiated another good piece of work by quickly passing out from the scrum to the three-quarters. The effort being ill-sustained, Bristol were soon back on the half-way line. Hunt giving Thompson the ball, the captain charged through the crowd and gained a try near the corner flag. Mackay made a game shot at goal, which just missed. Field's kicking came in very well when the game was once more set going, as Mackay was rushed down before he could return a second time, and Rogerson followed this up by a well-judged punting into touch. Their best effort was a dashing piece of passing, which Field started from the middle line. He sent to Davie, and receiving the ball back again transferred to Lias who threw it into the crowd when close to the visitor's goal. This was the last noteworthy incident, and the game ended in favour of Bristol by one goal and two tries to nothing. Teams:- Clifton: N.C.Cooper, back; C.A.Hooper, E.Field, T.Rogerson, and W.G.Davie, three-quarter backs; W.J.Lias (captain) and E.M.Panterdownes, half-backs; H.L.Norrington, B.H.Belson, W.Gwynn, L.Olivant, M.Blood, T.Jones, H.Bingham, and W.G.Grace jun., forwards. Bristol: W.A.Mackay, back; Chard, B.W.L.Ashford, W.Thompson, and E.Fenner, three-quarter backs; W.T.Pearce and F.W.Hunt, half-backs; W.H.Birch, A.W.Ford, W.Jarman, T.O.Davies, T.S.Duffett, P.F.Dewar, Capenhurst, and P.Lockyer, forwards. S.A.Ball refereed.

Bristol v Clifton: 10th April 1897, County Ground

This was the 16th fixture between the clubs. Bristol's superiority had been further extended, to the extent that to date Clifton had only won two and drawn two matches. Earlier in the season the clubs had played each other with Bristol running out 16-5 winners.

This match was much closer but still ended in a 6-5 victory for Bristol, achieved under disputed circumstances. A try was scored by Bristol just as the whistle was blown for full-time, Clifton claiming that the ball had been touched down after the game should have ended. The score stood and Clifton's players were thwarted once again by their closest and fiercest rivals.

The following season the fixture was controversially dropped by Bristol. It was reinstated in the 1898-99 season when Bristol won 19-0 and 28-5, following this up the next season with wins by 47-0 and 26-0.

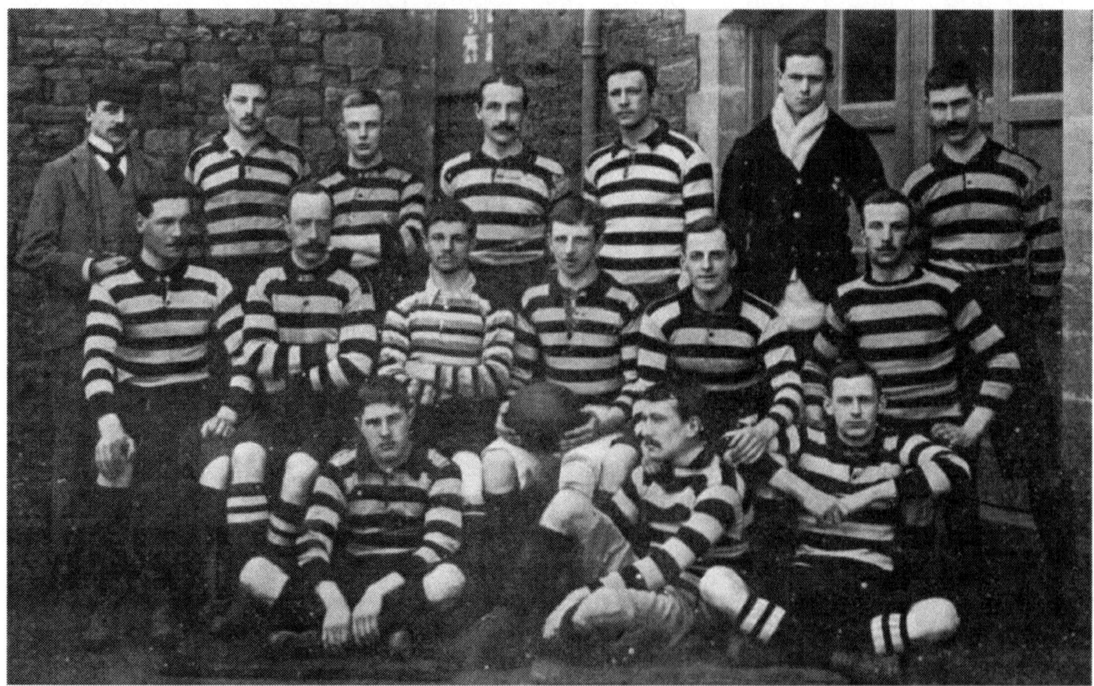

This photograph was taken just before the match against Bristol outside the pavilion at the County Ground on 10th April 1897. Standing (L-R): H.S. Sinnott, T.W. Baker, A.W. Board, W.J. Lias, W.H. Birch, T.W.H. Inskip, H. Mills. Sitting: J.M. Greenwood, T.S. Duffett, E.W. Baker, W.E. Paul, H.N. Spencer, C.W.W. James. On the ground: E.S.B. Smith, T. Taylor, A.B. Cridland.

Gloucester v Clifton: 26th September 1903, Kingsholm, Gloucester

The Gloucester club was a dominant force at this time, so with four regular first-team players missing Clifton could not possibly have expected what was arguably the club's most stunning pre-war victory.

The warm welcome at Kingsholm extended to the sale of so-called Death Cards, on this occasion bearing the message 'Death to Clifton' and on sale to an eager home crowd.

The *Bristol Times & Mirror* carried the following report on 28th September 1903:

Our heartiest congratulations to Clifton, who on Saturday achieved one of the finest successes of the club's history in defeating Gloucester, at Kingsholm, by five points to three. Not for many years have the town club been beaten by the Cliftonians on their own ground, and the match, which generally opens the Gloucester season, is looked upon more as a practice game than a serious encounter. This year, however, Gloucester have already played several games, whereas Clifton have not started their fixtures. Gloucester were without Romans and Smith, and Clifton had G.H. Beloe, D.A. Clark, H.C. Hicks, and T. Miller amongst their absentees. The two Bakers, however, who came in at half, did so well that it seems hardly just to send them back into the second fifteen next week, after filling the vacancies with such conspicuous success.

It may be argued that Gloucester under estimated their opponents, but if they did so, after the shock Stroud gave them last week, they deserved the reverse sustained. At the same time, Clifton made the most of their chances, except the shot at goal missed by Eddie Baker from a free, and defended splendidly; whereas Gloucester played raggedly, and did not show the finish the visitors did. From the records of the past two seasons it is evident that Clifton are treating football in a much more serious way than for many years past, and as a result the side has improved wonderfully. It is interesting to note that in 1899-1900 Gloucester secured 60 points against the Cliftonians, and in 1900-01 no fewer than 130. In 1901-02 the points were reduced to 94, last season to 53, and this year one would not be surprised to find that Clifton achieved a double success. It is the first time, at any rate, for many seasons that Clifton have commenced the year with points in hand, and such a big success should encourage Gardner and his men to many other victories during 1903-04.

Clifton playing against the full glare of a summer-like sun, went away with a dash which was irresistible, and at once got close down to the home line. The 'Cestrians, by strenuous effort, relieved the strain for the moment, but Clifton quickly carried play down to the Gloucester end again, and pressed with vigour which caused the supporters of the city club some anxiety. The defence, though clumsy, was dogged, and many clever bouts of passing by the Clifton back division were spoilt; but at length Eddie Baker, who was prominent throughout made a splendid opening for Eberle, the latter scoring in the corner, and Baker converting from a difficult position.

The second portion of the game was very similar to the first. Clifton had by far the best of the play. Their backs were clever, and the forwards worked well together. The display they gave was altogether finished, and in pleasing and striking contrast to the ragged play of the Gloucester contingent. Only Goulding among the forwards, and L. Vears at the back, played with intelligence. The former made some really brilliant efforts, and the latter was always cool, and tackled well, and kicked with good judgement, though failed at an apparently easy place kick, which if successful, would have given Gloucester the victory by one point. Stephens made several good attempts, but, taken altogether, the Gloucester play was weak. There were, certainly, as previously mentioned, two or three absentees, the captain, George Romans, being one; but it is extremely doubtful whether the result would have been different had he been in his old position at full back, as L. Vears proved an excellent substitute. For the visitors the brothers Eddie and Claude Baker, E. F. Eberle, and P. J. Slee were throughout conspicuous for good play, and the whole of the back division worked well together. Gloucester managed to score a try, so that Clifton only won by a couple of points; but this by no means adequately indicates their superiority.

Gloucestershire v Australia: 1st October 1908, Kingsholm, Gloucester

The Gloucestershire team included three Clifton players, Victor Fuller Eberle, Ellison Fuller Eberle and Worthington Wynn Hoskin. Australia won 16-0.

The Gloucestershire side that played Australia. (L-R) Back Row: C.E. Brown (Vice-President), R.A. Roberts (Hon.Sec.), E.S. Bostock Smith (President), H. Lowther, C.J. Woolf. Standing: ?, V. Fuller Eberle (Clifton), W.W. Hoskin (Clifton), F. Feltham (Bristol), A. Redding (Cinderford), H. Berry (Gloucester), A. Teague (Cinderford), J.H. Tratt. Seated: ?, E. Fuller Eberle (Clifton), J. Hyndham (Cinderford), W. Johns (Gloucester), A. Hudson [Captain] (Gloucester), ?, B. Davy (Cheltenham), W. Stichcombe (Lydney), M.A. Neale (Bristol), J. Hart (Hon.Treasurer). On the ground: D.R. Gent (Gloucester), ?.

The book "The First Wallabies" (Sharpham, 2000, p.43-45) has an account of the match:

The Wallabies travelled to Gloucester for the second match of the tour at the Kingsholm Ground on Thursday 1st October, where an expectant crowd of 8,000 paid £350 in gate money to witness the spectacle. In brilliantly fine conditions, described by one newspaper as 'tropical', Gloucestershire lost the toss and kicked off into the sun. The play at the outset was in the County half. The home forwards made good ground in the mauls but were constantly turned around whenever the Australian forwards fed the ball wide to their backs, who showed sizzling pace conditions, described by one newspaper as 'tropical', Gloucestershire lost the toss and kicked off into the sun. The play at the outset was in the County half. The home forwards made good ground in the mauls but were constantly turned around whenever the Australian forwards fed the ball wide to their backs, who showed sizzling pace. Carmichael took a clearing Gloucestershire kick which just failed to find touch on halfway and grazed the upright with his attempt at a dropped goal.

Fifteen minutes into the game the Australians won a line-out from a Gloucestershire throw-in and the ball sped along the back line for 'Boxer' Russell to cross wide out with opposing winger Hudson clinging to his shoulders. Carmichael converted from a difficult angle to make the score 5-0. The Wallaby eight were now dominating the mauls and winning tight heads from the Gloucestershire feed in the scrums by pushing the home forwards off the ball with ease. It seemed the visitors' set-positioning in the scrums was bearing fruit. The Australians were also dominant in the rolling mauls and short-passing rushes, which led to Russell's second try when Wood received a good ball from his forwards and sent the right winger careering down the blind side to score wide out. Carmichael's attempted conversion was just wide, so that the Australians led 8-0. Richards and Moran continued to dominate in broken play, reaching the loose ball at the breakdown of play well ahead of their opponents. The tourists were utilizing some clever tap-backs to Wood in the line out, a tactic that would eventually backfire on them in Wales. Wood and McKivat were creating reverse passing moves and run-around backing-up to create the extra man. From such a ploy Barnett received a short inside pass from McKivat and crashed over wide out. Carmichael's conversion attempt spun just wide of the goal posts, but the Wallabies went to the half-time break with a comfortable 11-0 lead.

Following the interval the Australian backs once again exhibited exceptional speed, but in their eagerness to score tries the passing was sometimes sloppy, causing the outside backs to overrun the leather. A revitalized Gloucestershire team attacked enthusiastically early in the second half but were repulsed by some fierce tackling. Winger Maurice Neale left the field with an injured shoulder leaving the County with fourteen players, Moran's offer of a substitute apparently not being taken up. Hickey and Mandible continually changed places in the centres in an effort to confuse the Gloucestershire defence but the home side grimly resisted wave after wave of backline assaults. (At that time the Australians normally played an inside and a specialist outside centre, while in Britain the centres remained on the left or right of the field.) Finally, just before full-time Wood scored a converted try following a reverse pass from five-eighth McKivat to make the final score Australia 16, Gloucestershire 0.

Australia 16 (Russell 2, Barnett, Wood tries, Carmichael two conversions) defeated Gloucestershire 0. Crowd: 8,000. Referee: T.D. Schofield (Wales).

Australia Backs: P.P. Carmichael, D.B. Carroll, E.F. Mandible, J.J. Hickey, C.J. Russell Halves: F. Wood, C.H. McKivat Forwards: H.M. Moran (captain), N.E. Row, T.J. Richards, S.A. Middleton, P.A. McCue, C.A. Hammand, T.S. Griffin, J.T. Barnett.
Gloucestershire Backs: B. Davy, A. Hudson (captain), M. Neale, V.F. Eberle, E.F. Eberle Halves: D.R. Gent, T. Elliott Forwards: W. Johns, H. Berry, A. Teague, A. Reading, J. Hyndman, W.W. Hoskin, W. Stinchcombe, F. Feltham.

Bristol/Clifton v Australia: 13th January 1909, County Ground, Bristol

Clifton provided six players to a joint Clifton/Bristol team that lost to Australia 11-3 at the Gloucestershire County Ground in front of a crowd of 5,000. The Clifton vice-captain A. J. Gardner was selected but was unable to play after being injured in the Gloucester Cup match with Saracens the previous week. W.W. Hoskin, also selected, was unavailable and was replaced by a Bristol player.

"The First Wallabies" (Sharpham, 2000, p.164-169) gives the following account of the match:

The Wallabies arrived in Bristol on the evening of Monday 11th January, to be welcomed by Stanley Bostock Smith, president of the Bristol Rugby Football Club, and other officials and supporters. The Bristol Evening News remarked:

'Tom Richards who played for Bristol last year, and has been perhaps, one of the most useful forwards of the Australian team, was soon hailed and given a hearty welcome. He looks wonderfully fit, and has played in nearly all the matches. Hand-shaking and words of welcome over, the visitors' baggage was transferred to cabs and breaks that waited outside, and the Wallabies were ready to drive off to the Queen's Hotel, Clifton, which had been selected as their headquarters.'

An entertaining programme had been planned for the tourists for the evening and the following day, their match against a combined Bristol and Clifton side being scheduled for the Wednesday of that week. The Bristol Evening News continued:

After dinner at the invitation of the management the Australians visited the Empire Music Hall, Old Market Street, where they were accommodated with 'boxes'. They seemed to find plenty of fun in the show - even though Tom Jones, the world-renowned Welsh comedian, figured on the bill - a rather cruel reminder to take the gilt off Saturday's gingerbread at Blackheath. They accepted the jest, however, as they accepted their reverse at Cardiff in the best of good humours. Mr McMahon was with them, and a glance at his face convinces one of his rare qualities for his position. His frank and kindly blue eyes; ever sparkling with fun; his winning smile; yet withal his firm mouth, are the hall-marks of a leader of men - a leader who can check and control, whilst inspiring with the fire of enthusiasm. They looked a jolly crew - those sun-tanned and virile figures, laughing in rollicking fashion in the depth of the boxes, showing beautiful sets of ivories, and ever and anon waving cheery greetings to friends. It happened that Adelaide Waldorf, 'the Australian gem', a lady with a really good voice, was down on the programme, and she was given a loyal greeting by her countrymen, her songs being heartily encored till time would permit no more, and with a wafted kiss she bowed them farewell. The performance over, the party took tram back to the Queen's and it was not long before the 'good-nights' were said, and the Wallabies sought rest. Several of their number are 'cripples', with stiff knees and bandaged legs - signs of wear and tear in the 25-odd matches they have played - but the majority seem fresh and keen as ever.

The Tuesday morning was spent at Fry's Chocolate Factory, where the tourists were shown through the workrooms and inspected the complex machinery involved in the process of converting raw cocoa beans from the West Indies into commercial chocolate. After a leisurely lunch at their hotel they then visited the enormous W.D. and H.O. Wills tobacco and cigarette factory. Ernest Booth reported: 'Miles of cigarettes in making came as a revelation to the team, who are mostly inveterate devotees of the weed. After an instructive inspection, the management received the whole company in their offices, and after refreshments and speeches, presented each with cigarettes and tobacco. In the evening a pantomime of 'Aladdin' was witnessed at the Princess Theatre. Thus finished a big day.'

For the match against Bristol and Clifton on the Gloucestershire County Ground on Wednesday 13 January, the Wallabies made three changes from the team which vanquished England at Blackheath. Bill Dix went to fullback to give Philip Carmichael a well-earned rest while Esmond Parkinson, having recovered from the injury which had kept him out of most of the tour, came in on the left wing. Charles Russell moved into the centres in place of Ward Prentice, who was injured at Blackheath, and Danny Carroll played on the right wing. The Bristol and Clifton team were more than capably led by Percy Down, a local farmer who had played with distinction against the tourists for England at Blackheath. He had also visited New Zealand and Australia in 1908 with the Anglo-Welsh side, but remained uncapped on tour. There were three late changes to the home side's fifteen listed in the match programme, F. Holbrook, J. Spoors and E. Kibbey replacing H.E. Shewing, C. Kingston and A.J. Gardner.

With the former Welsh international E. Gwyn Nicholls controlling proceedings, Percy Down won the toss and Row kicked off for Australia. The early play was all in the visitors' half of the field as the Bristol and Clifton forwards set up a series of dribbling raids while the 5000-strong crowd roared their approval. Holbrook appeared to cleanly intercept a Wallabies pass and set sail cornfield, then put the ball to his toe for winger Eberle to loom up outside and dive on it over the line. As the crowd celebrated Gwyn Nicholls was forced to bring the players back upfield for an earlier knock-on. The home forwards continued applying pressure with dribbling rushes, but the Australian backs fearlessly flung themselves onto the loose ball and saved the situation. The visitors were starting to dominate the scrums and McKivat set his outside backs moving at top pace. Carroll careered for the corner flag, but was just bundled into touch at the last moment by fullback W.R. Johnston. Soon after McCabe dodged through one opening, then another, before transferring to Middleton who put Gavin over the try-line out wide. Hickey missed with the kick and the Australians led 3-0. The Wallaby backs were receiving plenty of good ball but the home side's tackling was rock-solid. Soon it was Bristol and Clifton's turn to attack and only a last-ditch dive onto the loose ball by Carroll saved a certain try. Just before half-time scrum-half Spoors and Holbrook in the centres toed the ball towards the try-line, only to see it evade the former's spectacular dive in the in-goal area at the last moment.

On the resumption of play Carroll was seen at his best as he sprinted more than half the field for the try-line, but suddenly V.F. Eberle flashed across the field and tackled the flying St George winged in the shadow of the goal posts. Ten minutes' strenuous play ensued with both teams throwing caution to the winds and treating the crowd to some marvellous passing movements. During one of these McKivat shook himself clear of the defence and sent a well-timed pass to Hickey on the home side's twenty-five. Although three opposition backs attempted to halt his surge for the line, Hickey forced himself over near the uprights for Australia to go further ahead, 6-0. Hickey's attempted conversion of his own try swung wide at the last moment.

For a sustained period after this the Wallabies held good field position and with a surfeit of scrum possession looked certain to score again until George Percy cleared the home try-line with a grand dribble, more like a soccer player than a rugby forward, bringing the ball out between his twenty-five and halfway. From the ensuing maul Spoors on the right wing took a long pass and as he approached Dix at fullback, he kicked over his head, regathered the leather and touched down. The conversion just veered wide, leaving the Australians narrowly in the lead 6-3. Heartened by the try the hosts attacked again and were only thwarted from scoring at the last moment by Richards coming across in cover to pick up the rolling football and drive it into touch. Middleton and Barnett were dominating line-out possession and in the last ten minutes of the match the visitors remained camped in the Bristol and Clifton half of the field. From an untidy ruck midfield, McKivat, seeing McCabe unmarked out wide, threw a long spiralling pass and the five-eighth strolled in under the goal posts untouched. Hickey made no mistake with his conversion for the Wallabies to lead 11-3 as the whistle blew for full-time.

Australia 11 (Gavin, Hickey, McCabe tries, Hickey conversion) defeated Bristol and Clifton 3. Crowd: 5000. Referee: E.G. Nicholls, Newport.

Australia Backs: W. Dix, D.B. Carroll, C.J. Russell, J.J. Hickey, C.E. Parkinson Halves: C.H. McKivat (captain), A.J.M. McCabe Forwards: N.E. Row, K.A. Gavin, T.J. Richards, S.A. Middleton, P.A. McCue, M. McArthur, J.T. Barnett, C.A. Hammond.
Bristol and Clifton Backs: W.R. Johnston (Bristol), J. Spoors (Bristol), F. Holbrook (Bristol), V.F. Eberle (Clifton), E.F. Eberle (Clifton) Halves: G. Spoors (Bristol), H. Gardiner (Clifton) Forwards: P.J. Down (captain) (Bristol), J.L. Mathias (Bristol), N.

Moore (Bristol), F. Feltham (Bristol), G. Percy (Bristol), E.J.G. Higham (Clifton), E. Kibbey (Bristol), F.R.R, Rudman (Clifton).

The Welsh full-back Herbert Winfield, who watched the match, was reported by one newspaper as saying after the match "the Bristolians stuck to their formidable opponents very pluckily. They were beaten owing to the stronger individual play of one or two of the Wallabies". Percy Down exclaimed "from a player's point of view it was one of the finest games ever played on the County Ground. I was delighted with the way in which the side performed". Tom Richards, the Wallaby breakaway was quoted as saying "the Bristol forwards held the Colonials fairly well in the line-out, and we never got clear away from one of those moves, which was very exceptional. The Colonials, however, in their back division were superior to the home side".

More than one hundred players, officials and distinguished guests attended the sumptuous dinner in honour of the Wallabies which was held at the Royal Hotel, Bristol on the evening of the match. The Sheriff of Bristol was in the chair and his welcoming speech was answered by the Wallaby match captain Chris McKivat, who said: "I would like to say how thoroughly we all enjoyed the match. The game was fought out in the best traditions and in a sportsmanlike spirit. I cannot speak too highly of the Bristol and Clifton team for their plucky fight and we wish both teams great success in future contests". The menu included Cornish mussels, Scottish oysters, fresh lobster, local fish of all kinds and vintage white wines from Germany and France.

Before the end of the Wallabies' tour, 14 players had secretly signed contracts to turn professional in Rugby League.

Gloucestershire v Yorkshire: 9th April 1910, Kingsholm, Gloucester

Gloucestershire squeezed through the group stages of the competition, having had to replay matches against Somerset and Cornwall after the three counties had finished level on points. They then overcame Kent in the semi-final at Blackheath 6-3.

The team then beat a Yorkshire side missing a couple of key players 23-0, and thus won the County Championship for the first time in the county's history, since when Gloucestershire has won the championship more often than any other county.

Gloucestershire, County Champions 1909-10. (L-R) Back Row: J.A. Emery, A.C. Williams, H.S. Gould, A. Harris, W.T. Pearce (Vice-Pres), C.E. Brown (President), H. Lowther, E.S. Bostock Smith (ERU Referee), S.R. Carter (Ref.Sec.N.), H. Smith (Ref.Sec.S), J.L. Davis. Standing: W. Pearce, L.W. Hayward, H. Berry, G. Holford, J. Wright, A. Redding (Cinderford), V. Fuller Eberle (Clifton), G. Bowkett, W. Sawyer, W. Meredith, E.W. Moore. Seated: J.H. Tratt (Hon. Treasurer), T. Bagwell (Trainer), D. Hollands, J. Stephens, W.R. Johnston (Bristol), W. Johns (Gloucester), D.R. Gent (Captain), A. Hudson, J. Spoors (Bristol), M.E. Neale (Bristol), H. Uzzell, A.J. Gardner (Clifton), R.A. Roberts (Hon. Secretary).

Somerset v South Africa: 3rd October 1912, Recreation Ground, Bath

The first match played by South Africa on their 1912-13 tour saw the visitors triumph 24-3. Ronald Victor Knight of Clifton was in the Somerset side having only left school the previous year. Knight finished the season as Clifton's leading scorer, with eight tries, in a poor season for the club. The following season he was a reserve for England. After attending Bristol University he went to London to study medicine at Guy's Hospital. He would surely have played for England had war not broken out.

He lost his life during a flying accident at RAF Cranwell in 1917 – details in the World War 1 Roll of Honour chapter.

Somerset v Leicestershire: 14th April 1923 Bridgwater

Somerset won its first County Championship by a goal and try to two tries with the Clifton players W.F. Gaisford and E.H. Esbester in the team. The goal was converted by Gaisford. Despite winning the County Championship, none of the Somerset players appeared in an international side that season.

The Somerset XV that won the County Championship: (L-R) Back Row: W.H. Brown, S.M.J. Woods, Sir G. Duncan Grey, C.C. Wills. Standing: T.S. Bradford, W.F. Gaisford (Clifton), W.H. Sheppard (Bath), F.G. Spriggs (Bridgwater), W.S. Donne (Somerset President), P. Lewis (Bridgwater), A.J. Spriggs (Bridgwater), L.W. Bisgrove (Bath), G.V. Kyrke. Seated: F. West (Somerset Hon. Sec.), E.H. Esbester (Clifton), E.D.G. Hammett (Blackheath), A.E. Thompson (Wellington), R.G.D. Quick (Bristol), J. Jarvis [Captain] (Bridgwater), F.A. Meine (Bath), C.N. Manning (Bath), W.J. Growtage (Somerset Hon. Treasurer). On the ground: S.G.U. Considine (Bath), J. Reed (Bridgwater), H. Vowles (Bath).

England v Scotland: 15th March 1924, Twickenham

A golden period for English rugby saw one of the finest teams in the country's history win both the Calcutta Cup and the Grand Slam, defeating Scotland 19-0. England won all four championship matches with a points total of 69 scored against 19 conceded, the narrowest margin of victory being eight points against Wales in Swansea. This was England's sixth championship win in ten seasons, a period during which 33 of their 40 matches were won. Bunny Chantrill was a member of the victorious 1924 team – see the Famous Players chapter for more details.

The England team that won the Grand Slam. Image courtesy of the World Rugby Museum, Twickenham. (L-R) Back Row: W.G.E. Luddington (Devonport Services), B.S. Chantrill (Bristol), G.S. Conway (Rugby), R. Edwards (Newport) H.P. Jacob (Oxford University), H.C. Catcheside (Percy Park), H.M. Locke (Birkenhead Park), L.J. Corbett (Bristol). Seated: R. Cove-Smith (O.M.Ts), E. Myers (Bradford), W.W. Wakefield [captain] (Leicester), A.T. Voyce (Gloucester), A.F. Blakiston (Liverpool). On the ground: A. Robson (Northern), A.T. Young (Cambridge University).

Wasps v Clifton: 24th September 1938, Sudbury

Clifton played Wasps several times during the 1930s. In this match Clifton were leading 8-5 at half-time but eventually lost 18-8. The Wasps team included the Welsh internationals Powell and Bowcott.

The teams that day were:

Clifton RFC: W.T. Gresham, T.H.B. Burrough, A.L. Knight, K.G. Harvey, H.A.C.C. Hobbs, F.W. Grant, D.B.E. Paine, J. Moss, G.J. Dillon, M.E. White, O.D.F. Gardner, R.W. Sloan, A.G. Slator, R.A. Carrett, D.M. Fleming.

Wasps: M.H. Butcher, R.R. Szel, F.W. Peel, E.D. Shaw, D.M. Sleep, H.M. Bowcott, W.C. Powell, O.S. Ruane, H.C. Clarry, J.B. Bland, N. Compton, J. Oldfield, S.A. Paige, J.L. Blain, H.B. Bedwell.

Bristol v Clifton: 31st March 1954, Memorial Ground

The credit for this victory went squarely to the Clifton forwards who out-muscled a heavier and taller Bristol pack, Bristol's captain was England international and former Clifton player Jack Gregory. Perhaps crucially, Bristol's Glyn Davies had a cold and had to pull out at the last minute. A young John Currie played for Clifton and eight months later won his first Oxford blue.

Clifton won 8-5 with two tries by Johnson and Bradford (the latter just three minutes from time) and a conversion versus a penalty try and conversion for Bristol.

England v France: 26th February 1955, Twickenham

Having shared the 1954 Five-Nations Championship with Wales and France, the England team was disappointed to finish the 1955 campaign with a single victory (against Scotland) and fourth in the table above Ireland. Ex-Clifton player Peter Dalton Young led England, who were winning 9-8 with ten minutes to go but lost 16-9.

The England side that played France on 26th February 1955. (L-R) Back Row: Mr R. Mitchell [Ireland, Referee], D.St.G Hazell (Leicester), W.P.C. Davies (Harlequins), R. Higgins (Liverpool), I.D.S. Beer

(Harlequins), P.G. Yarranton (Wasps), F.D. Sykes (Northampton), J.E. Williams (Old Millhillians), Mr T.E. Priest [Touch Judge]. Seated: G.W. Hastings (Gloucester), R.C. Bazley (Waterloo), P.D. Young [Captain] (Dublin Wanderers), J. Butterfield (Northampton), N.A. Labuschagne (Guy's Hospital), D.S. Wilson (Metropolitan Police). On the ground: D.G.S. Baker (O.M.Ts), H. Scott (Manchester).

Above: Peter Young leads out England against France.

England v Wales: 21st January 1956, Twickenham

England came second in the 1956 championship despite scoring 18 points more than the winning country, Wales. Crucially, this fixture was lost 3-8 to a Welsh side with ten players from Newport. Wales won three matches by a margin of less than ten points, ironically losing only one to an Ireland team, by eight points, that England had thrashed 20-0 a month earlier.

John Currie, Clifton's most capped international (see Famous Players chapter) replaced another Cliftonian, Peter Young, in the England team. Currie was one of ten new caps in the side, which may explain any unfamiliarity amongst a team playing a hard-core of Newport team-mates.

The England side that played Wales on the 21st January 1956. (L-R) Back Row: Mr.R. Mitchell [Referee] (Ireland), P.G.D. Robbins (Oxford University), M.J.K. Smith (Oxford University), P.B. Jackson (Coventry), R.W.D. Marques (Cambridge University), J.D. Currie (Oxford University & Clifton), P.H. Thompson (Headingley), A. Ashcroft (Waterloo), Mr.H. Waldron [Touch-Judge] (Gloucestershire). Seated: W.P.C. Davies (Harlequins), J. Butterfield (Northampton), E. Evans [Captain] (Sale), D.L. Sanders (Harlequins), V.G. Roberts (Harlequins), C.R. Jacobs (Northampton). On the ground: R.E.G. Jeeps (Northampton), D.F. Allison (Coventry).

Currie was keeping good company in this match with, amongst others, the future Warwickshire and England cricket captain Mike Smith, and the legendary England scrum-half Dickie Jeeps.

England v New Zealand: 4th November 1967, Twickenham

From an England point of view the highlight of this match was a memorable try scored by Bob Lloyd (Harlequins) on his international debut after combining with Colin McFadyean of Moseley. Both players played for Clifton in the early 1960s.

On the day the All Blacks were far superior and won 23-11 with some ease.

England XV that played the All Blacks on 4th November 1967. (L-R) Back Row: D.C.J. McMahon (Referee), D. Rutherford (Gloucester), R.H. Lloyd (Harlequins), G.A. Sherriff (Saracens), J.E. Owen (Coventry), P.J. Larter (Northampton), R.E. Webb (Coventry), R.B. Taylor (Northampton), K.F. Savage (Northampton), A.D. Martin (Touch Judge). Seated: W.J. Gittings (Coventry), J.F. Finlan (Moseley), D.P. Rogers (Bedford). P.E. Judd (Coventry) (Captain), H. Godwin (Coventry), C.W. McFadyean (Moseley), A.L. Horton (Blackheath).

South & South West Counties v Australia: 27th October 1973, Recreation Ground Bath

The South & South West Counties scored a notable victory over Australia by 15-14. Clifton's Peter Johnson was stretchered off and taken to Bath Hospital during the match.

Two months later Johnson played in a trial for England, when the South Western and Southern Counties played the Metropolitan Counties on 15th December 1973 at Bristol.

South & South West Counties team that played Australia on 27th October 1973. (L-R) Back Row: E.J. Garland (Somerset Hon. Match Sec.), J. Scott (Devon), P.J. Colston (Coach), B.G. Nelmes (Glos), R. Hazzard (Som), J.A. Watkins (Glos), M.A. Burton (Glos), A. Brinn (Glos), R.C. Hannaford (Glos), J. Fidler (Glos), D.J. Tyler (Som), D.M. Rollitt (Glos), R. Swaffield (Bristol), J. White (Som), N. Vosper (Devon), A.O. Lewis (Som), Chairman Selectors, C. Williams (Glos). Front Row: A.F. Pearn (Devon), A.H. Nicholls (Bristol), C.B. Stevens (Cornwall), B.A. Tuttiett (President Somerset CRFU), J.V. Pullin [Captain] (Glos), P. Johnson (Glos), A. Morley (Glos), K.C. Plummer (Cornwall).

The Somerset president seated in the centre of the photograph, Ben Tuttiett, was Clifton RFC captain and scrum-half from 1952 to 1954.

Clifton v Sale: 11th February 1974 Eastfield Road

In perhaps the most memorable match to have been held at the Eastfield Road ground, Clifton took an early lead but lost with minutes remaining. A report in *The Times* carried the headline *Day when a try would have surprised the scorers* and continued:

Nothing was so appropriate as the composition of the score at Clifton, Bristol, on Saturday. Sale, who have rarely, if ever, played Clifton before, reached the quarter-final round of the national knock-out competition by beating them by two penalty goals (six points) to one penalty goal (three), and it would have been a mild surprise if either side had succeeded in scoring a try.

In any case, it was a day for kicking, not handling. The ground was soon ploughed into mud and a stiff breeze blew across the pitch. Passing movements usually died an early death and the wings, scarcely had a look-in. Sale adapted to the mud and wind slightly better than Clifton. But there was precious little else between them.

Barclay gave Clifton the lead in the first minute. But Toone made it 3-3 20 minutes later, the ball veering in on the breeze from right to left at the last moment. The decisive penalty came six minutes before the end. Sale held the ball in the back row at a set scrimmage, Cannon was tempted offside, and Toone never looked like missing. At one time or another, both sides were down to 14. Rule, the Sale Stand-off half, was off for ten minutes in the middle of the match having his right knee bandaged. He came back on the left wing and Midgelow moved to stand-off, where his clever kicking made a marked contribution to Sale's success. Polledri, one of Clifton's centres, was off for 15 minutes in the second half after being stunned in a tackle.

Sale had a weight advantage in the tight and Stagg was a handful for Brown in the middle of the lineout. Davies and Creed foraged far for Sale in the loose, but Watson and Donovan were not far behind. Both scrum halves could have played better. Smith, of Sale and England failed a fitness test and Morritt stepped in. Both full backs, on the other hand, played well, Barclay in particular. Near the end he stopped Drake with a head-on tackle when a try, for once, seemed possible.

Near the end, too, Rule, hobbled though he was, found a long touch in the right-hand corner with a left foot kick. But Sale, like Clifton, could not get over the line, however near it might be.

CLIFTON: P.Barclay; N.Bourne, P.Johnson, M.Polledri, K.Lowe; S.Gregory, J.Cannon; G.Mansfield, S.Luxmore; J.Raine, P.Donovan, P.Brown, D.Tope, G.Watson, G.Rogers.
SALE: C.Toone; J.Drake, S.Midgelow, W.Isherwood, G.Graham; S.Rule, A.Morritt; A.Newall, J.Lansbury, D.Ward, P.Stagg, R.Trickey, R.Creed, J.Davies, G.Ormond.
Referee: R.Eddy (Cornwall)

Harlequins v Clifton: 24th November 1990, The Stoop

There was a heavy media presence at this match. Sky TV was there to screen the rugby, but the majority of the coverage was related to a news event. Denis Thatcher was a keen Harlequins supporter, and the match took place two days after Margaret Thatcher had stepped down as Prime Minister.

The Harlequins side featured an all-international forward pack of Leonard, Moore, Mullins, Croker, Ackford, Skinner, Winterbottom (captain) and Chris Butcher, with David Pears and Will Carling providing more international calibre in the backs. For 20 minutes the teams looked evenly matched and the score stood at 4-4, upon which the floodgates opened and Harlequins ran away 56-4 winners.

Clifton v Bristol: 31st March 1992, Cribbs Causeway

The Bristol team selected for this match was very inexperienced. The front five, including Mark Regan, collectively had fewer than 20 senior appearances. Bristol had decided to rest the majority of the regular senior side for the match with London Scottish three days later. The Clifton side, packed with ex-Bristol players, was in no mood to take prisoners.

Kyran Bracken was making his debut for Bristol, as were four other Bristol players - the props, Nick Bartlett and Andy Crocker, full-back Paul McCormack and replacement Leon Blackman. Only Bracken was to appear for the first team again. Clifton led 10-0 inside 17 minutes and Doug Woodman's second try equalled the Clifton record of 33 in a season. Clifton won the game 23-7 and handed out Bristol's first and (to date) only defeat at Cribbs Causeway. This was the second time Clifton had beaten Bristol that season, having won 17-14 at the Memorial Ground on New Year's Day, although this had followed a 30-4 Pilkington Cup game defeat, also at the Memorial Ground, on November 30th 1991.

Clifton: A. Freeman, D. Cottrell, M. Brain, R. John, D. Woodman, S. Hogg, P. Jeffrey, A. Sharp, M. Patteson, P. Smith, S. Mills, T. Edbrooke, P. Polledri, M. Wyatt, W. Hone. Replacements: M. Trott, P. Brady.
Scorers: Tries - Woodman (2), Wyatt, Jeffrey. Conversions - Hogg (2). Penalty - Hogg

Bristol: P. McCormack, E. Thillet, R. Knibbs, K. Lock, D. John, P. Hull, K. Bracken, A. Crocker, M. Regan, N. Bartlett, A. Player, G. Lewis, S. Butt, I. Patten, J. Pearson. Replacements: P. Regan, F. MacMillan.
Scorers: Try - Lock. Penalty - Hull.

Clifton v Liverpool St. Helens: 11th December 1993, Cribbs Causeway

In winning the Courage Division 4 Shield, Clifton did not lose a single league match all season.

This match provided a seminal moment in persuading the team that it could win the league that year. Liverpool St Helens had the former England centre Kevin Simms in their team, and his Clifton opposite number Peter Naivalurua was very pumped up to be playing against him. On the day and perhaps against their expectations, Clifton finished comfortable winners by 35-21.

England v New Zealand: 6th December 1997, Twickenham

Clive Woodward was appointed coach on the 15th November and this was his fourth game in charge. He had selected David Rees for each of these games. The game was played at a furious pace and with about 5 minutes gone, New Zealand won a penalty in their own 22. The All Black fly-half Andrew Mehrtens kicked cross-field and found Rees on his right wing. Rees counter-attacked, chipped over the head of Lomu. He collected the ball, sidestepped round Zinzan Brooke's cover tackle and scored in the corner. The try sparked England on to a 23-9 half-time lead, though the All Blacks fought back in the second half with the match ending in a 26-26 draw. This game was seen by many as being the start of Clive Woodward's renaissance of English rugby that would eventually culminate in winning the world cup. David Rees joined Clifton in 2008 (see Famous Players chapter)

Clifton Ladies v Old Leamingtonians: January 2001

Welsh international Non Evans scored a world record 73 points when Clifton Ladies beat Old Leamingtonians 136-0. Unfortunately Old Leamingtonians couldn't complete their fixtures and the final league table excluded the result of all matches they played.

Non, from Llandaff in Cardiff, won two silver medals at judo in the Commonwealth Games and is a former world powerlifting champion. She has won 71 rugby caps for Wales.

Clifton Ladies went on to win the Premiership I league title for the first time in the club's history on 2nd May that year, beating Waterloo 83-5 in the final game of the season. Not only was this a first for the club, but it was also the first time the title went to a club outside London and the former 'big three' of Saracens, Richmond and Wasps.

Clifton Ladies v Nottingham Medocs: 2002, Franklin Gardens, Northampton

Clifton Ladies beat Nottingham Medoc Casuals 54-7 to win the RFUW *Rugby World* National Cup and again became the first club outside London to achieve the feat. The team included 12 internationals (eight Welsh, one Scottish and three English). The match took place at Franklin Gardens, the home of Northampton Saints; televised live on Sky Sports, it kicked off at 12:05 as a curtain raiser to the Northampton v Gloucester men's premiership clash. Clifton Ladies finished as runners-up in the Premiership that season.

The Clifton No. 8 Pip Minto won the Player of the Match award.

Clifton v Penryn: 23rd April 2005, Cribbs Causeway

Clifton finished the season with a flourish by registering a record 122-0 victory, Rob Viol scoring four tries to follow the eight he had scored in the previous home match against Gloucester Old Boys in the course of a 119-15 victory on 2nd April.

In spite of these big wins Clifton was not promoted that season, in part because the club (rather improbably, given the result of the return fixture) lost the first game of the season at Gloucester Old Boys.

Penryn was also safe from relegation, but went down the following season in spite of beating Clifton in the final game in Cornwall.

Richmond v Clifton: 29th April 2006, Richmond

After this play-off for promotion to National Division Three South, the *Bristol Evening Post* reported:

Clifton will return to the national leagues after four years next season following this play-off victory over highly-fancied Richmond.

Fly-half John Barnes was the key figure as he not only scored all Clifton 's points but his tactical kicking and skilful ball distribution kept the side going forward for long periods.

In front of a large crowd, Clifton had first use of a strong swirling wind and quickly found holes in the Richmond defence with breaks by centres Olly Sills and Barnaby Kent.

Despite dominating territorially they were unable to score a try due to the resolute defence. The opening score came after 22 minutes when following a drive from a line-out Clifton's pack worked play infield and when the ball came back from the driving maul Barnes dropped a goal.

During the first half Richmond looked dangerous on the break and centre Joe Ajuwa made several powerful runs.

Although outweighed up front Clifton continued to dominate and in the 35th minute Barnes was given his only opportunity to take a penalty kick and the ball flew between the posts from 40 metres. This was soon followed by his second drop goal.

After the break, Richmond put Clifton under tremendous pressure for 20 minutes. The visitors' defence was equal to the task though and they held firm, with their back row outstanding, and achieved turnovers at vital moments. The only reward for Richmond was a penalty from close range kicked by full-back Matt Hart.

On the hour Clifton survived a succession of close-range scrums and with that the Richmond effort began to fade. The game then turned Clifton's way through Barnes' tactical kicking and a string of turnovers.

With five minutes remaining, poor handling in the Richmond backs saw them concede a scrum close to their own line. The ball came quickly back on the Clifton side and scrum-half Dan Frost set up a position for Barnes to drop his third goal.

The kick took the game out of Richmond's reach and in the six minutes of injury-time they failed to threaten the Clifton line and the West Countrymen travelled home victorious.

Clifton: R.Voil; A.Bell, O.Sills, B.Kent, S.Kent; J.Barnes, D.Frost; R.White, T.Lambert, G.Shortman, M.Kempton, R.Cox, E.Smith, C.Steetskamp, J.Levis. Reps: B.Harvey, C.Trump, P.Morgan, C.James.

Clifton v Bracknell: 29th November 2008, Cribbs Causeway

Sometimes a team needs luck to win a league, and this game against fourth-placed Bracknell gave Clifton their 10th straight win to go six points clear at the top of the league.

The *Bristol Evening Post* reported:

Clifton 17 Bracknell 15: Clifton made it ten straight wins and opened up a six-point gap in South West One, but they were given an almighty scare by fourth-placed Bracknell.

Bracknell dominated most of the match and were very unfortunate not to be travelling back along the M4 with the points, while Clifton's nearest rivals, Redingensians, lost at home to Bournemouth.

Clifton looked short of ideas and leadership – they were missing their skipper Dan Frost and vice-captain John Levis.

The visiting team looked more like title contenders than their hosts until a blunder in second-half injury-time by fly-half Jervis Manupenu, who was otherwise faultless, handed an early Christmas present to the Henbury-based side.

Manupenu's fumble, in an attempt to clear his lines, fell nicely for Clifton lock Paul Reid, who dived on the loose ball to bring the scores level. Fly-half John Barnes converted to win the match.

Clifton scored first with a fourth-minute Barnes penalty, and it looked like business as usual with the home side in the ascendancy.

On the 20-minute mark the tide began to turn, though, as the visitors began to dominate. Centre Nick Shears glided in after Bracknell's pack repeatedly hammered at the Clifton line, and he converted his own try.

The hosts were unable to deal with the ferocity of the visitors' defence, which forced Barnes to direct Clifton from behind the advantage line or kick possession away.

A further Shears penalty made it 8-3 but on the stroke of half-time Bracknell lock Jason Borechard was yellow-carded for handling in the ruck.

Bracknell extended their lead when Manupenu danced his way past a mesmerised Clifton defence for a converted try to make it 15-3 with ten minutes of normal time remaining.

From the restart, hooker Joe Skelton was sin-binned for stamping; again reducing Bracknell to 14 men.

Clifton managed to work former England wing David Rees free to score out wide, with Barnes converting to reduce the gap to five points heading into injury time.

Shears was then yellow-carded for persistent infringement, and from the resulting penalty Clifton opted for a scrum but lost it against the head.

The game now looked over for the hosts but as the ball was passed back to Manupenu, he spilt possession and Reid pounced. Barnes converted to save Clifton's blushes.

The *Bracknell Times* was less complimentary and commented:

Teams have 'dirty wins' but this game plunged the term to new depths because on 73 minutes Bracknell were comfortably holding the league leaders and winning by 15-3. Then, referee Mr Adam Friend sin-binned the Bracknell skipper Ben Nowak to join hooker Joe Shelton following his yellow card on 68 minutes. But for the 13 brave Bracknell defenders left on the pitch it was a challenge too far as Clifton scored the winning points and the referee blew the final whistle.

Grounds

Clifton RFC has long had connections with Westbury-on-Trym and the surrounding area. All the Clifton grounds, with the exception of Horfield and Cribbs Causeway, have been sold for housing development. The club has never had a home ground in Clifton.

Over the course of 137 years, Clifton players have called ten grounds 'home', some for a very short period of time and others, as has thankfully been the case for the past 30 and more years, for rather longer. Surviving details of some grounds are scanty, whilst others are well documented. Here is a brief overview of Clifton's grounds to date.

1872-1882 Coldharbour Lane, Redland: it is difficult to know exactly where the pitch lay, as the only surviving detail is the description "on the corner of Coldharbour Lane, near the farmhouse".

It is not known whether the ground belonged to the farm or was outside its boundaries. However, some newspaper reports of the time do refer to the venue as Coldharbour Farm. In Coldharbour Lane itself there were just six cottages, the Cambridge Arms, then a small, two winged building, and the farm at the end. The cottages were occupied by two gardeners, a bootmaker, a coachman, a haulier and a laundress. John Martin from Chew Magna was the farmer, and he lived there with his wife, two unmarried daughters and a niece who worked as a dairymaid. The gamekeeper's cottage was empty. These people served the local area's wealthy families living in the large houses in Cambridge Park and facing the Downs.

The Cambridge Arms still exists, although the present building dates from 1900 and was designed by Edward Gabriel. Coldharbour Lane was re-named Coldharbour Road in 1904.

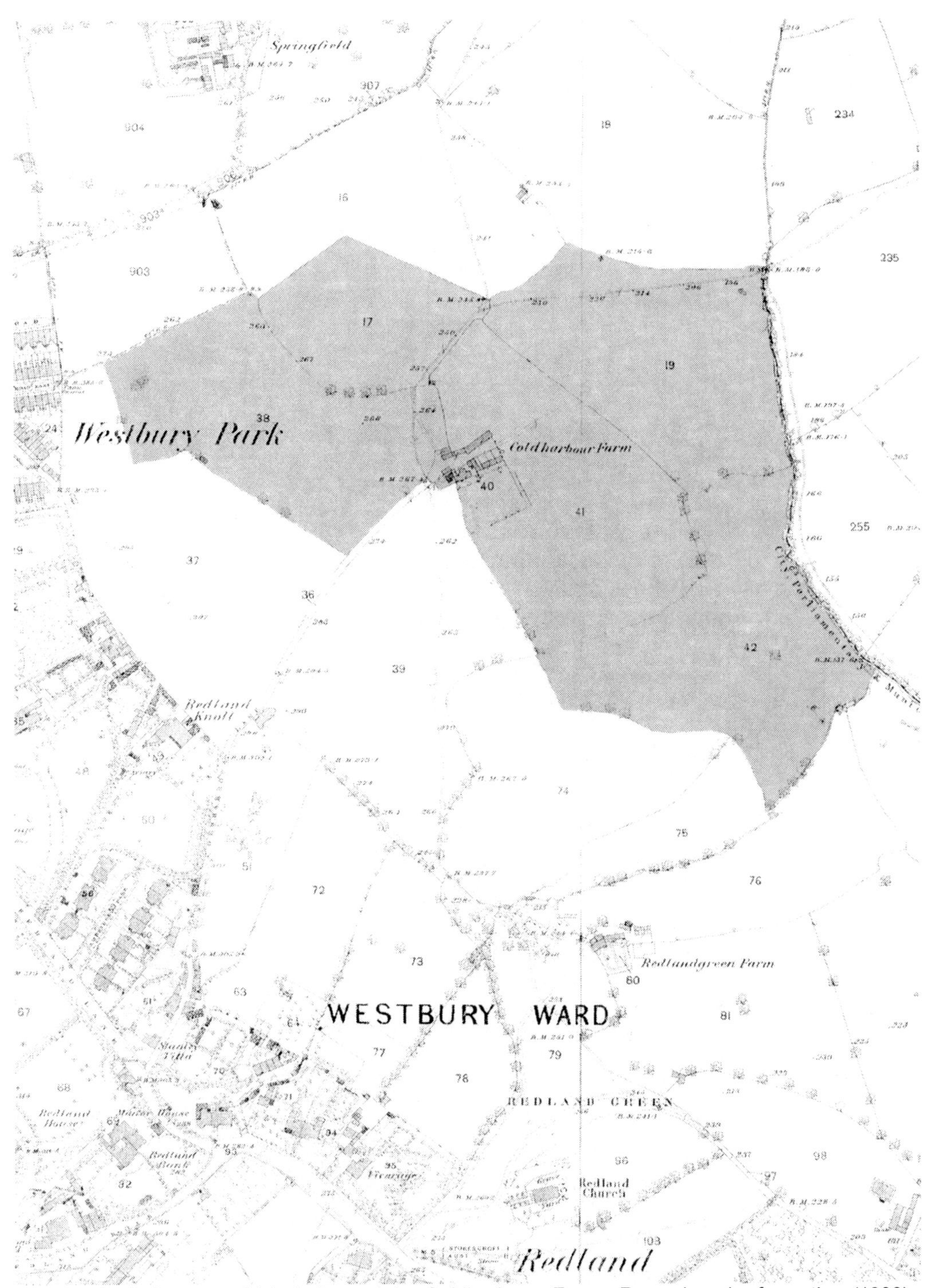

Land, shaded grey, which belonged to Coldharbour Farm. Reproduced from the (1883) Ordnance Survey map © Crown copyright

1882-1885 Durdham Down: the ground, comprising just over 12 acres, was owned by Mr. Henry St. Vincent Ames who lived at Cote House, Westbury-on-Trym. This house now forms part of St. Monica's Nursing Home.

The first match on this ground took place on 21st October 1882 against Bristol Medicals.

8063 11, Small Street, Bristol.

HIGHLY ATTRACTIVE

BUILDING LAND,

ON THE BORDERS OF

DURDHAM DOWN.

OWING TO NUMEROUS APPLICATIONS TO THE OWNER,

GEO. NICHOLS, SMITH, & ALDER have received instructions to SELL by AUCTION, at their SALEROOM, 49, BROAD STREET, Bristol, TO-MORROW (THURSDAY), August 13th, at Three o'clock in the Afternoon precisely,

All that Piece of Exceptionally Valuable

FREEHOLD BUILDING LAND

(formerly the Clifton Football Ground), containing

12A. 2R. 8P.,

or thereabouts, and Numbered 645 on the Ordnance Map, having a Most Important

FRONTAGE OF ABOUT 840 FEET

on the West or Durdham Down side, and

FRONTAGES OF 1280 FEET

to Henleaze Lane on the South and East sides.

It occupies a commanding situation for the erection of First-class Residences in the most healthy and fashionable neighbourhood of CLIFTON, and can be easily and advantageously developed, being nearly square in shape and having Roads on three sides of it.

The beds of Stone and other Minerals lying thereunder and the Ornamental Timber thereon will be included in the Sale.

THE PROPERTY IS FREE FROM TITHE AND LAND TAX

This presents a rare opportunity for the acquisition of very Valuable Building Sites immediately adjoining Durdham Down, where no others are now obtainable.

For further Particulars and Conditions of Sale apply to the Auctioneers, 49, Broad Street; or to

Messrs WANSEY & SON,

6783 Solicitors, Baldwin Street, Bristol.

In August 1896 the ground was sold to a housing developer for £16,500, and now lies beneath the buildings of Henleaze Gardens and Henleaze Avenue.

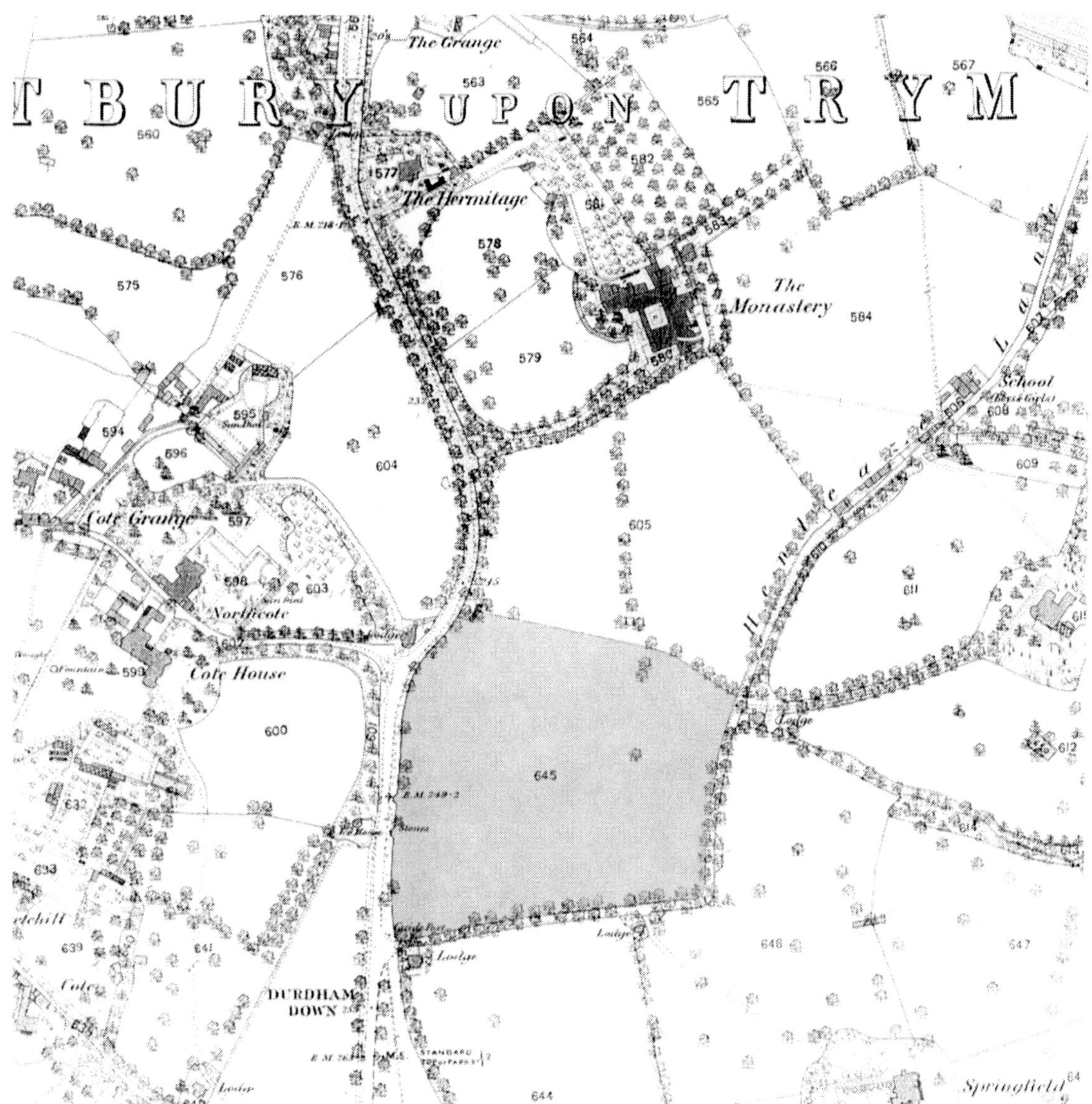

The ground at Durdham Down shaded grey. Reproduced from the (1881) Ordnance Survey map.© Crown copyright

1885-1892 Leach's Field, Westbury-on-Trym: thought to be next to Dorset Villas where John Leach lived. It's difficult to be precise about the location, but it is recorded that a charge was made for admission, so the assumption that the ground was fenced off to allow for this is probably reasonable. It was home to many important matches, the best-known being the first fixture against Bristol on 23rd March 1889 which the visitors won 4-0. Clifton would play Bristol four times at Leach's Field, recording a victory, a draw and two defeats.

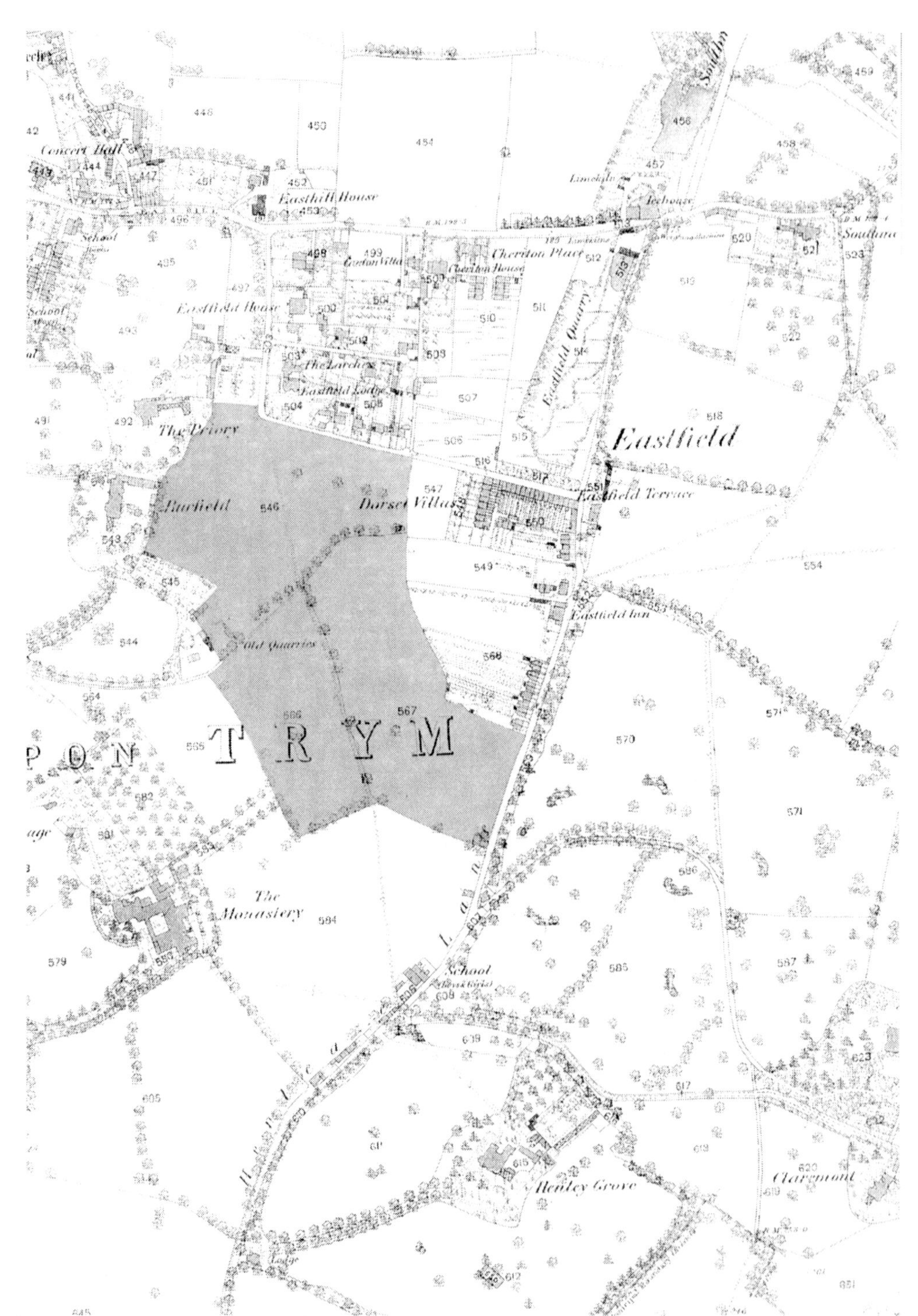

It is believed that the Leach's Field ground was on one of the fields shaded grey. Reproduced from the (1881) Ordnance Survey map © Crown copyright

1892-1893 Fishponds: we know from the report of the first match, versus Taunton on 24th September 1892, that this sloping ground was two minutes' walk from the railway station. These slim pickings represent the extent of the ground's surviving history.

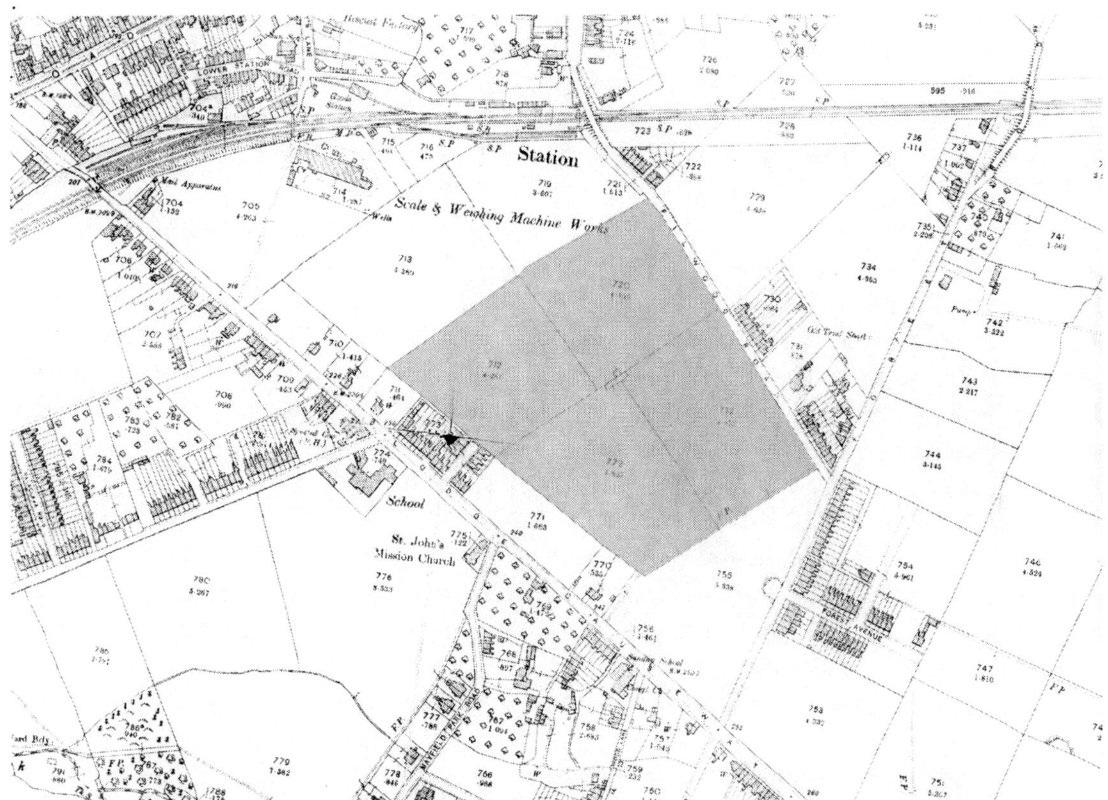

The Fishponds ground was probably situated on one of the fields shaded grey. Reproduced from the (1903) Ordnance Survey map © Crown copyright

1893-1896 Buffalo Bill's Field, Horfield: the club played for three seasons on a ground that acquired its unusual name when Colonel William "Buffalo Bill" Cody's Wild West Show was held there in 1892. Cody recruited famous people to perform in his show including Annie Oakley, Sitting Bull, Red Cloud and Frank North. The show included re-enactments of Custer's Last Stand and of Native American attacks on stagecoaches, as well as featuring cowboys showing off their skills.

The first match played there on 23rd September 1893 was against Bristol (see the Famous Matches chapter). The second fixture was held a week later with Bath as the opposition.

We know that this area of land was once part of the Horfield Court Farm Estate. John Leach and his family lived at the farm from 1898 to 1901, although it is believed that he bought the land several years earlier. He owned many parcels of land around Westbury-on-Trym and Horfield. Bristol took over the lease and built The Memorial Ground in 1921.

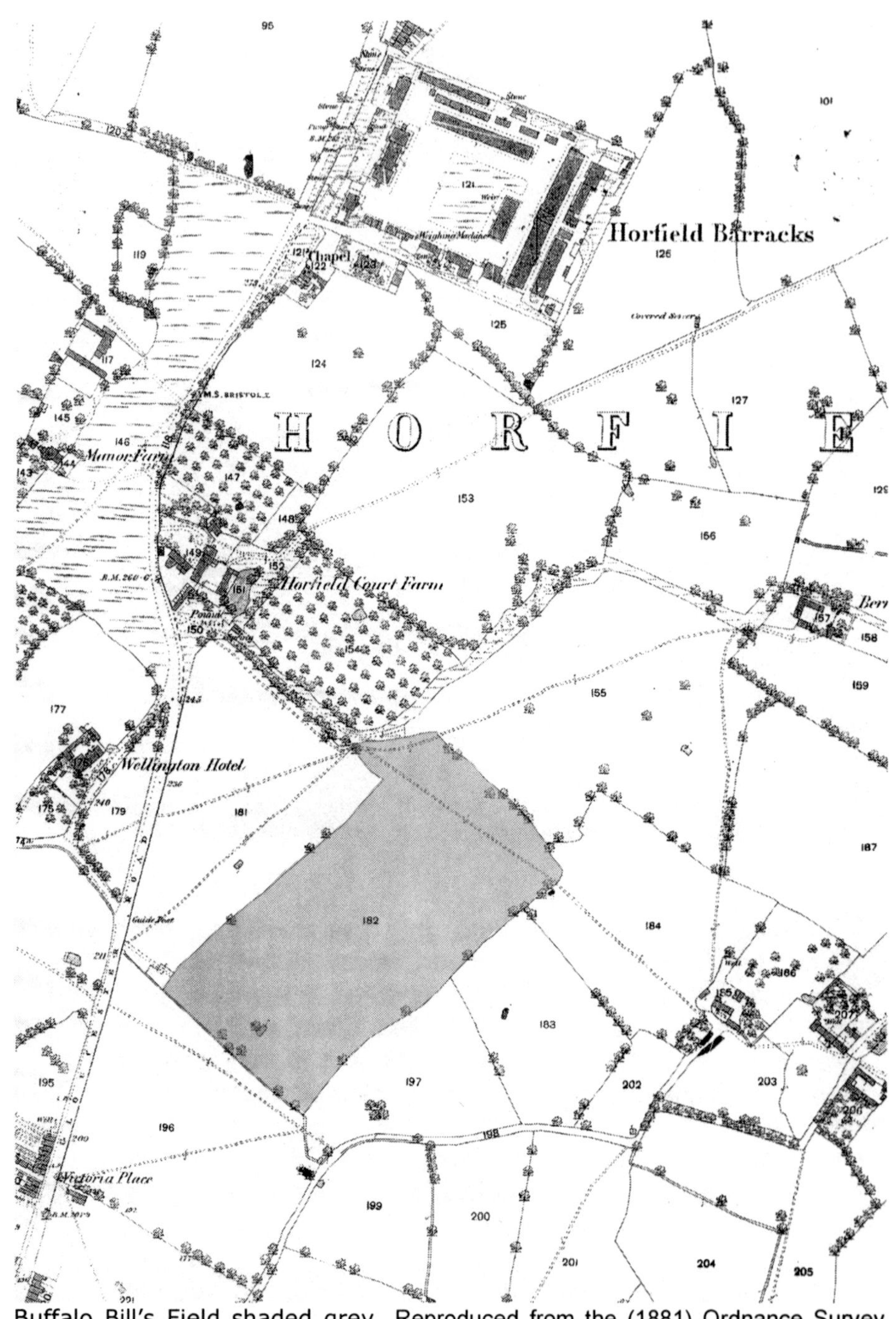

Buffalo Bill's Field shaded grey. Reproduced from the (1881) Ordnance Survey map © Crown copyright

1896-1899 Coldharbour Lane, Redland: the club managed to move back to its original ground on Coldharbour Lane for three seasons. The land was sold for housing sometime after 1900 and the development was originally named New Clifton.

1899-1914 North View, Westbury Park: at the time, this ground was just outside the City Boundary. Many team photographs survive from this period, but their close-up composition gives away little about the surroundings, other than that there may have been a clubhouse and a very small stand. There is sparse surviving documentation about the venue, and by the 1930s it was submerged under the Durdham Downs Garage, the Bristol School Of Motoring, houses and shops.

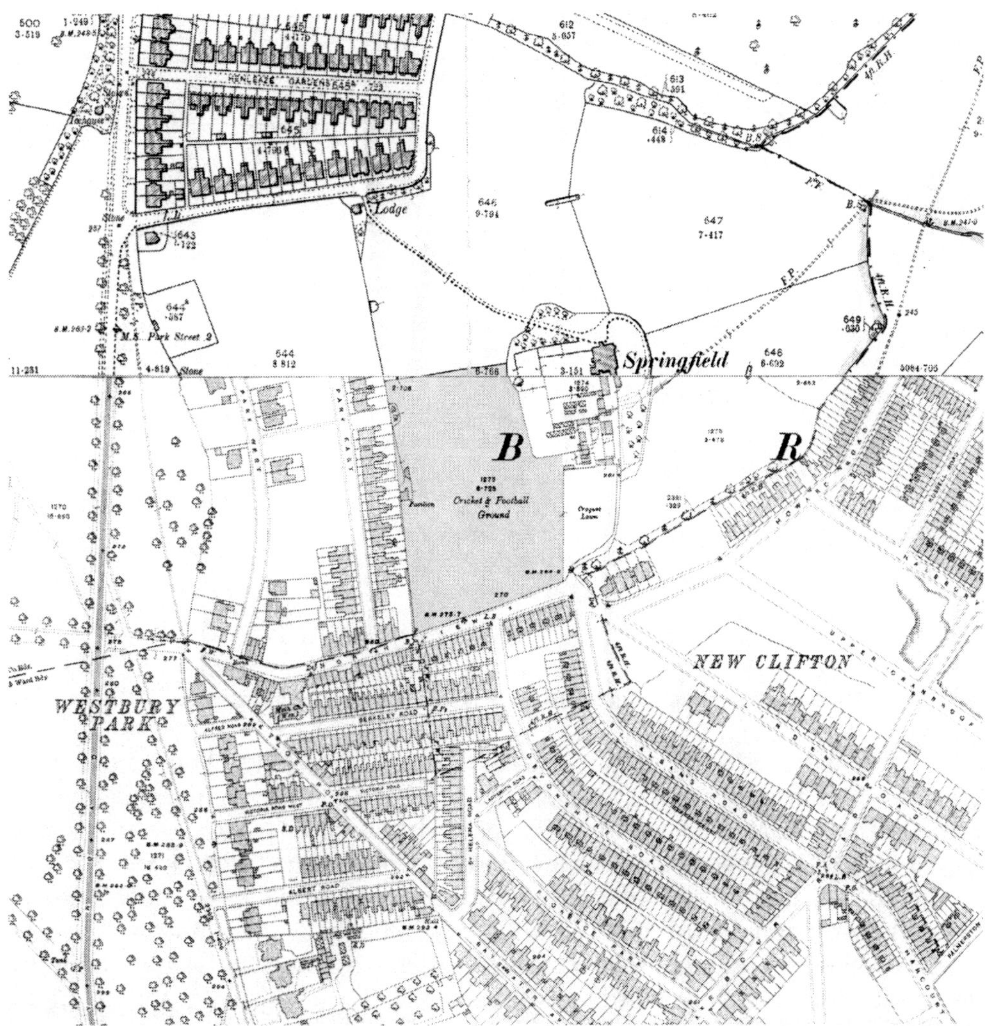

North View shaded grey. Reproduced from the (1903 & 1916) Ordnance Survey maps © Crown copyright

1919-1920 Redland Green, Redland: the ground at North View had been ploughed up and used for allotments during the First World War. The compensation paid for the damage to the ground was only £20, far from sufficient to cover the necessary repairs. A number of matches were played away until a suitable alternative could be found, and soon the club found a temporary home at Redland Green.

Redland Green shaded grey. Reproduced from the (1916) Ordnance Survey map. © Crown copyright

On 22nd November 1919 the Club unveiled the new ground. The Redland Green facilities were primitive: the changing rooms were housed in a wooden hut, five metres by three metres, situated in a farmyard with an old army portable canvas bath for washing. It was discovered just an hour before the first match, against the Tank Corps, that the posts had been mistakenly erected on the dead-ball line. A few weeks later, after cattle had grazed on the pitch and the surrounding ditches had overflowed, the pitch had become very muddy. A few tons of ashes were spread around, only for club officials to discover that they had been tipped onto the wrong field and so had to be moved across to the pitch by hand. The playing surface was now a mixture of hard ashes, mud and cow dung. Perhaps no-one was too dismayed that the club moved on after less than one full season here.

Clifton v Burnham, played on 7th February 1920 at Redland Green.

1920-1926 Eastfield: another temporary measure, the club sharing the ground owned by Westbury-on-Trym Cricket Club whilst a more permanent home was sought. The move to Eastfield was announced on 17th August 1920. The entrance to the ground was in Henleaze Road, about 100 yards beyond the Henleaze Congregational Church. It may have been very close to Clifton's third ground, Leach's Field, although its precise location has not been ascertained. The club's opening fixture here was on 9th October 1920 versus Bristol Grammar School.

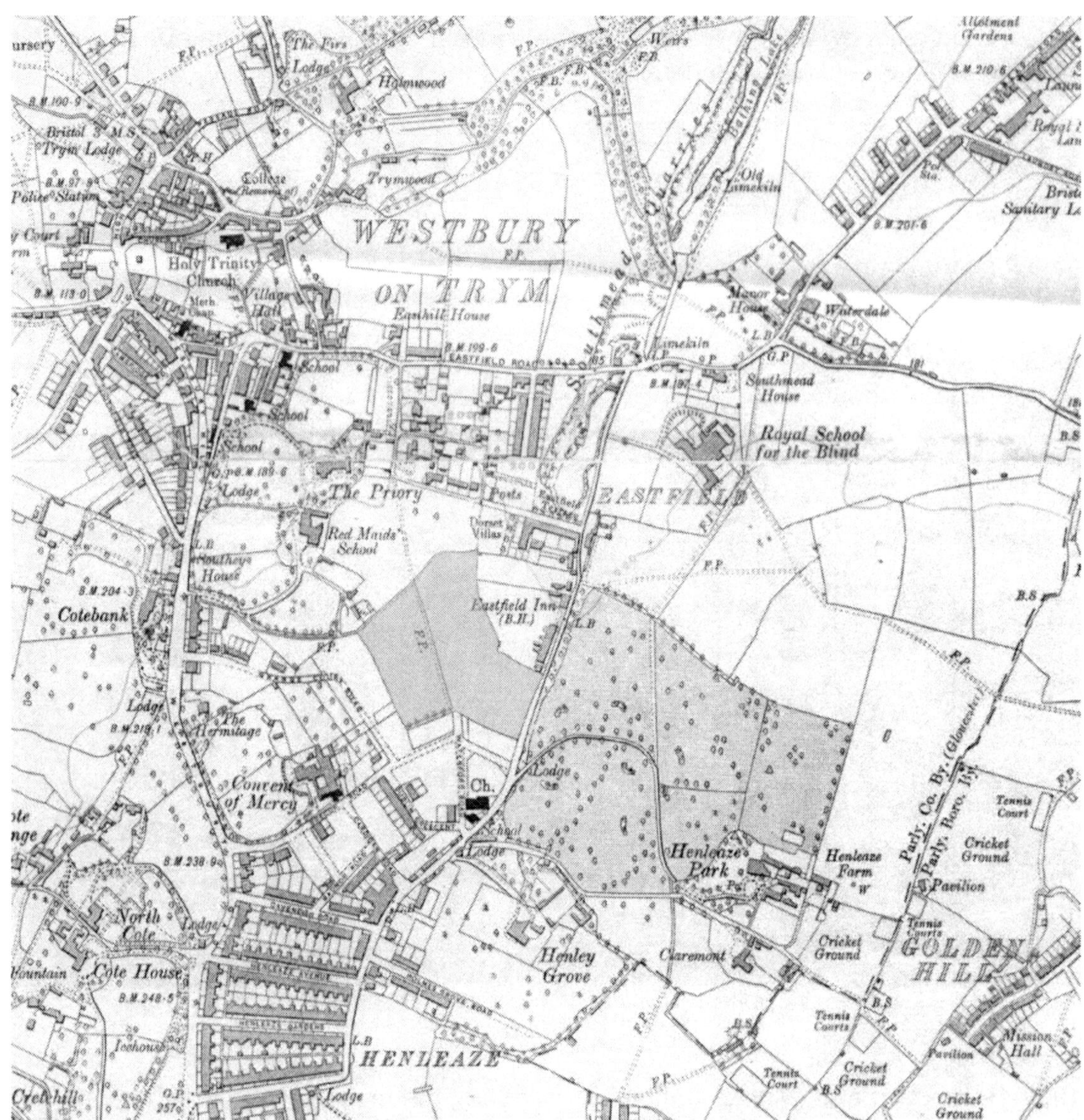

Land shaded grey thought to be the possible location of the Eastfield ground. Reproduced from the (1921) Ordnance Survey map © Crown copyright.

1926-1976 Eastfield Road: this ground was purchased in 1923 but it took three years to clear the site, lay the pitches and erect the new stand. The stand cost £3,000, paid for by a loan from the Rugby Football Union. Having moved ground twice in the eight years since the war and six times in the 42 years of the club's pre-war existence, it's safe to imagine that few would have predicted a stay of 50 years at this new home, albeit interrupted by six more years of war during which the ground was requisitioned as an anti-aircraft gun site.

Clifton's Eastfield Road Ground, taken about 1938.

The first fixture took place on September 11th 1926, a 6-35 loss to Bristol.

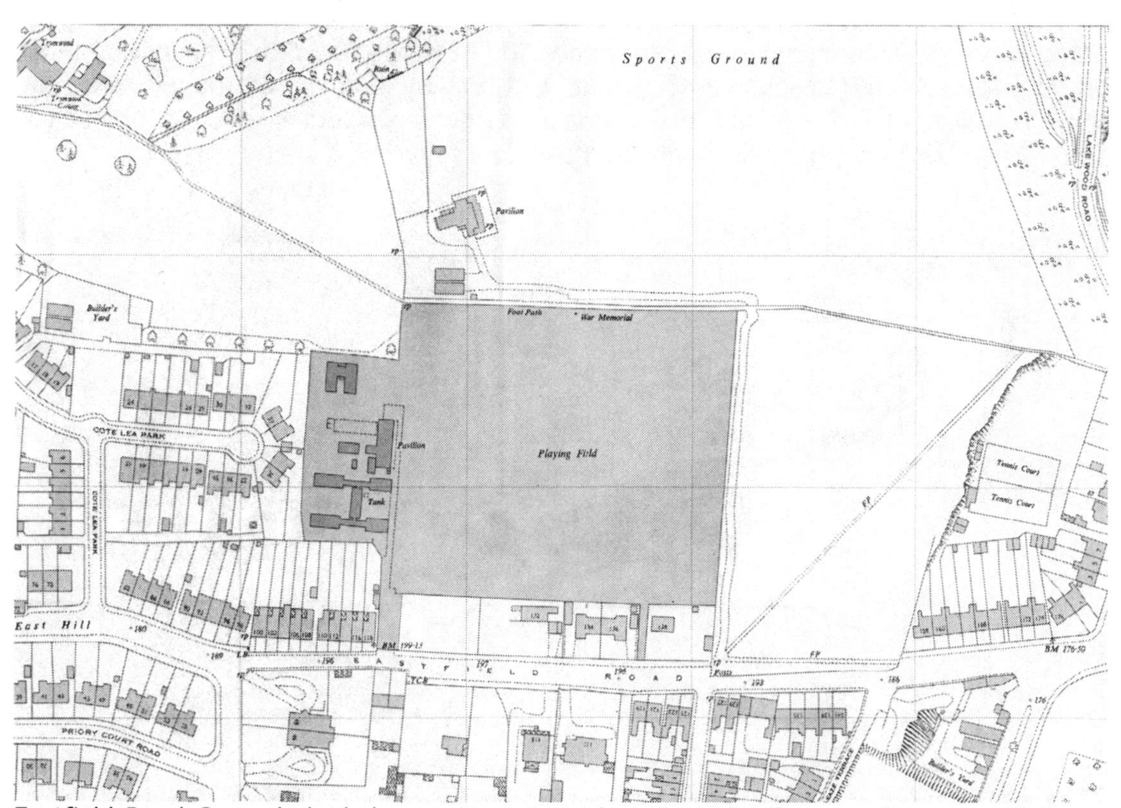

Eastfield Road Ground shaded grey. Reproduced from the (1951) Ordnance Survey map © Crown copyright

On the last match-day at Eastfield Road on 7th April 1976, it was planned that the swansong would be provided by the 1st XV, who lost that day to Bristol by the narrower margin of 15-17. In the event, with the referee's connivance it was the Clifton RATS who heard the final whistle at Eastfield.

1976 to the present day - Cribbs Causeway: when the club made its last move to date, two important and familiar artifacts also made the journey. A practical consideration prompted the removal of the structural steelwork from the old Eastfield Road stand; this was re-built and re-clad at Cribbs Causeway. A more reverent and spiritual motivation saw the War Memorial prominently re-sited on the approach to the new venue.

The first match played here on 5th September 1976 was a star-studded affair, producing a combined points total that was especially unusual in the days before a try earned five points. A Willie John McBride XV that included J.P.R. Williams, Alan Morley, David Duckham, Fran Cotton and Peter Wheeler, amongst other luminaries, beat Clifton 84-34. We haven't researched the club's history quite closely enough to determine on how many occasions Clifton has been beaten by 50 points, but it's entirely safe to assume that on no other occasion has a defeat of this magnitude been borne with such equanimity and indeed celebration. Clearly an auspicious new beginning, it heralded a period of the club's history which, not without its obstacles, sees Clifton RFC in rude health well into the 21st century.

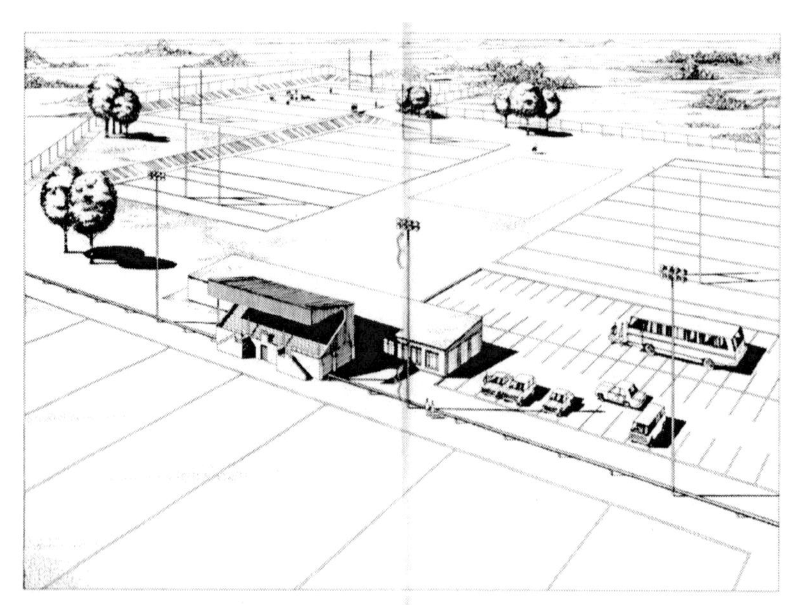

Architect's sketch of the new ground, featured in a brochure handed out at the last game at Eastfield Road.

Clifton Families

A number of families have produced three or more sons and relatives who played rugby for Clifton. Several of these families were related by marriage, for example the Fuller Eberle, Strachan, Wills and Fedden families and the Peck, Paul and Weston families.

In the **Baker** family, three brothers - Hiatt, Maurice and Lionel - and two cousins, Herbert and Roland, played for the club. Hiatt and Maurice turned out in the first match played against Bristol in 1889.

Herbert Midelton Baker was born on 24th April 1863 in Bristol, the eldest son of Thomas Baker. He was educated at Rugby School from 1877 to 1881 and joined Clifton RFC in 1896-7 aged 33. He died in 1943. His son Captain Geoffrey H. M. Baker was killed in Libya on 29th May 1942.

Herbert's younger brother Roland Midelton Baker, Thomas's seventh son, was born on 25th February 1876 in Clifton. He was educated at Rugby School from 1890 to 1894 and joined Clifton RFC in 1898-99 aged 22. He was a member of the Bristol Stock Exchange from 1903, and in 1931 was still living in Pembroke Road in Clifton.

Hiatt Cowles Baker was captain of Clifton and Gloucestershire and an England international (see the Famous Players Chapter for more details).

Hiatt's younger brother Maurice Mills Baker was born on 8th March 1867 in Bristol, the second son of William Baker. He was educated at St. Dunstan's College, London and Rugby School from 1881 to 1886 and at Oriel College, Oxford. A barrister, he joined Clifton RFC in 1886-87 and died on 22nd November 1936, in Southbourne, Hampshire.

William Baker's third son Lionel Gray was born in Bristol on 9th September 1880. He was educated at Rugby School from 1894 to 1896 and joined Clifton RFC in 1898-9. He died in Holborn, London in 1919, aged only 38.

The well-to-do **Watkins Baker** family produced seven rugby-playing brothers for the club in addition to the three daughters born to Julia and her solicitor husband Thomas. The family lived with a coterie of servants at Grove House on Tyndalls Park Road, Westbury-on-Trym. The eldest child, Thomas, was born on 30th August 1875. Also a solicitor, he joined Clifton RFC in 1896-97 and became captain the following season. He joined Bristol in 1901 but returned to Clifton six years later, at the same time serving as President of Bristol Saracens RFC between 1906-07 and 1908-1910. He then emigrated to Canada, became a rancher in Vancouver and married Lena Howard Freer on 13th April 1914 at Maple Ridge, British Columbia. He died on 23rd February 1949 in Haney, British Columbia.

Brother Dudley was born in 1877 and joined the club in 1901-02. Edward's birth followed in 1879 – clearly the most talented sportsman of the male siblings, he remains the only Clifton RFC member to have played for the Barbarians (see the Famous Players Chapter for more). Cecil Leecroft was born on 27th July 1881, educated at Clifton College from 1892 to 1897 and joined in 1900-01. Claude was born on 11th July 1883 and followed his brother to school from 1893 to 1899 and to the club in 1901-02. In 1920 he married the 17 year old Kathleen Helena Lee in Scarborough, Yorkshire. He became manager of a tea and rubber estate in Ceylon and died in 1958 at St. James's Hospital in Leeds.

The Watkins Baker brothers (L-R) Cecil, Claude, Dudley, Edward, Leonard, Lionel and Thomas

The family's children had continued to arrive at regular intervals, and Leonard Frere was born on 3rd August 1882. Also educated at Clifton College (1892 to 1896), he made his club debut in 1900-01. The last boy, although followed by one last sister, Lionel Charles was born on 3rd February 1886. Another Clifton College pupil (1899 to 1903), he went on to study at the University of Bristol, joining Clifton RFC in 1903-04. He married Irene Dempster on 18th February 1913 in Natal, South Africa.

The similarly affluent **Beloe** family is most notable for Henry Willoughby (Harry) Beloe's astonishing 34-year tenure as the club's President from 1891 until his death in 1925. Look at almost any 1st XV photograph during that span of years, and there is Harry sitting proudly centre-stage. Harry was a miller and corn-merchant, and lived at Home Lodge in Westbury-on-Trym, and later at Avonbank on Clifton Down, with his wife Ellen, three sons, a daughter and several domestic servants.

His eldest son Cecil, born 1876, had an undocumented association with the club. The next son Gerald Harry, born 21st November 1877, was educated at Marlborough College and joined the club in 1897-98. He also played cricket for Gloucestershire on six occasions, a left-hand bat with a top score of 52 not out. He died on 1st October 1944 in Clifton. Harry's youngest son Gilbert Charles, joined the club in 1898-99 after his Marlborough education. He became an adjutant in the 2/5th Gloucestershire Regiment from May 1916 to July 1917.

Gerald's son John Cecil Pochin ('Putch') Beloe followed his father and uncles to the club. Born on 2nd October 1919, he was educated at Clifton College from 1933 to 1937 and worked for W.D. & H.O. Wills. He died in August 2001 in Stafford. His son Iain continued the tradition by joining Clifton RFC in the 1970-71 season.

Harry Beloe

The **Bennett** family owned the Bedminster, Easton, Kingswood and Parkfield collieries. The head offices were at Easton Colliery, off Stapleton Road, and at Dean Lane, Bedminster. Alfred Henry Bennett was born in 1860 in Bristol and joined Clifton in 1880-81. He was the brother of John Ryan Bennett whose two sons also played for the club. Henry Ryan Bennett died in the Great War - more details in the Roll of Honour chapter. John Piers Bennett was born on 6th August 1898 and was educated at Clifton College from 1909 to 1916, and subsequently at Caius College, Cambridge. He joined Clifton RFC in 1919-20 and worked for the banking company N.M. Rothschild & Sons. He died in 1970.

Three **Boucher** brothers played for the club, the sons of John, a pharmaceutical chemist from Blackwell, Derbyshire, and his wife Julia. The eldest, Charles Edward, joined the club in 1909-10 when already 40 years old – presumably not in a playing capacity. George Herbert was born in Clifton in 1877 and was educated at Bristol Grammar School. He became a solicitor and joined Clifton RFC in 1901-02. George died on 2nd December 1970 at his home Maybank in Leigh Woods. Frank Treadwell, the youngest of four boys in the family of seven children, was born in 1883 and followed his brother to B.G.S. He joined the club in 1906-07 and qualified as a doctor. He died on 14th February 1958 in Exeter.

In sporting terms, the Boucher boys were eclipsed by their sister Edith, a tennis player who won two gold medals in the Indoor Singles and Mixed Doubles events at the 1912

Stockholm Olympics. Born on 28th November 1878 in Bristol, she married the Clifton player Francis Hannam who died in the Great War. After returning from a spell in Canada, where her husband had a timber business, she won ten Welsh titles between 1912 and 1923, as well as twice being a Wimbledon finalist, Singles 1911 and Mixed Doubles 1914. She died on 16th January 1951 in Bristol.

Four **Bush** brothers played for Clifton, the sons of Major Robert and Emily Bush. Their father's military career obviously took his growing family with him. The first three children were born in Australia and the fourth, the third son and first Clifton player James Arthur (See the Famous Players chapter), in Bengal. The marriage produced at least ten children - six sons and four daughters. The fourth son and second Clifton player Robert Edwin Bush had an interesting and varied career, also described in the Famous Players Chapter. The third son to join the club, James Paul (yes there really were two boys called James, which must have been confusing) was born on 30th June 1857 and educated at Clifton College from 1869 to 1876. He joined Clifton RFC in 1879-80. This James was a surgeon at Bristol Royal Infirmary, became Deputy Lieutenant for Gloucestershire and was appointed Officer of the Order of the Crown of Belgium. He married an Australian, Laura Robertson of Victoria, and was awarded the C.B.E in 1919. James Paul died on 7th October 1930 at 2 College Fields, Clifton. His funeral took place at Bristol Cathedral on 30th October 1930 - the last post was sounded by buglers of the 6th Battalion of The Gloucestershire Regiment. Details of the youngest boy, John Ernest, are also to be found in the Famous Players Chapter.

Nicholas John **Dunn** was Deputy Lieutenant of Pembrokeshire and County Magistrate, and his marriage to Emma, as well as producing at least seven daughters and another son, contributed three sons to the club. John Henry was born on 16th September 1857 at Penally House near Tenby and was a pupil at Clifton College in 1873. He joined Clifton in 1874-75 and became a solicitor with the practice of H. Cooke, J.B. Cooke and J.H. Dunn. It is a nice curiosity that he lived at 15 Victoria Square, Clifton, which later became the home of W.G. Grace. In 1878 John was elected as the first secretary of Gloucestershire Rugby Football Union. He died in 1915. His brother George was born in St. Florence, Pembrokeshire around 1863 and joined Clifton in 1879-80. A younger brother Edward Hutchins Dunn was born on 4th March 1866 in Cheltenham and attended Clifton College from 1877 to 1880, moving on to Sherborne School. He joined the club in 1882-83 and later became a farmer.

The **Fuller Eberle** family connection with the club stretches from its very beginnings to the present day. Admiral Sir James Fuller Eberle wrote this book's foreword and donated his father's extensive scrapbooks to the club's archive. His grandfather, also named James, was the club's founder and first honorary member, more can be found on him in the Foundation and Early Days chapter. The eldest and youngest sons of James and his wife Florence, George and Victor ("Admiral Jim's" father), are mentioned in the Famous Players chapter. The middle son Ellison was born on 4th July 1883 and schooled, like his brothers, at Clifton College. He joined Clifton RFC in 1899-1900, remained a first-team regular until the 1911-12 season, served as captain from

1907 to 1909 and represented Gloucestershire. All three brothers were still sufficiently hale and hearty to turn out for the Old Members XV in 1919-20. Ellison married Margaret, the daughter of Sir George Alfred Wills. In 1932, after Sir George' death, they bought Goldney House, Clifton from the trustees of his estate. In accordance with his late wife's wish, in 1956 he sold Goldney House to the University of Bristol and it was converted to student accommodation. Ellison Fuller Eberle died on 2nd May 1968.

A father and two sons came to the club from the **Edwards** family. Herbert George was born on 5th October 1853, was a pupil at Clifton College from 1863 to 1870 and joined the club in 1872-73. Herbert became Master of the Society of Merchant Venturers in 1899 and served as a member of Bristol City Council. He died in 1927. His son George Dall Edwards was born on 1st September 1883, educated at Clifton College from 1893 to 1900 and joined Clifton in 1901-02. He died in 1959. George's brother Philip, born in 1888, was one of those who died in the Great War and thus appears in the Roll of Honour chapter.

Three sons of John W **Egerton**, a merchant from Liverpool, and his wife Elizabeth followed the same Clifton College and Clifton RFC path. Thomas, aged about 22, joined the club in 1897-8, James in 1899-1900 at the same age and youngest brother Jack in the same season aged 18. James died at an early age in 1908.

Five sons of David **Evans** and his wife Susan found their way to the club. David had a tannery business and was a city councillor, whilst Susan was the daughter of Dr. Nicholson, the Deputy Inspector-General of Hospitals for the area. Eldest son Frank Evans was born about 1854 in Berkshire and joined the club in its earliest days of 1872-73, playing in the club's inaugural match against Sydney College, Bath. His brother Parker Nicholson Evans was born in Clifton in 1858 and joined the club in 1883-84. He died on 25th March 1927 at Brockley, Somerset. The middle son of the five, Herbert Lavington Evans, was a Scottish international and is covered in the Famous Players chapter.

The next brother, Ernest Dering Evans, was born on 21st August 1861 and educated at Clifton College from 1873 to 1879. He joined the club in 1879-80 and was another Clifton player good enough to play for Gloucestershire. He died in 1948. Howard Brinsby Evans was born on 5th February 1865 and put through Clifton College from 1880 to 1882. He joined Clifton RFC in 1884-85.

Three **Fedden** brothers, William, Nelson and Henry, produced between them four sons who played for the club. William's two sons Robert Agnew and Clement Agnew, born about 1863 and 1867, joined the club in 1882 and 1884 respectively. Clement died on 8th January 1920, aged 52, and was buried two days later at Mountain View Cemetery, Vancouver.

Nelson's son Robert was born about 1865 and joined the club in 1880. He died on 19th June 1943 at Pietermaritzburg, South Africa.

Henry's youngest son Sir Alfred Hubert Roy Fedden, usually known as Roy, was born on 6th June 1885 in Bristol. His father was a Bristol sugar merchant and his mother the daughter of the Revd Samuel Romilly Hall. Roy was educated at Clifton College from 1895 to 1904 and joined the club in the 1905-06 season. He appeared regularly for the 1st XV in 1907-08.

At a time when in certain social circles one was expected to join the church or the armed services, Roy Fedden decided he wanted to become an engineer and went to the Merchant Venturers College in Bristol. His chosen profession was often considered in those days little better than casual labouring. It was expected that he would marry Norah Carew, but upon hearing of Roy's ambitions, her mother was horrified and no longer wanted him in her house and suggested if he did call again that he used the tradesman's entrance at the rear of the house. His interest in engines was stimulated by his father's purchase of a car in 1903, registration number AE4; he was only the fourth person in Bristol to own one, and the fiftieth in all of Britain. In 1906, when his apprenticeship was complete, aged only 21 Roy designed his first car, the successful Straker-Squire Shamrock. He established the engine-building department of the Bristol Aeroplane Company in 1920, where he was chief engineer until 1942. Initiating a famous range of piston engines, including the Pegasus and Hercules, he was also notable for his unique development of the sleeve-valve engine. He held a variety of governmental and international posts until 1960, and was president of the Royal Aeronautical Society in 1938, 1939, and 1945. For his role in creating some of the most successful aircraft engines of the era, Roy was knighted in 1942. At the height of his career in the 1930s, Roy's aero engines powered Britain's national airline, more than half the Royal Air Force, and about half the other airlines and air forces of the world.

Although Roy had created a long line of hugely successful engines for Bristol, he had fought constantly with management over funding priorities. His draughtsman Leonard Butler, with whom he had worked inseparably since 1915, left the company to recuperate from the stress of wartime production needs. Without Butler's support Roy apparently found it difficult to continue, and shortly after being knighted he left Bristol to take up a variety of positions within the Government. For much of the remainder of the war, he travelled in the United States with another Bristol employee, Ian Duncan, to study American production line techniques in order to improve their own.

On his return he set up Roy Fedden Ltd in 1945 with Ian Duncan. A couple of early projects found little interest. Finally they decided to design their own car, powered by a three-cylinder air-cooled radial, but they found it had serious handling problems and tended to flip over when being cornered hard. After this, Fedden worked for a time consulting with George Dowty (another inventor and draughtsman), but soon retired and spent his time teaching at the College of Aeronautics at Cranfield University.

Roy was the uncle of the prominent British artist Mary Fedden, who taught painting at the Royal College of Art from 1958 to 1964, the first woman tutor to teach in the painting school and whose pupils included David Hockney and Allen Jones. She was President of The Royal West of England Academy from 1984 to 1989.

Roy Fedden died on 21st November 1973 at his home, Buckland Old Mill, by the River Usk in Breconshire. A memorial service was held at St. Clement Danes, London, on the 6th February 1974.

Two **Fry** brothers, Albert Magnus and George Falconer (who died within a week of each other), were sons of Albert Fry who owned the Bristol Wagon & Carriage Works Company Ltd and was part of the Quaker Chocolate family. Albert and George both played for the club, as did two cousins.

Albert was born 13th May 1857 and educated at Clifton College from 1871 to 1874. He joined Clifton RFC in 1877-78 and played for Gloucestershire, later becoming a director of J.S. Fry and Sons. George was born on 4th February 1863, followed Albert to Clifton College from 1874 to 1876 but then completed his education at Uppingham School in Rutland – perhaps his brother preceded him there too. George went on to University College Bristol and became a mechanical engineer, having joined the club in 1884-85.

George died on 13th September 1938, and Albert precisely a week later, his burial taking place at All Saints Church, Easter Compton.

Their cousin Francis Rhodolph Fry was born in Clifton in 1862, the son of Francis James and Elizabeth, and joined the club in 1883-84. Leslie Harrington Fry, a second cousin of Albert and George, was the son of Charles Alfred Harrington and Kate. He joined the club in the 1913-14 season and died in the Great War – see the WW1 Roll of Honour chapter for more.

It is just possible that the **Gardiner** family associated with the club for many years was connected to the Venetian explorer John Cabot, for a John Gardiner sailed with him to America in the late 15th century. Another John Gardiner was Warden of the Merchant Venturers in 1626. In the 19th century the family established a business - Gardiner & Sons - which manufactured trench mortars, bombs and aeroplane parts during the Great War.

In 1970 the company was taken over by Canton Industries, now part of Hawker Siddeley, and the manufacturing part of the business was discontinued. The builders' merchants line continued to expand, with branches at Cirencester and Shepton Mallet, and Haskins joined the firm on a franchise basis in 1972. The last Gardiner left the firm in the 1950s. The company is known today as Gardiner Haskins.

The Gardiner family around the turn of the century. (L-R) Back Row: Ernest, Enid, Hubert, Edward Lucas. Seated: Agnes, Thomas Chapple, Sarah, Florence, Ethel, Alfred

In all, six family members represented the club. Edward, the eldest son of Thomas and Sarah appears to have eluded the club's grasp, but his three younger brothers all played, and appear together in the Ist XV team photograph of 1904-5. Ernest, the second son, was killed in the Great War and is covered in the Roll of Honour chapter. Hubert was born on 26th July 1881 and spent eleven years at Clifton College from 1889 to 1900, subsequently taking a degree at University College, Oxford. He boxed for the university at middleweight against Cambridge. Hubert became an accountant and joined the club in 1903-04. He died on 27th September 1934 in London and is buried at Putney Vale Cemetery.

Alfred was born on 7th November 1882 and educated at Clifton College from 1891 to 1900. He began playing for the club in 1900-01. The toss of a coin decided that he, not Ernest, would stay home and help run the family business during the war; as happened so often at the time, a local woman, believing that he should have gone to war, sent him a white feather. Alfred later joined Harlequins and died in 1959.

Christopher John was born on 2nd June 1907, the son of Edward and nephew of Alfred, Ernest and Hubert. He followed the family's Clifton College tradition from 1919 to 1926 and played for Clifton during the 1920s and 1930s, appearing regularly for the 1st XV for several years. Christopher worked for the family business.

The Harrow-educated Michael Gardiner, a cousin of Alfred, Ernest and Hubert, also appeared for the club. His son Peter, born on 26th December 1907, was at Clifton College from 1922 to 1925 and appears next to his cousin Christopher in several team photographs. Peter ran a letter service for players during World War II from the family engineering firm, Midland Works, in the St. Philips area of Bristol.

Two **Gibbs** brothers, George Herbert and Arthur Ronald played for the club, as did their cousin. George was born on 18th December 1888 in Bristol and Ronald, as he was known, following three years later in 1891. They were the sons of Herbert and Marian. Their father was a gun and rifle manufacturer and had city centre offices and a showroom in Corn Street. George was educated at Clifton College from 1900 to 1905 and joined the club in 1908-09, Ronald following in 1910-11. George was the father of the Bristol and England player (two caps) George Anthony Gibbs (1920-2001) and the Harlequins and England player (two caps) Nigel Gibbs (born 1922), who was also a cricket blue at Oxford University and head teacher at Bristol's Colston's School in 1965.

George and Ronald's cousin, George Percy Vernon Gibbs, was born on 14th August 1894 in Clifton, the son of George and Catherine Gibbs. His father was a partner in the family gun business, and inventor in 1911 of the .505 Gibbs round, intended for hunting elephant and cape buffalo or for stopping lions. His own father George, founder of the family firm, had been involved in the invention, patenting and distribution of the Gibbs-Farquharson-Metford hunting rifle in 1877. This rifle had a successful and long-lived career, eliciting the following testimonial, written in Kenya in the 1920s, from today's perspective may seem heartless,

On the 5th of this month while on safari, I was called at 5.30 a.m. as a native informed me that elephant were raiding his garden, so I rushed out, picked up the .505, and in half an hour came to a herd of seven elephants in the long grass just clear of the village. I got up to within 12 yards of them and dropped two, the rest made off and I followed, and owing to there being natives around, did not go far, and in a few minutes I came up to them again and dropped four more; only one was left and he returned to the first two, and I shot him at 6—7 yards. I think this is the finest christening any rifle ever had. Seven elephant before breakfast!

Not surprisingly, George Gibbs, son of the founder, was a crack shot who represented England and who once scored 57 consecutive bullseyes in front of King Edward VII in 1909. His father and uncle had both joined the Bristol Rifle Volunteers when they were re-formed in 1859 (Bristol's 1798 Volunteers were the first in the country), and a craze for rifle drill and shooting-ranges resulted; when the Drill Hall was built at the top of Park Street in 1861, there were some one thousand members in ten companies, and the firm of George Gibbs had the contract to supply them.

His father became Colonel of one of the Volunteer Corps, and he would, as a birthday treat, let his little daughter head the parade on a big horse. The Colonel, a keen sportsman, started the Clifton Beagles, and was a friend of W.G. Grace. He once became the talk of the town for shooting down an effigy of a parliamentary candidate, hung by pranksters from the Suspension Bridge.

George Percy Vernon was educated at Clifton College from 1908 to 1912 and joined the club in 1912-13. He worked in the family business and was notorious for rifling the barrels of many of the firm's firearms.

Ernest Hain **Greenslade** was born on 18th December 1872 in Clifton, Bristol and educated at Clifton College from 1887 to 1890. He joined Clifton RFC in 1897-98 and was a boot manufacturer. His brother William was a partner with John Acraman in the Bristol firm of Greenslade & Acraman on Thomas Street, Bristol, which was already listed in Pigot's Directory of 1830 as makers of bellows, brushes, sieves and mops, later diversifying into chandlery. William's sons followed their uncle to the club. Arthur Acraman Greenslade was born in 1894 and is covered in the World War II Roll of Honour chapter. His brother Donald Acraman was born on 16th February 1895, was educated at Charterhouse School and joined the club in 1913-14. He joined the Gloucester Regiment in the Great War and became a Major, surviving capture and imprisonment in a P.O.W camp in Poland. Donald died of a heart attack in the early 1940s.

Walter Gouldsmith **Gribble** was born on 20th April 1855, the son of Henry Gribble. He was educated at Clifton College from 1868 to 1872, joined the club in 1872-73 and played in the club's first fixture after its foundation. Walter became a solicitor and died in 1929. His younger brother Herbert Willis Reginald was born on 23rd December 1860 and followed Walter to Clifton College from 1871 to 1878, where he was a member of the cricket XI and captain in 1878. Between 1878 and 1882 he played in 29 first-class cricket matches for Gloucestershire and also played rugby for his county. He joined the club in 1879-80 and lived in Clifton until about 1888, when he moved to Courthorpe Villas, Wimbledon, and became a member of the London Stock Exchange. He died at Teddington in Middlesex on 12th June 1942.

Their nephew Henry John Carew Gribble was born on 19th June 1885, the son of Henry Ernest Gribble. He was, inevitably, also educated at Clifton College - from 1899 to 1903 - and joined the club in 1903-04. Another solicitor, he died in 1959.

Joseph John Leech **Harvey** was the eldest of three brothers to play for Clifton. Born on 15th April 1883, he was educated at Clifton College from 1892 to 1902, and then took a degree at Queen's College, Oxford. He joined Clifton RFC in 1902-03 and later became a solicitor of Straits Settlements, a group of British territories which have since become Singapore and parts of Malaysia. His brother Charles Alfred Leech was born on 31st March 1884 and became a wine merchant in Bristol and Kidderminster. He joined the club in 1901-02 and died on 25th October 1938. The youngest of the three, Lt. Col. Robert Bleeck Leech Harvey was born on 19th August 1887 and joined the club in the 1905-06 season.

The **Inskip** family moved to Bristol in the middle of the 19th century and became a famous local name. Two brothers played for the club, the sons of James Inskip and Constance Sophia Louisa Hampden.

The Rt. Hon. Sir Thomas Walker Hobart Inskip was born on 5th March 1876 in Clifton. He attended Clifton College from 1886 to 1894 and then graduated from King's College, Cambridge, joining Clifton RFC in 1895-96. He was MP for Central Bristol from 1918 to 1929 and for Fareham from 1931 to 1939, and was knighted in 1922.

Despite an exclusively legal track record, in 1936 he became the first Minister for Coordination of Defence. His appointment to this particular office was highly controversial. Winston Churchill had long campaigned for such an office and when its creation was announced, most expected Churchill to be appointed. When Inskip was named, a famous remark (often but possibly wrongly attributed to Churchill himself) was that "this is the most cynical appointment since Caligula made his horse a consul"' His appointment is now regarded as a sign of caution by Prime Minister Stanley Baldwin who did not wish to appoint someone like Churchill, because it would have been interpreted by foreign powers as a sign of the United Kingdom preparing for war. Baldwin anyway wished to avoid appointing such a controversial and radical minister as Churchill.

Thomas Inskip became Viscount Caldecote of Bristol in 1939, served as Leader of the House of Lords in 1940 and Lord Chief Justice from 1940 until 1946. He held many other positions of influence and note throughout his life.

He died on October 11th 1947 at his home in Godalming, Surrey, and was buried at Caldecote, near Baldock in Hertfordshire, whence his grandfather had come to Bristol a century earlier.

Sir John Hampden Inskip was born on 16th December 1879, also in Clifton. He followed in his brother's footsteps to Clifton College from 1890 to 1898 and then to King's College, Cambridge. He joined Clifton RFC in 1901-02 and was a first-team regular for several seasons after the turn of the century. John Inskip worked as a solicitor, held the office of Lord Mayor of Bristol in 1931 and of Alderman of Bristol in 1932. He was invested as a Knight Commander, Order of the British Empire (K.B.E.) in 1937 and died on 8th April 1960.

John Arthur **Osborn** was killed in the 2nd World War and is covered in the Roll of Honour chapter. His brother Dennis Charles was born on 9th September 1911 and educated at Clifton College from 1925 to 1929. He became club captain in the 1930s and managing director of Osborn and Wallis Ltd of Hotwells, Bristol who shipped coal from South Wales. He died in 1974.

Dennis's two sons Mark and Robert were also involved with the club, Mark was an active non-playing member and Robert as No. 8 in the 1st XV of the mid-1970s.

Two **Paul** brothers were founder members of the club, both joining in that first season of 1872-3. Walter Stuckey was born on 4th November 1849 and educated at Clifton College from 1863 to 1866; he was good enough to play for Gloucestershire. He became a Bristol architect and surveyor and died in 1925. Arthur Clifford was born on 10th August 1854 and also educated at Clifton College (1864 to 1873). He worked as a clerk and died a year before his brother.

Walter's son Courtenay Talbot St. Paul joined the club in 1905-06. He died in the Great War and is covered in the Roll of Honour chapter.

Three sons of William **Peck**, a Bristol wine merchant, all played for the club. Francis Samuel was born on 1st April 1858 and educated at Clifton College from 1871 to 1875. He joined the club in 1873-74 aged only 15. Francis had a varied career as a Lieutenant-Colonel in the Indian Medical Service and Professor at the Calcutta Medical College, re-surfacing in Burma in 1886. In 1908, while home on leave, he met with a serious accident at Sheringham while crossing the railway by the golf course; he was knocked down and run over by a passing train. Although not fully recovered from the accident, he returned to India to resume his official duties. His health was clearly still fragile, and on the next homeward voyage to England he died.

Herbert Withers Peck was born on 30th July 1859, was educated at Clifton College from 1872 to 1874 and joined the club in 1873-74 aged only 14. He also played for Gloucestershire. Herbert followed his brother into military service and became a captain in Pulleine's Irregulars during the South African Wars of the 1870s. He subsequently went on to command the Sarawak Rangers for Raja (Sir James) Brooke, and was later the Raja's Resident in Labuan and formed the Sarawak Civil Service. Herbert retired in 1901 and died in 1916.

Edward Surnam Peck was born on 23rd March 1866, followed the family's Clifton College tradition from 1878 to 1884 and went on to Christ's College, Cambridge. He joined Clifton RFC in 1884-85 and became a major in the Army. He died in 1934.

Four **Pocock** brothers, sons of a Bristol cleric, played for the club in the 1870s and 1880s. All of them, as was the case with the other five children of the family were given the second name Innes, and the name mutated into a double-barrelled surname which survives to this day. The most prominent of the sons, Edward, played twice for Scotland and is covered in the Famous Players chapter. His brother Walter was born on 25th September 1859 in Clifton. Academically gifted, he took an M.A. as a Scholar of Trinity College, Dublin and became Higher Division Clerk of the Local Government

Board in Ireland between 1882 and 1900. Walter joined Clifton RFC in 1884-85 but presumably, given his employment, must have been an infrequent player. He died on 26th June 1913 in Clifton.

Herbert Innes Pocock

Herbert was born on 2nd June 1861 in Clifton, and was educated at Bristol Grammar School, Lancing College and Bristol University. He joined the club in 1879-80. Herbert became a colonel in the R.A.M.C. and was appointed C.M.G. He died on 21st August 1947 in Newquay. The youngest of these four Pococks, Reginald, was born on 4th March 1863 in Clifton. He joined the club in 1883-84 and was employed as a zoologist and author in the London Zoological Gardens. He died on 9th August 1947 in London.

The three **Bostock Smith** brothers who played for the club were sons of Samuel Smith, an erstwhile wholesale grocer who became a well-to-do sugar merchant. He added Bostock – perhaps his mother's maiden name – to the name of each of his six or more children and, as in the case of the Innes Pococks, the family name thus acquired a lustre more befitting of the family's status.

The eldest child Charles Henry was born in Clifton in 1874 and joined the club in 1896-97. He and his brother Stanley both became merchant clerks, probably in the sugar business, although their father died in the 1890s. Brother (Edward) Stanley was born in Clifton in 1876 and joined the club a year after Charles, later moving into rugby administration as Chairman of Bristol Rugby Club and President of Gloucestershire Rugby Football Union. He died in 1937. Their youngest sibling Claude was born in 1891 and started his club career in the 1908-09 season. He was killed in Belgium towards the end of the Great War and is covered in the Roll of Honour chapter.

Richard Ellison **Strachan**, a merchant, was born about 1817. He was one of the founder members of Clifton Rugby Club in 1872, and the father of the club's first captain Charles (of whom more in the Famous Players chapter). Richard died in 1892.

Charles's brother Walter was born on 22nd September 1856 in Cheltenham and was a pupil at Clifton College from 1868 to 1874. He joined Clifton RFC in 1872-73 and played for Gloucestershire in 1882. Walter became a barrister and died on 14th June 1936. He married rather late in life and his son Richard Gething was born on 31st March 1911 when his father was already 54 years old. Richard was also educated at Clifton College (1915 to 1929) and played for the club during the 1930s. He became a solicitor with David Johnstone & Co. in Bristol and died in August 1992.

Walter Strachan

Three sons of, at least, nine children of David **Walsh**, a wholesale clothing merchant, and his wife Sarah played for the club, all joining in the inaugural season 1872-3. Little is known about Henry Furze, also a wholesale clothier, who was born about 1842 and died on 22nd November 1874, nor about his brother Alexander, born on 29th June 1851, educated at Clifton College from 1863 to 1864 and who died in 1900. The family's third son David Henry was born on 17th October 1852 and attended Clifton College from 1863 to 1871. He played in the first Clifton fixture in 1872 and served as the club's first vice-captain. David was an academic high-flyer and became a pioneering radiologist, a founder and first honorary secretary of the Röntgen Society. With David Greenhill he co-authored in 1897 the seminal work "The Röntgen Rays in Medical Work". He studied and worked in Edinburgh and Dundee, and was later senior physician at the Western Skin Hospital and tuberculosis medical officer at St George's In The East in London. David Walsh died in 1943.

The **Wills** name is perhaps the most famous of all those closely associated with the city of Bristol. In all, seven members of the Wills tobacco family played for the Clifton club.

Stephen Prust Wills was born in 1847, the eldest son of Henry Overton Wills II and his second wife Mary Seccombe. Stephen played for the 1869 Clifton side and later, married with several children, worked as a stockbroker in Swansea. He died in 1922.

His younger brother Sir Frank William Wills was born on 17th August 1852, the fourth son of Henry and Mary. An architect, he married Sara Dobell who died in 1930. Sir Frank was Lord Mayor of Bristol in 1910-11 and knighted in 1912 when the King visited the city to open the Edward VII Memorial Building at the Bristol Royal Infirmary. He played for the 1869 Clifton side and for the new club founded in 1872. He died on 26th March 1932.

Stephen and Frank's nephew Henry Herbert was the eldest of six sons of Henry Overton Wills III, himself the eldest of nine children from his father's first marriage to Isabella Board. Very nearly 30 years separated the birth of the eldest child of the first marriage and the youngest of the second. Henry was born on 20th March 1856 and was educated at Mill Hill Grammar School, and then at Clifton College from 1872 to 1874. He joined Clifton RFC in 1879-80 and later became a director of Imperial Tobacco. Henry's name is particularly associated with the University of Bristol. He was responsible for meeting the funding needed to build Wills Hall, a hall of residence for Bristol University students, and also funded the building of the H. H. Wills Physics Laboratory situated in Royal Fort Gardens. With his brother George Alfred, he was responsible for the building of the Wills Memorial Building, a landmark building of the University, in memory of his father. Henry married Mary Cunliffe-Owen in 1886 but there were no children. He died on the 11th May 1922, aged 66, at his home at St. Vincent's, Clifton Park. A requiem was held at All Saints Church, Clifton and the funeral service at Bristol Cathedral. He was buried at Canford Cemetery in Bristol. Henry's brother Maitland Wills was born on 7th December 1857. He was educated at Clifton College from 1871 to 1877 and graduated from Trinity College, Cambridge. He joined the club in the 1883-84 season. Maitland was killed in an accident while on holiday in North Wales on 6th April 1885 when he slipped and fell mountaineering at

Capel Curig. His funeral took place at Redland Park Church on 14th April 1885 and his body was taken in a procession to be buried at Arnos Vale Cemetery.

Frank Oliver Wills

Three of Sir Frank William's sons also played for the club. Henry William Seccombe was born in 1877, trained as a surveyor and joined in 1900-01. Frank Oliver was born on 3rd April 1882 and joined in the same season. He went into the family tobacco business, became Sheriff of Bristol in 1924 and died in 1972. Hugh Cecil was born on 5th July 1884 and joined in 1903-04. He died in 1970.

Associated Organisations

Sporting Links

Whilst rugby has been the main priority of most club players, many have participated in other sports, especially during the summer months.

Ariel Rowing Club was founded in 1870 and is the oldest in Bristol. Several Clifton RFC players rowed for Ariel, including Alan Caldicott (who died in the Great War - see Roll of Honour chapter), S.D. Withers, John Holloway, who was captain in many seasons between 1910 and 1925, and W.I. Gunn who later became Vice-Chairman of the Imperial Tobacco Company and was the great-grandson of H.O. Wills.

The club is now known as Bristol Ariel Rowing Club and is based in St. Anne's, which was also home to Clifton College Rowing Club.

Bristol & Clifton Golf Club was founded on the 14th February 1891 at the Imperial Hotel in Clifton. Golf had originally been played on the Downs, where there existed a nine-hole course belonging to Clifton Downs Golf Club; this was at the top of Blackboy Hill along Upper Belgrave Road in the direction of the Zoo. Owing to problems between the players and the public, a meeting was held to establish a club and course elsewhere. The Clifton RFC players involved at this St Valentine's Day meeting were Edmund Judkin Taylor, who became the first Secretary of the Club, William Octavius Moberly, L. Danger, Edward James Barff, Michael Arthur North, James Monteath and Walter Fairbanks, who became the Golf Club's first captain (see the Famous Players chapter for more details of Fairbanks and Moberly). Fairbanks emigrated to the United States in 1898 and became a famous golfer on the American circuit. Moberly, Fairbanks, Barff and North all taught at Clifton College.
A nine-hole course was soon opened later in 1891 at Failand, on land owned by Sir Greville Smythe, and extended to eighteen holes in 1895. The club still plays on the original course. Later, other Clifton rugby players became involved, including William Stanley Alston Brown (B&CGC captain 1922-23) and George Fuller Eberle (President B&CGC 1955-71).

Bristol Rugby Club's fortunes have been linked with those of Clifton from an early stage. Clifton RFC had been the premier rugby club in the south-west for 16 years by the time the Bristol club was formed in 1888. Local interest in rugby increased with the rivalry generated by the formation of Bristol Rugby Club and its relationship with

Clifton, with newspaper reports in the 'Bristol Times and Mirror' becoming a regular feature from 1888 onwards.
The Clifton versus Bristol fixture became an annual event that generated more interest amongst supporters than any other fixture. Clifton gate receipts from this one match used to exceed the combined total for all the other matches played that season.

The establishment of the Bristol Combination in 1901 was intended to promote Rugby Union and the wellbeing of its clubs in the area. The reality was that it provided the 'senior Clubs' - Bristol and Clifton - with a pool of players upon which to call, and in time this increasingly worked to Bristol's advantage as the club was better placed than Clifton to draw on the majority of the pool of local players. There has always been a tension between the local side, the ambitious player and these 'senior clubs'. Professionalism, Leagues and National Cup Competitions have only served to accentuate this situation.

When Bristol Rugby Club resumed activities after the Great War, the County Ground was no longer available. Clifton RFC, which owned land on Radnor Road in Horfield, leased it to Bristol Rugby Club. The ground was not ideal, and occasionally the Bristol club would play at Bristol Rovers' Eastville Ground and at Ashton Gate, home of Bristol City. The club played at Radnor Road for two seasons from 1919, until the Memorial Ground was opened on land that had been home to Clifton RFC from 1893 to 1896. The land was given anonymously.

Latterly, professionalism had an effect on Clifton as it did on the Bristol club. Clifton cut its cloth to suit, whilst Bristol went all out to compete and - in July 1998 - went into receivership. The club lost the ownership of the Memorial Ground to Bristol Rovers FC. Nowadays the administrative headquarters of Bristol Rugby Club are based at Clifton's ground at Cribbs Causeway, where the Bristol club trains and the Bristol United club plays.

Clifton Association Football Clubs early days are associated with the Clifton Rugby families Wreford-Brown and Pocock. Its most famous goalkeeper in those days was ex-Clifton and England Rugby international James Arthur Bush. He played for Clifton AFC in the late 1880s and early 1890s. Perhaps his most famous season was 1889-90 when Clifton became football champions of Gloucestershire, beating St. George 5-0 on 22nd March 1890 at the St. George's ground in front of 2,500 spectators. That team also included the former Clifton RFC Reginald Innes Pocock. It went on to beat the champions of Wiltshire, Swindon Town, 2-1 away on 29th March 1890 in front of 1,000 spectators.

Clifton AFC was a founder member of the Western League, then called the Bristol and District League, in 1892, and was instrumental in the creation of the Gloucestershire Cup competition in 1888. That year, the Clifton AFC captain was Charles Wreford-

Brown who later captained England in 1893 and 1894. He is credited with inventing the word "soccer" as a synonym for association football.

During the 1890s Clifton AFC played for several years in the FA Cup. In 1891-92 the club beat Reading 8-2 in the 3rd Round (Southern Division) although in the next round they were knocked out by Luton Town. Clifton also played Reading in the FA Cup in 1892-93 and 1894-95.

In the 1892-93 season Clifton AFC was forced to leave its County Ground home, also home of Gloucestershire County Cricket Club. Bristol Rugby Club became the sole tenant at the County Ground – the club's fortunes had improved, and consequently the attendance at its matches. Clifton AFC moved to Kingswood; its attendances dwindled and ultimately led to the club's demise.

Clifton Cricket Club played its first match on 12th August 1819 in Captain Thornhill's field (Sydenham Meadow), Lower Bristol Road, Bath. The Clifton Club beat Bath in one innings by 191 runs. They played their home games on Durdham Downs, initially at the Sea Walls and then, from 1847, at Hollybush Lane. In 1930 the club moved close to Arnell Drive in Henbury. After World War II they played on Clifton RFC's ground at Eastfield Road and then at Cribbs Causeway.

W.G., E.M. and G.F. Grace all played games for Clifton, and from July 30th to August 1st 1868 they played together for the Clifton Cricket Club XX against an All England XI on Clifton College Close.

From 1872 many early members of Clifton RFC, most of whom also played for Gloucestershire CCC, played for Clifton CC, including J.A. Bush, R.E. Bush, W.O. Moberly, E.J. Taylor, W. Fairbanks and J. Cranston. Subsequent generations of Clifton RFC players such as V. Fuller Eberle, W.W. Hoskin, Tom Burrough, Michael Corbett, David Cecil Mills and many others also spent summers with Clifton CC.

Between 1919 and 1926, Clifton provided the cricket captains of Gloucestershire: F.G. Robinson, P.F.C. Williams and D.C. Robinson. The county was captained by B.O Allen in 1937-38 and 1947-50. Foster Gotch Robinson also played for Clifton RFC from 1905-6.

Many members of the rugby club rowed for **Clifton Rowing Club** during the summer.

Rule 1 of the 1883 rulebook stated that "this club be called the 'CLIFTON ROWING CLUB' and Gentlemen Amateurs only be eligible as members". This philosophy of sport being for pleasure and not for financial gain was also deeply rooted in the ethos of Clifton RFC.

Of the nine members of Clifton Rowing Club listed on its Great War memorial, eight also played for Clifton RFC: R.H. Down, N. Durant, P.A. Edwards, L. Harrington Fry, E. Gardiner, F.A. Haycroft, P.T. Rowe and H.E. Rudman. There were also two mutual members who died in the Second World War, J. Burrough and R. Sloan.

The clubhouse of Clifton Rowing Club during the Saltford Regatta in 1908. The clubhouse has since been demolished.

In 1963 the Clifton and Redcliffe rowing clubs merged to become the Bristol Rowing Club. In 1973 the new club then merged again with Avon Rowing Club to become Avon County Rowing Club. Its headquarters are at Saltford, close to the site of the old Clifton Rowing Club.

There is no Bristol newspaper report of 1869 or early 1870 to indicate the official formation of **Gloucestershire County Cricket Club**, but certainly in 1870 the County played two first-class games against Surrey and another game against the MCC at Lord's, and the club confidently celebrated its centenary in 1970.

There has long been an association between Clifton College and Gloucestershire CCC, dating back to the days of W.G. Grace and former pupils of the College who played both cricket and rugby. Many Gloucestershire county cricketers have played rugby for Clifton, from Victorian times to more recently in the case of Chris Broad and James Averis (who also played rugby for Bristol).

During the 1924-25 season Clifton played and defeated **Moseley Rugby Club** for the first time by 10 points to 8. Soon afterwards, Moseley proposed the formation of a new club called Mosecliff. This appears not to have been taken any further - why this was proposed and where they would have played is not recorded.

Westbury-on-Trym Cricket Club was founded in 1858, but the association with Clifton RFC only began in 1900 when the club shared Clifton's ground at North View until the start of the Great War. Many Clifton RFC members played cricket for Westbury, including W.S. Alston Brown, J. Cranston, E.J. Taylor and E.W. Ball, all of whom also played cricket for Gloucestershire. W.E. Lambert played for both clubs and was responsible for the cricket club sharing the Clifton RFC ground for five years from 1920 onwards. In 1996 Westbury-on-Trym Cricket Club merged with Old Bristolians CC and is now based at Failand.

Woodford Rugby Club in Essex was founded on 4th August 1924 by Clifton's Frank Ellerton, and the club still wears the same colours as Clifton. In 1938 Woodford sported a team capable of beating Wasps. The club ground is close to Epping Forest.

Charitable Links

The Society of Merchant Venturers evolved from a guild of merchants dating back to the 13th century, but are now primarily involved in supporting greater Bristol through enterprise and charitable activity. At one time the Society was practically synonymous with the Corporation (local government) of Bristol and for many years had effective control of Bristol's port.

Its past Masters have included many Clifton players over the years, notably G.H. Beloe, V. Fuller Eberle, E. Fuller Eberle, H.C. Baker, F.O. Wills and many others.

Its own charity donates around £200,000 per year to various good causes; the largest trust it controls, St. Monica's Trust, has an annual turnover of over £6 million.

The Merchant Venturers are sponsors of the Merchants' Academy, Withywood, which is co-sponsored by the University of Bristol, and also of Colston's Girls' School which was converted into a City Academy in 2008.

The Grateful Society is a charity which raises funds to help elderly ladies who, through no fault of their own, are experiencing financial hardship.

Past presidents of the Society include F.R. Cross, H.W. Peck, J. Fuller Eberle, G. Fuller Eberle, F.O. Wills, E. Fuller Eberle, F.J. Press, G.H. Beloe and several others who either played for Clifton or helped with its foundation. The current President is Grant Watson, a former president of the rugby club.

The Ancient Society of St. Stephens Ringers comprises a group of businessmen, successors of a society dating back to the time of Queen Elizabeth I and probably the oldest surviving ringing society in the world.

The Society was founded in 1620. Although peal boards in the tower testify to the fact that peals were still being rung under its banner into the last 20 years of the 19th century, it seems most unlikely that these participants were members of that society.

By this time the Society had become entirely a social club, and its work was dedicated solely to the maintenance of the fabric of the Church. There have been several Clifton players amongst its members.

Statistics

Abbreviations. Date (day, month, year) followed by opponents. An: Andorra, A: Australia, AG: Arabian Gulf, Ar: Argentina, Au: Austria, Bo: Bosnia, Bu: Bulgaria, Cr: Croatia, De: Denmark, E: England, F: France, Ge: Germany, Hu: Hungary, I: Ireland, IC: Ivory Coast, Ke: Kenya, La: Latvia, Li: Lithuania, Lu: Luxembourg, Mo: Moldova, M: Morocco, Na: Namibia, NZ: New Zealand, Po: Poland, S: Scotland, SA: South Africa, Se: Serbia, Sw: Sweden, Ne: Netherlands, W: Wales.

Internationals

England

James Arthur Bush 5/2/1872 S, 3/3/1873 S, 8/3/1875 S, 13/12/1875 I, 6/3/1876 S
William Octavius Moberly 5/2/1872 S
Arthur James Budd 11/3/1878 I, 10/3/1879 S, 24/3/1879 I, 19/2/1881 W, 19/3/1881 S
William John Penny 11/3/1878 I, 10/3/1879 S, 24/3/1879 I
Herbert George Fuller 6/2/1882 I, 4/3/1882 S, 16/12/1882 W, 5/2/1883 I, 3/3/1883 S, 5/2/1884 W
Hiatt Cowles Baker 8/1/1887 W
Richard Thomas Dutton Budworth 15/2/1890 W, 3/1/1891 W, 7/3/1891 S
Edwin Field 7/2/1893 W, 4/2/1893 I
Charles Alexander Hooper 6/1/1894 W, 3/3/1894 I, 17/3/1894 S
Bevan Stanishaw Chantrill 19/1/1924 W, 9/2/19024 I, 23/2/1924 F, 15/3/1924 S
John Arthur Gregory 15/1/1949 W
Peter Dalton Young 16/1/1954 W, 30/1/1954 NZ, 13/2/1954 I, 20/3/1954 S, 10/4/1954 F, 22/1/1955 W, 12/2/1955, I, 26/2/1955 F (captain), 19/3/1955 S (captain)
Victor H. Leadbetter 20/3/1954 S, 10/4/1954 F
John David Currie 21/1/1956 W, 11/2/1956 I, 17/3/1956 S, 14/4/1956 F, 19/1/1957 W, 23/2/1957 F, 16/3/1957 S, 18/1/1958 W, 1/2/1958 A, 8/2/1958 I, 1/3/1958 F, 15/3/1958 S, 17/1/1959 W, 14/2/1959 I, 28/2/1959 F, 21/3/1959 S, 16/1/1960 W, 13/2/1960 I, 27/2/1960 F, 19/3/1960 S, 7/1/1961 SA, 20/1/1962 W, 10/2/1962 I, 24/2/1962 F
Stephen Brookhouse Richards 16/1/1965 W, 13/2/1965 I, 27/2/1965 F, 20/3/1965 S, 7/1/1967 A, 11/2/1967 I, 25/2/1967 F, 18/3/1967 S, 15/4/1967 W
Colin William McFadyean 12/2/1966 I, 26/2/1966 F, 19/3/1966 S, 7/1/1967 I, 25/2/1967 F, 18/3/1967 S, 15/4/1967 W, 4/11/1967 NZ, 20/1/1968 W (captain), 10/2/1968 I (captain)
Robert Hoskins Lloyd 4/11/1967 NZ, 20/1/1968 W, 10/2/1968 I, 24/2/1968 F, 16/3/1968 S
David Llewellyn Rees 15/11/1997 A, 22/11/1997 NZ, 29/11/1997 SA, 6/12/1997 NZ, 7/2/1998 F, 21/2/1998 W, 5/12/1998 SA, 20/2/1999 S, 6/3/1999 I, 20/3/1999 F, 26/6/1999 A
Alex Brown 11/6/2006 A, 26/5/2007 SA, 2/6/2007 SA

Scotland

Edward Innes Pocock 19/2/1877 I, 5/3/1877 E
Herbert Lavington Evans 21/2/1885 I, 7/3/1885 I
Robert Kenneth Gillespie MacEwen 9/1/1954 F, 13/2/1954 NZ, 27/2/1954 I, 10/4/1954 W, 14/1/1956 F, 4/2/1956 W, 25/2/1956 I, 17/3/1956 E, 12/1/1957 F, 2/2/1957 W, 23/2/1957 I, 16/3/1957 E, 1/2/1958 W
Alan Sharp 5/2/1994 E, 5/3/1994 I, 19/3/1994 F, 4/6/1994 Ar, 11/6/1994 Ar, 19/11/1994 SA

Ireland

Maurice John Daly 12/2/1938 E

Wales

James Alfred Bevan 19/2/1881 E
Glyn Davies 1/2/1947 S, 20/12/1947 A, 17/1/1948 E, 7/2/1948 S, 21/2/1948 F, 13/3/1948 I, 15/1/1949 E, 26/3/1949 F, 20/1/1951 E, 3/2/1951 S
Gareth Lloyd Evans 5/2/1977 F, 18/3/1978 F, 17/6/1978 A
Rhys Oakley 16/8/2003 I, 30/8/2003 S

Zimbabwe

Paul Johnstone 3/7/1993 Ke, 7/7/1993 AG, 10/7/1993 Na, 14/6/1994 Na, 16/6/1994 M, 18/6/1994 IC.

Malta

Oliver Sacco 23/11/2002 Li, 30/11/2002 Au, 29/3/2003 Lu, 5/4/2003 Bo, 17/4/2003 Se, 24/4/2004 La, 22/5/2004 Hu, 29/5/2004 Mo, 6/11/2004 Po, 9/4/2005 Se, 16/4/2005 Bu, 28/5/2005 De, 28/10/2005 Ge, 15/4/2006 Cr, 28/10/2006 La, 4/11/2006 Cr, 12/5/2007 An, 19/5/2007 Po, 10/11/2007 Cr, 17/11/2007 La, 10/5/2008 Po, 17/5/2008 An, 25/10/2008 Cr, 1/11/2008 Sw, 18/4/2009 La, 25/4/2009 Ne.

Switzerland

Yves Bellanger

Hong Kong

Alan Dixon

Rugby Blues

Oxford University

William Octavius Moberly 10/2/1872 (captain), 27/2/1873, 3/12/1873
Reginald Wynn Rucker 12/12/1874, 11/12/1876
Graeme Vassall Cox 10/2/1879
Charles Cyril Bradford 14/12/1887
Richard Thomas Dutton Budworth 14/12/1887, 12/12/1888, 14/12/1889
George Heinrich Frederick Cookson 16/12/1891, 14/12/1892 (captain)
George Strachan Fuller Eberle 11/12/1901, 13/12/1902
Christopher William Wordsworth 13/12/1902
Worthington Wynn Hoskin 13/12/1904, 12/12/1905, 11/12/1906, 10/12/1907 (captain)
Charles James Gardner 12/12/1905, 11/12/1906
Edward Turk Benson 11/12/1928
Charles Anthony Langdon Richards 6/12/1932
John David Currie 7/12/1954, 6/12/1955,11/12/1956, 10/12/1957
Stephen Brookhouse Richards 11/12/1962
Andrew Christopher Thomas 11/12/1979
James Maxwell Michael Averis 10/12/1995
Adam Reuben 9/12/1997, 8/12/1998
Andrew Stanley Collins 8/12/1998, 7/12/1999

Cambridge University

Walter Fairbanks 3/12/1873, 12/12/1874
James Alfred Bevan 12/12/1877, 14/12/1880
Herbert George Fuller 10/2/1879, 25/2/1880, 14/12/1880, 13/12/1881, 14/2/1883, 12/12/1883
Edwin Field 14/12/1892, 13/12/1893, 12/12/1894
Charles Alexander Hooper 3/3/1891
Glyn Davies 7/12/1948, 6/12/1949, 5/12/1950 (captain)
Peter Dalton Young 6/12/1949
Victor H. Leadbetter 12/12/1951
David Cecil Mills 9/12/1958
Ross Blake 12/12 2006, 6/12/2007 (captain)
James Lumby 6/12/2007

Bibliography

Books

Allan, Walter, 1994. The Official History of the Melrose Sevens. Mainstream.

Atkinson, C.T., 1931. The History of The South Wales Borderers 1914-1918. The Medici Society.

Barnes, A.F., 1930. The Story of the 2/5th Battalion Gloucestershire Regiment 1914-1918. Crypt House.

Barstow, Harry W., 1986. Gladiators of a Roman City, A History of Bath Football Club. Bath Football Club and Corsham Publishing.

Beacall, Philip J., 1971. Birkenhead Park, The First Hundred Years. Willmer Brothers.

Belsey, James, 1986. The Forgotten Front. Bristol at War 1914-1918. Bristol: Redcliffe Press Ltd.

Billot, John, 1970. History of Welsh International Rugby. Ron Jones.

Bowker, Barry, 1976. England Rugby. Cassell.

Bowker, Barry, 1970. North Midlands Rugby, A Jubilee History of the North Midlands Football Union. NMFU.

Bracken, Kyran, 2004.Behind The Scrum. Orion.

Budd, John, 2002. Chickens on the Lawn. Redcliffe Press.

Burrell, J.F., 1983. Sides & Squares, Clifton Cricket Club 1819-1983. Triangle Press.

Burrough, T.H.B., 1970. Bristol. November Books.

Bye, Maurice, 2003. Castle Park Before the Blitz. Stroud: Tempus.

Christie, O.F., 1935. History of Clifton College. Bristol: Arrowsmith.

Collins, Tony, 1998. Rugby's Great Split. Routledge.

Coughlan, Kevin, Hall, Peter, & Gale, Colin, 2003. Before The Lemons. A History of Bath Football Club RFU 1865-1965. Stroud: Tempus.

Couglin, Ken, 1994. A.G.Neale A 'Tiny' Glimpse. Oxford Instant Printing Service.

Croome, A.C.M., 1913. Fifty Years of Sport at Oxford, Cambridge and the Great Public Schools. London: Walter Southwood & Co.

Croxford, W.B., 1967. Rugby Union in Lancashire and Cheshire. Littlebury Bros.

Currey, R.F., 1955. St. Andrews College Grahamstown 1855 – 1955. Basil Blackwell Oxford.

Darter, Adrian, 1914. The Pioneers of Mashonaland. 1977 edition. Books of Rhodesia.

Davidson, John McI., 1994. A Compendium of Scotland's Matches. Polygon.

Davies, Jack, 1960. Newport Rugby Football Club 1875-1960. Newport Athletic Club.

Davey, F.A., The Story of the Devon Rugby Football Union.

Devins, Joseph H., 1968. The Vaagso Raid. Chilson. 1983 edition. Bantam.

Douglas, Derek, 1997.The Thistle, A Chronicle of Scottish Rugby. Mainstream.

Ducker, Chris, 1988. Rugby, Bristol Fashion. Bristol Rugby Football Club.

Dunnill, Michael, 2006. Dr. William Budd. Bristol: Redcliffe.

Dunning, Eric & Sheard, Kenneth, 1979. Barbarians, Gentlemen and Players. New York University Press.

Eberle, Sir James Fuller, 2007. From Greenland's Icy Shore. Roundfruit Publishing.

Eberle, Victor Fuller, 1973. My Sapper Venture. Pitman Publishing.
Edgell, Tim, & Sandles, Geoff, 2005. Gloucestershire Pubs and Breweries. Stroud: Tempus.
Esbeck, Edmund Van, 1986. The Story of Irish Rugby. Stanley Paul.
Eveleigh, David J., 1996. Bristol 1850–1919. Sutton.
Fox, Dave & Hoskins, Mark, 2001. Bristol Football Club (RFU) 1945-2001. Stroud: Tempus.
Fox, Dave & Hoskins, Mark, 2003. 100 Greats Bristol Rugby Football Club. Stroud: Tempus.
Frith, David, 1978. The Golden Age of Cricket 1890-1914. Omega Books.
Frost, David, 1988. The Bowring Story of the Varsity Match. Queen Anne Press.
Giles, Tony, & Hutt, Horace, 1972. One Hundred Years with the Clifton Rugby Football Club. Bristol: J.W. Arrowsmith.
Godwin, Terry, 1987. The Complete Who's Who of International Rugby. Blandford Press.
Grace, W.G., 1980. W.G. Cricketing Reminiscences & Personal Recollections - First published in 1899 when Grace last played for England. Reprinted by Hambledon Press.
Green, David, 1990. The History of Gloucestershire County Cricket Club. Christopher Helm.
Griffiths, John, & Cleary, Mick, 2003. International Rugby Yearbook 2003-2004. Collins Willow.
Griffiths, John, 1982. The Book of English International Rugby 1871-1982. Willow Books.
Griffiths, John, 1987. The Phoenix Book of International Rugby Records. Phoenix House.
Gunston, Bill, 1991. Fedden, the life of Sir Roy Fedden. Rolls-Royce Heritage Trust, Historical Series No. 26.
Hammond, Dave, 1999. The Club - The Life and Times of Blackheath FC.
Hammond. N.G.L., 1962. Centenary Essays on Clifton College. Arrowsmith.
Harkin, Trevor, 2007. War Memorial Park. War Memorial Park Publications.
Hawkins, Frank C., 1909. History of Clifton Rugby Football Club 1872-1909. Bristol: J.W. Arrowsmith.
Hawkins, Frank, & Seymour-Bell, E., 1922. Fifty Years with the Clifton Rugby Football Club. J.W. Arrowsmith.
Hayes, Dean, 1998. Gloucestershire County Cricket Club. Sutton.
Herbert, Alfred, 1980. The Natal Rugby Story. Shuter & Shooter.
Hignell, Andrew, & Thomas, Adrian, 2002. 100 Greats - Gloucestershire County Cricket Club. Stroud: Tempus.
Hill, C.P., 1951. The History of Bristol Grammar School. Pitman.
Hoskins, Mark, & Fox, Dave, 2000. Bristol Football Club (RFU) 1888-1945. Stroud: Tempus.
Hoskins, Mark, & Fox, Dave, 2001.Bristol Football Club (RFU) 1945-2001. Stroud: Tempus.
Hoskins, Mark, 2008. Classic Matches, Bristol Football Club (RFU). Stadia.

Hutt, Horace, 1978. The Centenary History of Gloucestershire Rugby Football Union (1878-1978).
Jenkins, John M., Pierce, Duncan, & Auty, Timothy, 1991. Who's Who of Welsh International Rugby Players. Bridge Books.
Jones, Brian, 1993. Bath Ace of Clubs. Breedon Books.
Ladd, James, 1978. Commandos and Rangers of World War 2.
Lewis, Steve, 1999. Newport Rugby Football Club 1874–1950. Stroud: Tempus.
Lewis, Steve, & Griffiths, John, 2003. Wales, The Essential History of Rugby Union. Headline Books.
Lewis, Steve, 2005. The Priceless Gift - 125 Years of Welsh Rugby Captains. Mainstream Publishing.
Littlewood, Peter R., 2005. Gallantry Awards to the Gloucestershire Regiment 1914-1918. Spink.
Loosley, S.G.H., 1982. Wycliffe College, The First Hundred Years 1882–1982. Wycliffe College.
Lyes, John, 2003. Bristol 1914-1919. The Bristol Branch of the Historical Association Local History Pamphlets.
Mace, John, 2000. The History of Royal Air Force Rugby 1919-1999. The Royal Air Force Rugby Union.
Macroy, Jennifer, 1991. Running with the Ball, The Birth of Rugby Football. Collins Willow.
Malin, John, & Griffiths, John, 2003. England, The Essential History of Rugby Union. Headline.
Marsh, John, 2006. The Lion Rampant, A History of Rugby at Emmanuel College Cambridge. John Marsh.
Marshall, Howard, 1951. Oxford v Cambridge, The Story of the University Rugby Match. Clarke & Cockeran.
Marshall, Rev. J., 1894. Football – The Rugby Union Game. Cassell and Company.
Massie, Alan, 1984. A Portrait of Scottish Rugby. Polygon.
Maule, Raymond, 1992. The Complete Who's Who of England Rugby Union Internationals. Breedon Books.
McDonald, Rhona, 1991. Winning The Gascoyne. Hesperian Press, Carlisle, Western Australia.
McWhirter, Ross, & Noble, Sir Andrew, 1969. Oxford University Rugby Football Club 1869-1969 Centenary History. OURFC.
Medworth, C.O., 1984. History of Natal Rugby.1870–1964. Howard Timmins.
Messenger, H., 1923. Colston's School and The Great War 1914-1918. W. Bennett.
Middlebrook, Martin, 2006. The First Day of The Somme. Pen & Sword Military.
Miles, Dr G., 1941. The Epic of Lofoten. Hutchinson & Co.
Miller, C.C. Hoyer, 1929. Fifty Years of Rosslyn Park. Wyman & Sons.
Montgomery, The Viscount of Alamein, 1973. El Alamein to the River Sangro. Hutchinson.
Morgan, Paul, 2003. A History of Rugby. Green Umbrella.
Mortimer, David, 2003. Classic Rugby Clangers. Robson.

Oswald, Nick, & Griffiths, John, 2003. Scotland, The Essential History of Rugby Union. Headline.
Owen, O.L., 1955. The History of the Rugby Football Union. Playfair Books.
Parker, A.C., 1970. The Springboks 1891 – 1970. Cassell.
Parker, Graeme, 1983. Gloucestershire Road, A History Of Gloucestershire County Cricket Club. Pelham Books.
Parry-Jones, David, 1988. Rugby Remembered from the Pages of the Illustrated London News. Partridge.
Pelmear, Kenneth, 1960. Rugby Football in the Duchy, The Official History of the Game in Cornwall 1884 - 1959. Cornwall RFU.
Pelmear, Kenneth, & Morpurgo, J.E., with an introduction by G.L. Owen, 1958. Rugby Football An Anthology. George Allen & Unwin Ltd.
Perry, C. Bruce, 1981. The Bristol Royal Infirmary 1904-1974. Portishead Press.
Peters, Robert. 1988. Letters to a Tutor, The Tennyson Family Letters to Henry Graham Dakyns (1861-1911). Scarecrow Press.
Potter, Jeremy, 1998. Headmaster, The Life of John Percival. Constable.
Proudfoot, C.L., 1976. History of the 16th Light Cavalry (Armoured Corps) - Hooghly Print. Co.
Rae, Simon, 1998. W.G.Grace A Life. Faber & Faber.
Raeburn, Wallace, 1971. A History of Rugby. Arthur Baker.
Raeburn, Wallace, 1975. The Men In White, The Story of English Rugby. Pelham.
Rea, Chris, 1977. Rugby, A History of Rugby Union Football. Hamlyn.
Reed, John, 1978. Surrey Rugby, 100 Years. The Surrey County Rugby Football Union.
Rhys, Chris, 1987. Guinness Rugby The Records. Guinness.
Richards, Alun, 1980. A Touch of Glory, 100 Years of Welsh Rugby. Michael Joseph Ltd.
Richards, Huw, 2007. A Game For Hooligans, The History of Rugby Union. Mainstream.
Rickman, John, 1990. Old Tom and Young John. Allborough Press.
Robinson, Derek, 1986. The Combination. Bristol and District Rugby Football Combination.
Robinson, B.F., 1896. Rugby Football. Innes & Co.
Royds, Admiral Sir Percy, 1949. The History of the Laws of Rugby Football. Walker & Co.
Ryan, Greg, 1993. Forerunner of the All Blacks. Canterbury University Press.
Salmon, Tom, 1983. The First Hundred Years, The Story of Rugby Football in Cornwall. Cornwall RFU.
Sampson, Walter Adam, 1912. History of Bristol Grammar School. Bristol: Arrowsmith.
Savory, John, 1989. A Man Deep in Mendip: The Caving Diaries of Harry Savory. Alan Sutton Publishing.
Sharpham, Peter. 2000. The First Wallabies. Sandstone Publishing.
Shipley, Rev. S. Paul, 1989. Bristol Siren Nights. Bristol: Redcliffe Press.
Smith, David, & Williams, Gareth, 1981. Fields of Praise. Official History of the Welsh Rugby Union 1881-1981. University of Wales Press.

Smith, G. Munro, 1917. A History of the Bristol Royal Infirmary. Bristol: J.W. Arrowsmith.
Starmer-Smith, Nigel, 1986. Rugby, A Way of Life, An Illustrated History of Rugby. Stanley-Paul.
Starmer-Smith, Nigel. 1977. The Barbarians. MacDonald-Futura.
Stembridge, P.K., 1969. Goldney - A House and a Family.
Stocks, Mary D., 1945. Fifty Years in Every Street - The Story of Manchester University Settlement. University of Manchester.
Symes, J. Odery, 1931. A Short History of the Bristol General Hospital. John Wright & Sons.
Tamlyn, W.H., 1945. Seventy Years of Somerset Rugby. Hy Bryant & Sons.
Thomas, Clem, 1997. The History of the British Lions. Mainstream.
Thomas, J.B.G., 1980. The Illustrated History of Welsh Rugby. Pelham.
Thorburn, Sandy, 1980. The History of Scottish Rugby. Johnston & Bacon.
Thorncroft, Nick, 2007. Gloucestershire and North Bristol Soldiers On The Somme. Stroud: Tempus.
Tonkin, Marguerite, 2005. Henbury Dynastie. Bristol: Redcliffe Press Ltd.
Tyson, Dick, 2008. London's Oldest Rugby Clubs. JJG Publishing.
Wakelam, H.B.T., 1954. Harlequin Story. Phoenix House.
Warner, Philip, 1991. The Harlequins, 125 Years of Rugby Football. Breedon Books.
Wemyss, A., 1955. Barbarian Football Club – History And Complete Record Of Results & Teams 1890-1955. Playfair Books.
Winch, Jonty, 1983. Cricket's Rich Heritage. A History of Rhodesian and Zimbabwean Cricket 1890-1982. Books of Zimbabwe Publishing Co.
Winterbottom, Derek, 1990. Clifton After Percival. Bristol: Redcliffe.
Winterbottom, Derek, 1991. A Season's Fame. Bristol Branch of the Historical Association of the University of Bristol.
Woodward, Clive, 2005. Winning! Hodder.
Woolgear, Jason, 1999. England, The Official RFU History. The Rugby Football Union.
Wyrall, Everard, 1931. The Gloucestershire Regiment in the War 1914-1918. Methuen.
Wyrall, Everard, 1927. The Somerset Light Infantry 1914-1919. Methuen.
Young, Brigadier Peter, 1958. Storm From The Sea. Corgi Books paperback. First published by William Kimber & Co.

Various Authors

Cheltenham College Register 1841-1910.
Clifton College Registers 1862-1887, 1862—1912, 1862-1947, 1862-1962, 1962-1978.
Clifton College - Twenty Five Years Ago 1879-1904. The Diary of a Fag. F.E. Robinson 1904.
Collins Schoolboys Annual - London & Glasgow Collins Clear-Type Press 1925.
County History & Centenary Year Programme 1983-1984. Hampshire Rugby Football Union.
Famous Rugby Footballers 1895. Yore Publications 1997.
Football Records of Rugby School 1823-1929. George Over (Rugby) Limited 1930.

Our Heroes. London Stamp Exchange 1916.
Rugby School Register 1675-1875, 1874-1905.
The Story of the 2/5th Gloucestershire Regiment 1914-18. Crypt House Press in 1930.

Directories, Journals, Newspapers and Magazines

BAT News Spring 1983. British American Tobacco.
The Bristol Football Club Jubilee Book 1888-1938.
Bristol Football Club – 75th Anniversary 1888-1963.
Bristol Mercury - Various Years 1878-1900
Bristol Times and Mirror - Various Years 1888-
Clifton Chronicle - Various Years
Clifton Rugby Football Club - A Few... Snapshots 1906-07. Published by Bristol Times and Mirror Ltd.
Clifton RFC 1907-08 Review of Season
The Cliftonian. Several Years.
Daily Telegraph - 2000-2009
Double Gloucester, The City and County of Gloucester, part of the World of Rugby 1972.
Early Days - Journal of the Royal Western Australian Historical Society. Volume 8, Part 6 – 1982
Evening Post - Various Years
The Future of Rugby by William John Lias - an article from the 1897 annual edition of the Badminton magazine.
Gloucester RFC 125 Glorious Years. Arrow
Gloucestershire Rugby Football Union Handbook. Various dates.
Kelly's Directory. Various Years.
Melrose 1883 – 1983. The Sevens Centenary.
One Hundred Years of Rugby Football. A History of Rosslyn Park Football Club 1879-1979.
Oxford Dictionary of National Biography
Rugby World. Various dates.
The Times - 1872-2009
TRY, An Anthology to Celebrate the WRU Centenary 1881–1981. Welsh Rugby Union 1980.
Western Daily Press - Various Years
Wright's Directory. Various Years.

Personal Collections

Thomas Hedley Burrough Collection. Courtesy of Clifton Rugby Club.
Friedrich Willhelm Bartelt Collection. Courtesy of Gathorne Girdlestone.
Gilbert Castle Collection. Courtesy of Clifton Rugby Club.
Ellison Fuller Eberle Collection. Courtesy of Clifton Rugby Club.
Victor Fuller Eberle Collection. Courtesy of Sir James Fuller Eberle.

Barcroft Joseph Leech Fayle Collection. Courtesy of Geg Fayle.
Peter Johnson Collection. Courtesy of Peter Johnson.
J. Harry Savory Collection. Courtesy of Richard Savory.

Websites

Adopt an Anzac - http://horowhenua.kete.net.nz/adopt_an_anzac
Ancestry - http://www.ancestry.co.uk/
Bath Rugby Club - http://www.bathrugby.com/
Blundell's - http://www.blundells.org/
Bristol and Avon Family History Society - http://www.bafhs.org.uk/
Bristol Grammar School - http://www.bristolgrammarschool.co.uk/
Bristol Libraries - http://www.bristol.gov.uk/ccm/navigation/leisure-and-culture/libraries/
Bristol Record Office - http://archives.bristol-city.gov.uk/
Bristol Rugby Football Club - http://www.bristolrugby.co.uk/
Clifton College - http://www.cliftoncollegeuk.com/
Clifton Rugby Football Club - http://www.cliftonrugby.co.uk/
Colonial Rugby - http://www.colonialrugby.com.au/
Cricket Archive - http://cricketarchive.com/
Ebay - http://www.ebay.co.uk
Friends of Arnos Vale Cemetery - http://www.arnosvalefriends.org.uk/
Fryer Library, University of Queensland - http://www.library.uq.edu.au/fryer/
Gloucestershire County Cricket Club - http://www.gloscricket.co.uk/
Gloucestershire Rugby Football Union - http://www.grfu.co.uk/
Great War Forum - http://1914-1918.invisionzone.com/forums/
Historical Directories - http://www.historicaldirectories.org/hd/
Marlborough College - http://www.marlboroughcollege.org/
Military Genealogy - http://www.military-genealogy.com/
National Archives - http://www.nationalarchives.gov.uk/
Newsbank - http://infoweb.newsbank.com
Old Cliftonian Society - http://www.cliftoncollegeuk.com/ocs/
Ovalballs - http://www.ovalballs.com/
Rugby Football History - http://www.rugbyfootballhistory.com/
Rugby Museum of New Zealand - http://www.rugbymuseum.co.nz/
Rugby Relics - http://www.rugbyrelics.com/
Rugby School - http://www.rugbyschool.net/
Society of Merchant Venturers - http://www.merchantventurers.com
Somerset Record Office - http://www.somerset.gov.uk/Archives/
St. Stephens Church, Bristol - http://www.saint-stephens.com
The British Library - http://www.bl.uk/
The Commonwealth and War Graves Commission - http://www.cwgc.org/
The Times Digital Archive 1785 - 1985 - http://infotrac.galegroup.com/
Twickenham World Rugby Museum - http://www.rfu.com/microsites/museum/
World War One Photographs - http://www.ww1photos.com/

Authors

Patrick J. Casey

Patrick Casey was born in Loughborough, Leicestershire in 1955. He was educated at Henry Mellish Grammar School in Nottingham and Heriot-Watt and Napier Universities in Edinburgh. He has been a life-long supporter of Nottingham Rugby Club since the glory days of the 1980s when they supplied many members of the England team. His parents and brother still live in Nottingham and support the club. Patrick coached rugby at Clifton RFC from 2002-2007, was Vice-Chairman of the Junior Section at Clifton from 2004-2005 and Chairman of the Junior Section from 2005-2006. He started the Clifton Rugby History website in 2002. His son played for Clifton u-7's to u-12's from 2001 to 2007.

He lives in Bristol with his partner Debra, son Daniel and step-daughters Kayna and Dulcie.

Patrick has previously worked on rugby-related chapters of books about Bertram Fletcher Robinson and George Turnavine Budd. He has plans for a re-issue of the 1896 book 'Rugby Football' by Bertram Fletcher Robinson in 2010, and after that a biography of former Clifton player and President of the RFU, Arthur Budd.

He works as an IT Manager for a firm of architects in Bristol.

Dr. Richard I. Hale

Richard Hale was born in Bristol in 1960 and educated at Bristol Grammar School. He played rugby for the school and subsequently for Keynsham RFC, Old Bristolians RFC, Leicester University RFC and Leicester Tigers 2nd XV, and captained the Law Society RFC. An enthusiastic amateur, he played first team rugby spanning four decades. He is a fourth generation hooker, his father Ian, grand-father William (Bill) and great-grandfather Walter all having played in the front row for Bristol FC. He lives in Bristol with his wife Shan, and his two sons Oliver and William have played junior rugby at Clifton RFC and at Clifton College, creating a fifth generation of hookers.

Professionally Richard is a management development consultant and author (www.richardhaleassociates.com), working with corporations supporting their educational strategies for the development of leaders in business. He works on the faculty of several universities, promoting the benefits of work-based action learning. Richard works with Bristol-based polar adventurer Alan Chambers MBE, and with former Welsh rugby captain and manager of the Welsh Rugby Football Union academy Phil Davies, linking inspirational leadership and coaching in sport with business: see www.adventurousbusiness.com.

Richard Hale and Patrick Casey. Photograph by Kayna Clarke.

Index

C

D

E

F

G

H

I

J

K

L

M

N

O

P

R

S

T

U

V

W

Y

Lightning Source UK Ltd.
Milton Keynes UK
16 October 2009

145026UK00002B/2/P